## HEARTBEAT OF THE ABSOLUTE

BY THE SAME AUTHOR

The Heart Sutra
No Water, No Moon
The Mustard Seed
Meditation, The First and Last Freedom
Tantra: The Supreme Understanding
Vedanta: Seven Steps To Samadhi
A Must For Morning Contemplation
A Must For Contemplation Before Sleep
The Zen Manifesto
*and many more*

# HEARTBEAT *of The* ABSOLUTE

*Discourses
on the
Ishavasya Upanishad*

# OSHO

## ELEMENT
Shaftesbury, Dorset • Rockport, Massachusetts
Brisbane, Queensland

This edition published in Great Britain in 1994 by
Element Books Limited
Longmead, Shaftesbury, Dorset

Published in the USA in 1994 by
Element Inc
42 Broadway, Rockport, MA 01966

Published in Australia in 1994 by
Element Books Limited for
Jacaranda Wiley Limited
33 Park Road, Milton, Brisbane 4064

Editing by Swami Anand Siddhartha,
Ma Prem Maneesha, S.R.N., S.C.M., R.M.N.
Design by Ma Deva Sandipa
Typesetting by Swami Dhyan Vimukta
Photography by Osho Photo Services

Printed and bound in Great Britain

British Library Cataloguing in Publication
data available

Library of Congress Cataloging in Publication
data available

ISBN 1-85230-490-1

*Spontaneous talks
given to disciples and
friends of Osho
in Mount Abu,
Rajasthan, India.*

# Contents

# Introduction

*A*ll is God! This, I am told, is the meaning of *Ishavasya*. But what does it mean that all is God? There is a story that Osho once told, of a man who had devoted many years to the search for the meaning of life. His quest had led him through the worlds of university research and esoteric practices, through psychedelic drugs and psychotherapy, but still the answer eluded him. Then, one day, when he had almost given up hope, he was told of a sage living in a remote and inaccessible region of the Himalayas, who knew the meaning of life. Convinced after much questioning that this sage must indeed hold the answer, the man settled his affairs, packed his bags, and set off on his great trek to find the sage.

The journey was arduous – planes and trains, buses that became more rickety and ancient as the roads became rougher and bumpier under them, and a long and often precarious climb on foot into the forbidding, uncivilized interior of the Himalayas. After many weeks the man finally reached his destination. Sure enough, there was the tiny village, and just beyond it the very hut in which, so he had been told, lived the sage. It was with a sense of immense antici-pation that the man entered the hut, as he saw himself drawing together all the energy of his life's work into this single moment.

There sat the sage, and the air of serenity that pervaded every-thing about him spoke of his great wisdom. In tremendous excite-ment, having been invited to sit with the sage, the man put his burning question: "Tell me," he said, "what is the meaning of life?"

The sage sat silent for some minutes, while his visitor waited with heart pounding and bated breath. Then the sage spoke. "Life," he said, "is a flowing river."

After fifteen minutes of stunned silence, the visitor finally exploded, bursting with rage: "You mean that I have disturbed my whole existence, struggling my way here after countless years of devoted inquiry, facing extremes of hardship and peril on the way, and with nothing more at times than my belief in your wisdom to keep me going, just to be told that life is a flowing river?"

The sage looked at him with an expression of great surprise on his face: "You mean it isn't?"

Likewise *Ishavasya* – all is God! And likewise also the sutra with which the *Ishavasya Upanishad* begins and ends. Between the first and last sutra only one word is changed – the word 'perfect' is substituted for the word 'whole', and is there any difference between what is perfect and what is whole? In the opening paragraph Osho says that for those who fully understand this one sutra, no more is needed. Like "All is God" and "Life is a flowing river," the sutra says all there is to be said. "For those who have come to the peaks of understanding, this is the end of the *Ishavasya*; but for those who are still climbing, it is only the beginning." And in taking us through the sutras between the beginning, and the end that is also the beginning, Osho takes us on an extraordinary journey.

What I love about the story of the man searching for the meaning of life is his journey. What a journey it must have been! And this is what awed me reading and coming to know intimately these discourses of Osho's on the *Ishavasya*. The journey through these chapters to the destination from which we set out is breathtaking. It is an inward and upward journey, the journey of Everyman through all the layers of existence, the journey of man and woman through all that being a human being can possibly mean – through innocence, ignorance, knowledge, love, death, hell, heaven, attachment, grief, sex, surrender, truth, desires, freedom, meditation, helplessness, prayer, bliss – through and through, not sequentially as I have to write them down, but as insights contained within insights.

What Osho reveals to us are the inner visions. Like the journey into the Himalayan interior, the scenery becomes ever more spectacular, the atmosphere ever more rarefied. But the magic lies for me in the *inwardness* of the journey; the truth revealed in its simple beauty is captivating. But Osho's voice whispers, "Look into it! See where you are going. Look! Look!" and, looking through his wisdom, the truth we are looking at opens, and we are guided into the truth that lies hidden within it – a pearl within a pearl, and containing its own hidden pearl. Traveling thus in and in, we find we are moving upwards too. This is the journey into consciousness!

Heartbeat Of The Absolute is the record of a similar journey. But it is not merely a record; it is an alchemical work, a song that can turn your path inwards and upwards, if you let the music in!

As he says in the final discourse, "Whatever I have been telling you was with the purpose of making a diving-board for you. *The purpose was the jumping.* This is why we entered into meditation at the end of each sutra, so that you might experience its significance by taking a jump into it."

Swami Anand Rajen

# All
# Is A Miracle

**1**

Om.
*That is whole, and this also is whole.*
*For only the whole is born out of the whole;*
*and when the whole is taken from the whole,*
*behold, the remainder is whole.*
*Om. Peace, peace, peace.*

THE ISHAVASYA UPANISHAD begins and ends with this sutra, and in it is declared all that can ever be said. It is quite unique. For those who fully understand it, no more is needed; the rest of the Upanishad is for those who do not. Thus the peace prayer, which usually brings the Upanishad to its close, is here invoked at the end of the very first sutra. And for those who have come to the peaks of understanding, this is the end of the Ishavasya; but for those who are still climbing, it is only the beginning.

Part of its uniqueness lies in the clarity with which it distinguishes between the Eastern and the Western methods of thinking and reasoning. Two schools of reasoning have flourished in the world – one in Greece, the other in India. The Greek system of logic gave birth to the whole of Western science, while from the Indian system emerged religion. The first and most fundamental of the differences between the two lies in the Western – Greek – method of progressing towards a conclusion. Whenever we seek the truth of a matter, an initial inquiry will lead via research to an eventual conclusion; first, thought and inquiry, then conclusion.

The Indian way is exactly the opposite. India affirms that what we are going to investigate is always there. It does not take shape as a result of our inquiry, but is already present even before our investigation begins. The truth which will become manifest was there before we were in existence. It was there before we discovered it just as much as it is there once we have done so. Truth is not formed or constructed through our research; what research does is to bring it within the realm of our experience. Truth is ever-present. That is why the Indian way of reasoning declares the conclusion in the beginning, and afterwards discusses method and procedure; first conclusion, then method. The Western way puts method first, then investigation, and finally conclusion.

One important point should be kept in mind: the Western method is very appropriate for those who look for truth by thinking about it. This method of reasoning is like trying to find something on a dark night with the help of a small lamp. The night is pitch black, and the light sheds its light dimly over three or four feet of ground. Only a small patch is visible, most remains unseen; and conclusions arrived at about that which is seen will be tentative. After a while, as one proceeds with the lamp, a little more becomes visible, and it is needed to revise or change the conclusion. As one progresses further and further, new things continuously become visible and so the conclusion is altered again and again.

Following as it does the Greek school of logic, Western science can never reach a final conclusion. All its conclusions are therefore tentative, temporary, and based on the knowledge acquired up to the present time. If something new is discovered tomorrow, there will be a change in the conclusion. That is why no truth arrived at by the West is absolute. It is not total. All its truths and conclusions are imperfect. But truth can never be imperfect or incomplete, and whatever is imperfect will be untruth. The conclusion we are required to alter tomorrow is in reality not the truth even today! It simply appears to be the truth. That alone can be truth which we never need to change. So the conclusions which are declared as truths by the West are really untruths based on the knowledge acquired so far and needing alteration according to the knowledge obtained tomorrow.

The Indian system of reasoning is not like investigating truth with the help of a lamp. It is like investigating the dark night in the dazzling brilliance of a lightning flash, when everything becomes visible simultaneously. Not that something – a part – is seen now, sometime later another part, later again something more, and so on; no, the Indian way is not like that. In the Indian system of investigation, the revelation of truth takes place all at once; everything is discovered at one and the same time. All the roads extend to the horizon, and all – whatsoever – is seen simultaneously in the flash of lightning. There is no scope for any change in the future because the whole has been seen.

The Western method called logic investigates truth by the process of thinking. The Indian way, which we call experience or wisdom, discloses all things at one time like the lightning flash, with the result that truth comes out as it is, in its totality, leaving no room for change or alteration. As a result there is no potential for change in what Buddha or Mahavira or Krishna has said. But Western thinkers – inclined to doubt and worry – question whether what Mahavira said twenty-five hundred years ago can still be true today. It is reasonable for them to raise such doubts; over such a period of time we should expect twenty-five *thousand* changes if we have been looking for truth with a torch! New facts will appear every day, and we will be compelled to alter or transform the old ones. But the truths declared by Mahavira, Krishna or Buddha are revelations. They are not truths found by lamplight; they have been seen and known and revealed in the dazzling lightning flash of a still mind – a mind devoid of thoughts. The truth which Mahavira knew was not discovered by him step by step; otherwise he could not have known the total truth. He knew it in its totality in a single moment.

What I want to tell you is that everything revealed in its totality through the wisdom of the East is included in this short sutra. It is there in its totality. This is why we in India declare that the conclusion is first and the inquiry follows. The announcement of the truth is made in the beginning, then we discuss how the truth can be known, how it has been known, and how that can be explained. This sutra is an announcement – a proclamation. The rest of the book is not essential for those who can comprehend the full meaning from the announcement. Nothing new will be stated in the entire Upanishad: the truth will be retold again and again in various ways. The remainder of the book is for those who are blind to the dazzling flash of lightning, and stubbornly insist on searching for truth with the help of a lamp. By the light of this lamp, the truth can be picked out line by line in the Ishavasya sutra; but first the subject is presented in its entirety in this great sutra. That is why I told you this sutra is so unique: it says everything. Now let us try to understand it.

It declares that the whole is born out of the whole, and yet that which remains behind is always whole; in the end the whole is absorbed into the whole, and even then the whole increases not at all, it remains as it was before. This is a very great antimathematical statement. P. D. Ouspensky has written a book called Tertium Organum. He was a renowned mathematician of Russia, who in later years, as a disciple of a remarkable western master, Gurdjieff, became a mystic himself. He was a mathematical genius, his intelligence penetrating the heights and depths of his subject.

The first statement he makes in this wonderful book is that there are only three great canons of thought in the world. The first, entitled Organum, is by Aristotle, father of the Western science of logic. Organum means the principle of knowledge. The second book is by Francis Bacon and is called Novum Organum – the new principle of knowledge. And the third one is his own book, which is called Tertium Organum – the third principle of knowledge. He follows this statement with a short sentence that has puzzled many people: "Before the first existed, the third was." That is, the third principle was already in the world before the first principle was discovered. The first book was written by Aristotle two thousand years ago, the second by Bacon three hundred years ago, and the third one was written some forty years ago. But Ouspensky says the third existed in the world before the first was written, even though he wrote this third book only forty years ago. When anyone asked him the meaning of this crazy, illogical statement, he replied, "Whatever I have written is not written by me. It was already in existence; I have simply proclaimed it."

The earth was under the influence of gravity before Newton was born. The earth attracted a stone before his birth in the same way that it has done ever since. Newton did not invent the principle of gravitation, he only revealed it. He opened what was hidden, he made known what was unknown. But gravity was already there before Newton; otherwise Newton himself would not have been there. Newton could not have been born without gravity. Gravity can exist without him, but he cannot exist without the earth's gravity. It existed already but was not known in the world.

Ouspensky says his third principle existed before the first was known. It is quite a different matter that it was not known; and perhaps it is wrong to say it was not known, because what Ouspensky has said throughout his book is contained in this small sutra. His Tertium Organum is a very valuable book. His claim that there are only three such great books in the world – and the third his – is not false. He does not say so out of vanity, it is a fact. His book is as important as that. If he had not said so, his silence would have been a false humility. It is a fact, his book is that important. But everything he says in it is there in this small sutra of the Ishavasya Upanishad.

He has tried throughout his book to prove that there are two kinds of arithmetic in this world. One is that which says two and two are four. This is simple arithmetic which we all know, a simple calculation which verifies that if we add up all the parts of a thing, they can never be greater than its whole. Simple arithmetic states that if we break a thing into pieces and then add up those pieces, their sum can never exceed the whole. This is a simple, direct fact. If we change a rupee into one hundred paise, the sum of these one hundred paise can never be more than one rupee. Can it ever be? It is simple arithmetic that addition of parts can never be greater than the whole. But Ouspensky says there is another, higher, mathematics, and that is the mathematics of life. In this mathematics, it is not necessary that two plus two should equal four. At times, two and two may make five – or three. In life, he tells us, the sum of the parts sometimes exceeds the whole. We shall have to understand this a little more clearly, because if we cannot understand it we shall not be able to comprehend fully the significance of this first and the last sutra of the Ishavasya.

An artist paints a picture. Suppose we evaluate the cost of his materials. How much would the colors cost? Not much, certainly. And a canvas? Again, not so much. But no great work of art, no beautiful painting, is merely a mixture of colors added to canvas: it is something more.

A poet composes a poem, a song. All the words used in it are quite ordinary words which we use every day. Perhaps you might meet a word or two in it which is less frequently used; even so, we know them. Yet no poem is simply a collection of words. It is something more than the collection and arrangement of words. A person plays a sitar; the effect produced in our hearts on hearing the notes of the sitar is not merely the impact of the sound. Something more touches us.

Let us understand the phenomenon in this way. Shutting his eyes, a person touches your hand lovingly. Again, the same person touches your hand with great frustration. The touch in both cases is the same. As far as the question of physical, bodily touch is concerned, there is no basic difference between the two. Yet there is certainly some distinctive element in the feel of someone touching us lovingly: the touch of one who is angry is quite different from the loving touch. And again, when someone touches us with complete indifference we feel nothing in the touch. Yet the act of touching is the same in all these cases. If we were to ask a physicist he would reply that the degree of pressure exerted on our hand by another person's touch could be measured – even the amount of heat passing from one hand into another could be worked out. Nevertheless, all the heat, all the pressure, cannot disclose in any way whether the person who touched us did so out of love or anger. Yet we *experience* the distinctions among touches that are qualitatively different. So certainly, the touch is not merely the sum total of the heat, pressure and electrical charge conveyed in the hand: it is something more.

Life depends on some higher mathematics. Something quite

new, and full of significance, is born out of the sum total of the parts. Something better than the sum of the parts is created. Something important is born out of even the lowliest things. Life is not just simple arithmetic – it is a far more profound and subtle arithmetic. It is an arithmetic where numbers become meaningless, where the rules of addition and subtraction become useless. The person who does not know the secret of life, which lies beyond the ordinary arithmetic of life, does not understand the meaning and purpose of life.

There are many wonders to this great sutra. It is said:

> *When the whole is taken from the whole,*
> *behold, the remainder is whole.*

From the point of view of ordinary arithmetic this is absolutely incorrect. If we remove some part of a thing, the remainder cannot be the same as it was originally. Something less will remain. If I take ten rupees from a safe containing millions of rupees, the total will be something less. It will be less even if ten paise are taken out. The remainder cannot be equal to the amount as it originally was. However great the fortune may be – even Solomon's or Kubla's treasure – it is reduced if just ten paise are removed from it; it cannot be the same as it was before. Similarly, however great the fortune may be, ten paise added and it is still greater. But according to this sutra the whole may be taken from the whole – not just ten paise but the entire fortune – and still the remainder is whole.

This seems like the babbling of a madman whose knowledge of arithmetic is nil. Even a beginner knows that a thing will be less if something is taken from it, no matter how little is taken; and if the whole is taken, there will be nothing left at all. But this sutra declares that not just something, but the whole, remains. Those who know only the logic of the money-box will certainly not understand this phenomenon. Understanding appears from an altogether new direction.

Does your love decrease when you give it to someone? Do you

experience any shortage of love when you give it totally? No! 'Love' is the word we need to come to an understanding of this sutra; this is the word we shall have to use. However much you may part with your love, what you are left with remains as much as it was originally. The act of giving it away produces no shortage. On the contrary it grows, increasing as you give it away, entering you deeper and deeper as you distribute it more and more. As you give it freely away, the wealth of love within you begins to grow. One who gives his total love, freely and unconditionally, becomes the possessor of infinite love.

Simple arithmetic can never comprehend that when the whole is taken from the whole, the remainder is whole. Only love can find the meaning in this statement. Einstein cannot help. To seek that kind of assistance will be useless. Go instead to Meera or Chaitanya; through them you may perhaps find your way to understanding, for this is a subject relating to some other, unknown dimension, in which nothing decreases when given away. The only experience you have that can enable you to understand this in a sudden flash of insight is love – and out of every one hundred, ninety-nine of you are blind to this experience. If, having given your love, you experience a sense of loss, then know that you have no experience of love at all. When you give your love to someone, and feel within you that something has disappeared, then know that what you gave must have been something else. It cannot be love. It must be something belonging to the world of dollars and pounds. It must be a measurable thing which can be valued in figures, weighed in a balance and estimated in meters. Remember, whatever is measurable is subject to the law of diminution. Only that which is immeasurable and unfathomable will remain the same no matter how much is taken from it.

Have you experienced that love, when it is given, diminishes? Almost everybody is familiar with it. If someone loves me, I want that she love no one else, because my reasoning says that love divided is love diminished. So I seek to become sole owner and possessor of her love. My demand is that the person loving me give not even a loving glance to anyone else; such a glance is poison for me, because "I know" that now her love for me will begin to diminish. If I cling to this notion of the love diminishing, I need to accept that I have no idea what love is. If I had any appreciation of true love, I would want my beloved to go out and give it freely to the whole world, because through so giving it she would come to understand its secrets and its mysteries, and as she fell deeper and deeper into love, her love towards me, too, would be overflowing.

But no, we are ignorant about higher mathematics. We live in a world of very simple mathematics where everything diminishes through distribution; so it is quite natural that everyone should be afraid of the act of giving. The wife is afraid of the husband giving his love to someone else, and the husband fears that his wife may fall in love with another man. Actually, to talk about the husband or wife falling in love with someone else is beside the point, for the dilemma already exists within the family. When the mother shows her love towards her son, her husband is jealous; and when the father shows his love for his daughter, his wife is jealous. Tension breeds in such circumstances, for true love is absent. That feeling which we are given to calling *love* is not true love.

The real test of love lies in whether it is beyond the laws of quantification. Love is immeasurable. Drop your delusion that true love diminishes when it is shared. The stumbling block is the fact that all the other experiences available to us are measurable. Whatever we have can be measured; our anger, our hatred, and all other feelings can be measured.

The only experience which is beyond measurement is love; and love is unknown to you. This is why you find it so hard to understand what God is. One who understands what true love is does not worry about understanding God, because if you know love you know God – they are part and parcel of the same arithmetic, they belong to the same dimension. One who has understood true love will say, "It's all right even if I don't know God. I have known love, it is enough. My purpose is served – I have known! I am initiated into that higher world, that world where sharing brings no decrease, where the things freely and abundantly given remain with the giver."

And remember, when you feel within you a kind of love which remains whole even after it has been given in its totality, then your need of love from others disappears, because your own love cannot increase however much love you receive. Bear in mind that the thing which cannot be diminished through giving it away cannot be increased through receiving it. These phenomena happen simultaneously. So be aware also that you have no experience of love as long as you need to demand it from others.

It is not only the children but the grownups too! – all of us demand love, and go on demanding it. Throughout our lives we beg for love. Psychologists say there is only one problem in our lives, and that is our anxiety about how to get love from others. All our tension, all our cares, fears and anxiety are attributable to this single dilemma; and when we can't find love, we search for substitutes. Throughout our lives we strive after love; we are hot on its scent, and in constant pursuit. Why? In the hope that our stockpile of love will increase if we get it. And all this means is that we have not yet known love, for that which increases in the getting is not love. No matter how great the amount of love received, love will remain as it was.

So the person who understands this sutra of love fully also understands these two facts. First, however much I give of it, my love will not diminish; and secondly, however much love I receive, the love in me will not increase. Even if the whole ocean of love rushes into me, my love will not increase one iota, nor diminish one iota if I give it all away.

> *And when the whole is taken from the whole,*
> *behold, the remainder is whole.*

This entire universe comes out of God. It is not small – it is endless, limitless, without bounds. It has no direction, no beginning, no end. God remains whole even though such immensity has been born out of him. And even when all this vast universe returns into that highest totality – existence – and is once again immersed in it, God will remain whole. There will be neither increase nor decrease in it.

Let us try to understand this phenomenon from another direction. We know the ocean: it is an experience seen and felt by our sense organs. It can diminish, and it can be augmented. Vast as it is, it is not limitless. Rivers flow into it continuously, and never re-emerge. The clouds of the sky go on taking up its waters and showering them back onto the earth. There is never any deficiency of water in the sea. And yet it does diminish, for though it is vast, it is neither endless nor limitless. The thousands of rivers flowing into it make hardly a difference of an inch in its volume, it is so vast. It defies the imagination to conceive of the amount of water thrown into the sea every moment by great rivers like the Brahmaputra, the Ganges, the Amazon. Yet to all appearances the sea remains the same. Day by day the sun's rays drain off its water, and the clouds in the sky are born out of it. In spite of all these operations the sea appears to remain constant in volume, but it is not in actual fact in a condition of no increase or decrease. It diminishes and it increases, but it is so vast that we know nothing of the changes.

If we turn our faces to the sky and look up into space, we encounter an experience of a different kind. Everything that exists, exists within space. The very meaning of space is that element in which everything is contained. Space is that in which all things are included. So take note, that space cannot exist within any other element. If we start thinking that space must itself be contained within some other element, we have to conceive of the idea of some greater space. The situation becomes difficult, and we are forced into the fallacy that logicians call infinite regression. This is to embark on an endless foolishness, in which we now have to determine the nature of the greater space in which space is contained. The question becomes endless, because forever we must now ask, "And what is the nature of the surrounding element?"

No, we have to accept that everything is contained in space, and space is uncontained. Space surrounds all and is unsurrounded. Therefore everything happens within space, but it is not added to by the happening; and though everything within it comes to an end, space is undiminished. Space is as it is. It remains in its suchness; it remains in its own condition. You construct a building, a magnificent palace; after a time, your palace will crumble in ruins. So palaces that reach for the skies are reduced to earth again. Space will be unaffected; it was not lessened when you built your palace, and it will not increase when your palace falls down. The palace is constructed within space, and will likewise crumble within space. The events cause no difference in space. Perhaps, then, space brings us closer to existence: this I intended to explain to you.

Space is beyond our reach, it is insubstantial: and yet, while constructing a building or making any other thing, we have the sense of space increasing or decreasing. You cannot occupy the seat where I am sitting, because I have occupied this space. There was space here which you could have used if I had not filled it. On one spot we can construct only one building; we cannot raise another building on the same spot. Why? – because the building constructed by us has consumed that space. Now if this building has consumed that space, there is a sense in which space can be said to have decreased. We are compelled to build skyscrapers precisely because the surface space of the earth is decreasing day by day. As the cost of land increases, so the buildings are raised higher and higher, and the land has become more expensive because more and more of it is being occupied. So, as the available space diminishes, the buildings climb higher and higher. Soon we will start constructing buildings underneath the ground, because there is a limit to the height to which we can build.

We are busy filling our sky space, our atmosphere. More and more we encroach upon the sky, devouring ever more space. So much has empty space decreased.... It is true that endless space spreads into the void on all sides. There is really no shortage of space at all. But no other space can be created on the land on which we are sitting. Wherever buildings stand, space is consumed. There is that much less land space available to us.

God is unbounded. God does not diminish. The ocean, so vast to us, is such a tiny drop of what God is. Yes, it is huge compared to great rivers like the Ganges and the Brahmaputra. All their flowing into the ocean makes no visible difference to it; and yet there *is* a difference, though it cannot be weighed or measured. So much greater again than our seas and oceans is the sky; yet for us, this too has limits. To reach the concept of God needs one more jump, in which all logic, ideas and imagination will have to be discarded.

God means existence, being – what simply is: isness is God's attribute. Whatever we may do, it makes no difference to his isness. Scientists have another way of stating this truth. They say, "Nothing can be destroyed." This means that we cannot remove anything from its isness. If we wish to destroy a piece of coal, we can turn it into ash, but that ash will exist. We can even throw the ash into the sea; it will blend into the water and will no longer be visible, but whatever its form now, it will still exist. We can destroy its forms, but we cannot destroy its isness. Its isness will remain for ever. Whatever we go on doing with it, will make no difference to its isness. Isness will remain. Of course, we can alter its shapes and forms; we can give it a thousand different shapes – we can transform it again and again – but we cannot change what is within it. That will remain. It was wood yesterday, it is ash today. It was clay yesterday, today it is coal. Yesterday it was coal, today it is diamond. Always, it is. Nothing makes any difference to it: it remains.

God is the isness in all things – their being, their existence. Things may be created in any number, but there will be no addition to that isness; they may be destroyed in any number and still there will be no reduction in that isness. It will remain the same – unsullied, unattached and untouched.

When we draw a line on water, even though it vanishes no sooner than it is drawn, something has happened. Not even a line as momentary as this can be drawn into existence – not even this much is possible. The sutra says that this whole has come out of that whole. That is unknown; this is known. This which is seen has come out of that which is unseen. This which we know has come out of that which we do not know. This which we experience has come out of that which lies beyond our experience.

Understand this phenomenon properly. Whatever falls within our experience always comes from that which lies beyond our experience. Whatever is seen by us emerges from that which is invisible. What we know comes from the unknown; and whatever is familiar to us derives from that unfamiliar. If we plant a seed, a tree grows from it. If we break the seed and crush it into pieces, there will be no tree. There will be no trace of the flowers which should have blossomed. There will be no trace of those leaves which should have appeared. From where do they come?

They come from the invisible. They are created by the invisible. Every moment the invisible is being transformed into the visible, and the visible is being lost into the invisible. Every moment the limitless enters into the limited and returns every moment from it. It is just like our breathing process – breathing in and breathing out. The whole of existence is continuously inhaling and exhaling. Those who know the secret of the breathing process of existence call it creation and annihilation. They say the creation takes place when existence inhales, and the annihilation when existence exhales, and between the two breaths we pass through endless lives. As existence breathes once in, then out, we go through endless births, times without number we come and go.

Two things this sutra says. First, that the whole comes out of the whole and what remains is whole. Second, that when the whole is absorbed into the whole, it is still whole. That whole remains always virgin, always untouched. Nothing affects its virginity. This is a very difficult matter to understand. It is like this: a child is born, but its mother remains a virgin. Such a story is told of Jesus and his mother, Mary. Having given birth to Jesus, Mary is called the blessed virgin. The story prevails through those who knew and understood Jesus and Mary, and it is exactly like the birth of existence; the whole comes out of the whole.

Christianity is unable to explain this event. Christians are baffled by the concept of the virgin birth. They are ignorant of that arithmetic which can leave the mother a virgin after she has conceived and borne a child. They know nothing at all of that arithmetic; they are totally ignorant about higher mathematics. Christianity is greatly puzzled. Christians ask, "How can we explain this phenomenon? It is impossible – it is a miracle! It is absolutely impossible but it has happened, God has shown us a miracle."

Whatever miracle is shown by existence in this world is shown by its every moment. No miracles take place in this world – or, to see it the other way, the happening of every moment is a miracle. All is a miracle. When a tree grows from a seed, it is a miracle; and when a child is born from a mother's womb, it is a miracle. No, there is nothing strange here: this vast universe is born out of the whole, yet that from which it comes is untouched. If a mother goes so deep that she is absorbed – in the meaning of this sutra – in the whole, then where is the difficulty in her remaining virgin after childbirth? If a woman merges into this sutra, becoming one with it, she can become a mother *and* remain a virgin.

But the seeker has to understand this sutra correctly – and I am saying this because I see your desire to attain. You want to achieve something. The true seeker does not talk about all this: after all, what can happen by just talking? He knows that he does not know; and in any case what can happen through just knowing? He lives it. He is conscious. Perhaps you will understand more easily through a personal experiment than you will through my words. So experiment. Involve yourself in a small, routine action, and be conscious all the time: It is happening – I am not doing it. Test it. See it, while doing anything. See it while eating, see it while walking along the road, see it when you are angry with somebody. And be aware that the thing is happening. Stand behind and be a witness to the thing happening – then you will discover the secret of this sutra. You will hold its secret key in your hand. You will understand that something is happening outside and you are standing behind, untouched and unconcerned. As you were before doing it, so you remain after, and the thing happening in between comes as a dream, and passes away as a dream.

To existence, *samsara* – the wheel of life – is no more than a dream. If it becomes a dream to you too, then you become inseparable from existence. I repeat: to existence, samsara is no more than a dream; and as long as samsara is more than a dream to you, you will be less than existence. The day on which samsara becomes as a dream to you, you are existence. You can then say, "I am the Brahman."

This is such a profound sutra. No one knows how many secrets are implied in it. The remainder is whole even when the whole is taken from it. Bear both in mind – the whole remains, and the whole is taken: it goes totally, it remains total! What does this mean? It means that every individual also is existence, in toto. Each and every individual, and each and every atom, is total existence. It is not that an atom is partial existence – no, it is existence in toto. Because this is unknown in our ordinary arithmetic, it is a little hard to understand.

If you have understood that the whole comes out of the whole, and still the remainder is whole, then I can tell you more. The endless whole comes out of the whole, and still the remainder is whole. If, after one whole emerges, there is no possibility for another whole to appear, it means that some deficiency is caused by the birth of the first whole. But if, after the first whole emerges, the second to appear is as much the whole, and the third also – if successive wholes keep emerging and still there is always as much potential for the emergence of wholes – then the remainder is in truth the whole.

Therefore it is not that you are a part of existence; to say this is mistaken. Whoever says you are a part of existence is wrong. He is again talking of lower mathematics. He is talking of that world where two and two make four. He is talking of the world of weights and measures. I tell you, and the Upanishads tell you, and those who have ever known the truth tell you, that you are existence in toto. This does not mean that your neighbor is not existence in toto also.

No, the fact cannot be altered. A rose blossoms on a bush – and blossoms to the full; but the totality of its blossoming does not hinder the blossoming of its neighboring bud. Help and cooperation become possible, but there is certainly no hindrance. A thousand roses can bloom to their fullest capacity: the totality of existence is endless totality. Out of endless totality, endless wholes can be born. Each individual is existence in toto. Each atom is this vast universe in toto; there is not an iota of difference between it and the whole. If there is any difference then it can never be the whole, then there is no way to make it whole; and if it is ever going to become the whole then it is whole right now – we are just ignorant of the fact. The deficiency is simply in our knowledge.

Keep this sutra in mind during these days of our *sadhana* – our work together. Repeat to yourself, "The whole comes out of the whole, and the remainder is whole. When the whole is absorbed in the whole, the whole still remains the whole." It all makes no difference! Remember this, and go on humming it within you with every breath you take. Every day its many interpretations will be revealed in various forms and in various ways. Keep the sutra in mind, and as we go on discovering it, keep going deeper and deeper into its meaning, and into your remembrance of it. Let these processes go on working within you. During these seven days it is possible that at any moment something may happen – all of a sudden this sutra may tumble from your lips, and you will feel the whole coming out of the whole, and the whole remaining. The whole is lost in the whole and yet the whole remains the whole. There is no difference at all. All this takes place like a dream and yet nothing really happens. All this happens like play-acting, and yet the whole remains as undisturbed and untouched as ever.

To remember the sutra as much as you possibly can will help you. Try to live in its spirit twenty-four hours a day.

The substance of the Upanishads cannot be understood through the mind alone; it must be comprehended by living it. This sutra is not proclaiming theories; it presents certain sadhanas, certain practices. It does not consist just of conclusions arrived at with the help of knowledge; it proclaims experiences. When you live these experiences within yourself – giving them birth within yourself, allowing them to enter your blood, bones, flesh and tissues, allowing them to merge into your breathing; when you live in listening, remembering and humming them while going through your daily routine of waking, standing, sitting and sleeping – then, and only then, will their secret, their doors, begin to open to you.

You are given only the first announcement in this sutra. They must have been remarkable people to have said, as they did, all there is to be said in this one sutra. It comes to an end declaring the quietening of the three forms of pain:

*Om. Shanti, shanti, shanti.*

What relation can this sutra have to the quietening of threefold pain? Have anybody's miseries ended by chanting certain formulas? No, but the sage says, "Om!" and that finishes the matter. Can all your miseries be over, can you become free from them all by chanting this sutra?

If it is chanted in all sincerity, with full understanding, it is possible. If it is merely read from the book, it is never possible. This is to say that if it is chanted with the attitude, "I have already read this – I have already heard it," then nothing is possible. But for those who have said, "Om!" with all their courage and daring, all problems are over. All the miseries of people who have realized the truth are ended. All the afflictions of their body, mind and soul disappear. Such people go beyond affliction.

You think, "There must be some significance when he says this with such ease, such confidence." The significance is this: whoever lives this sutra, whoever gives birth to it within himself, will experience himself free from all afflictions, because there is only one kind of affliction, only one pain – whether on the mental, physical or spiritual level; there is only one kind, and that is ego. "I am doing this – this is done by *me*," is the only affliction, the only obstacle. "This insult is directed against *me* – I am abused thus...." All these happenings accumulate around this I. But when such a vast universe makes no difference to existence, and leaves it unaffected, do I have to allow such insignificant things to affect me? Can I not also remain untouched? Can I not stand aside and say, "The insult given was not given to me"; and, "Whatever I did has been done. I have not done it." If I become a witness to the actions that come to me and proceed from me – if I cease to be the doer – then wonderful secrets begin to unfold.

So try to live this sutra during these seven days. While I am talking on the Ishavasya Upanishad you will hear this sutra interpreted from various perspectives. If you just try to live according to the interpretation I have given today, understanding will certainly come to you; not otherwise.

This is enough on the sutra. Now I shall give certain instructions regarding meditation, because tomorrow morning we shall begin to practice meditation. The first thing to keep in mind is throughout the day to breathe as totally as possible and, whenever you remember, to inhale as deeply as you can. Hyperoxygenate! The energy you liberate for your work will be in direct proportion to your intake of breath. A great deal of energy lies hidden in your body. It must be aroused and activated towards meditation; it must be channelled into meditation. So the first meditation sutra I give you is to activate that energy. The nearest and the easiest means available to you is your breathing activity.

As soon as you wake up in the morning and come to your senses, begin to breathe deeply, sitting on your bed. When you are walking along the road, breathe as deeply as you can. Do it slowly, don't overexert yourself, be comfortable and joyful – but remember, your breathing should be deep. Bear in mind all the time that it will be easier for you to go into meditation if you take in as much oxygen as possible. The more oxygen you have in your blood, in your heart, the easier you will find your meditation. The more you expel carbon dioxide, the easier it will be for you. The impurities decrease as you increase the amount of oxygen in your body. It is interesting to know that the mind finds it difficult to function if the basis of bodily impurity is removed. The opportunity for thoughts to flourish in your mind will lessen as you absorb more fresh air; and as I told you, this will enhance the potential for sutras like this to blossom and flower within you.

So the first thing is: hyperoxygenate. Let there be an abundance of oxygen in you. Remember this throughout these seven days. Two or three things will happen if you do this, but don't be afraid of them. When you start breathing deeply, your sleep will become shorter. This is not something to worry about. When sleep is deep and sound, its duration decreases, and as you begin to breathe more deeply, the depth of your sleep will increase also. This is why those who do hard physical work sleep so soundly at night. The depth of your sleep will increase in proportion to the depth of your breathing, and as the depth of your sleep increases, so its duration will decrease. Do not worry about this. If you sleep seven hours now, it will become four or five hours. Don't be anxious about it – you will wake up in the morning more refreshed, more joyful and healthier from these five hours' sleep than you used to after sleeping for eight hours. So when your sleep comes to an end in the morning – and this will begin to happen earlier if you have been breathing deeply – you should get up immediately. Don't miss that blissful moment of the morning; use it for meditation.

The second point to remember is that the less food you eat, and the lighter it is, the better it is for you. Reduce the quantity as much as is comfortably possible. The pace of your meditation will be quicker and easier the less you eat. Why is this? There are some sound reasons for it. Our bodies have certain settled habits. Meditation is not one of them; it is new work for the body. The body has fixed associations. If the settled habits of the body are interrupted at any point, then our body and mind can form new habits easily. Suppose you are worried, and begin to scratch your head out of habit. Now if your hands are tied down at that time so that you cannot scratch your head, then you cannot remain worried. This is very puzzling. You might ask, "What is the relation between worrying and scratching?" The answer is habit. The body holds its habits fast and functions through them.

Eating is the most deep-rooted habit of the body; it is the deepest because no life is possible without it. Bear in mind, it is stronger and more potent than sex. Among all the deep-rooted habits of life, the food habit is the most profound. It begins from the first day of life and continues till the last day. The very existence of life, the body itself, depends upon it.

So, if you want to change the habits of your mind and body, then weaken their deepest habit at once. As soon as you do this, all the fixed physical routines and arrangements of your body will be disturbed, and you will find it easier to enter new regions, and to go in new directions with your body in this disturbed condition; otherwise you will find it more difficult. So commit yourself as much as you can in this direction. You may choose to fast, or perhaps to eat once a day. Do as you choose; there is no need for rules. Quietly, and at your own pace, follow the path which is easiest for you.

The third point is concentration. You have to breathe deeply twenty-four hours a day, and at the same time be aware of your breathing. Pay attention to your breathing, and concentration will easily take place. When walking, bring awareness to walking, bring awareness when taking a shower. Concentration can easily be achieved – even walking along the road. In this way: breathing in, observe that the breath from without is entering within – be attentive! Keep on observing the inhaling and also the exhaling of your breath. If you are attentive you will also be able to breathe in deeply. If you are not attentive you will forget to watch, and your inhaling process will become shallow. If you go on taking deep breaths you will be able to remain attentive because you will have to be attentive to do the deep breathing. So associate meditation with breathing. While you are doing certain jobs, if you feel it is not possible to keep your attention on your breathing, then keep your concentration on your task. For example, when you are eating your food, concentrate fully on the act of eating. Take every mouthful with full concentration. When you are taking a shower, concentrate on the water pouring over your body. Walking along the road, concentrate on each step you take.

Immerse yourself in concentration for twenty-four hours a day during these seven days. The meditation we shall do here is quite separate, but I am explaining to you the background of what you should do during the rest of the time. So practice this third point: great attention, great concentration – and especially on your breathing, because breathing is a ceaseless, twenty-four-hours-a-day process. No one can go on eating or swimming or walking for twenty-four hours, but breathing goes on ceaselessly, so concentration can be practiced on it all the time. Concentrate on it! Forget that there is anything else going on in the world. Live as though only one thing is happening in the whole world, and that is the breath coming in and the breath going out. It is enough; follow this process of the breath entering and leaving like the beads of a rosary. Concentrate just on this.

The fourth point is sense deprivation. Three things are to be done. If you feel able to observe silence for the whole day, then begin immediately; and if you find this hard, then be telegraphic in your speech. Understand that you are paying a price for each word you speak. So don't speak more than twenty words during the course of the day. Speak only when it is absolutely necessary, when it is unavoidable – like a matter of life and death! You cannot imagine how beneficial it will be for you to observe total silence – its value is incalculable.

So let yourself be totally silent; you will not find it hard. Keep a paper and pencil with you and if you find it absolutely essential, write down your message and show it to someone. Remain utterly silent. Your total energy will be accumulated within by observing silence. This energy will help you to go deeper in meditation. More than half of man's energy is consumed by words. So stop using words completely. To your utmost capacity, observe silence; and take great care that nobody else's silence is broken because of you. If yours is broken, it is your misfortune, it is your own responsibility; but see that nobody else's silence is broken by you. Don't ask anyone useless questions, don't make unnecessary inquiries, don't raise useless questions, don't try to drag anybody into conversation. Cooperate and help others to observe silence. If somebody asks a question, signal him to keep silence. He needs reminding.

Leave aside talking absolutely for seven days. You have talked a great deal up to today, and you will do so again in seven days' time. But for this one week, give up talking completely. Everyone should try his best. If you can remain silent for the whole seven days it will help you tremendously, and you will have no need for the excuse, "I cannot meditate." If you follow the five guidelines I am giving you, you will have no cause for complaint. If you create problems by ignoring these points, you only are responsible. So observe total silence, and if you cannot do this – if you are weak, if you lack determination, if your intelligence is not strong enough – then make do with as little talking as possible. If you have some intelligence, some willpower, some strength, some self-confidence, then observe total silence.

Silence is the first essential of a sense-deprivation program. The second is a blindfold. Make one, and begin using it from tomorrow morning. Your eyes must be completely covered. The eyes are the door through which you go out. The more you keep them closed, the better it will be for you. Even when you are just sitting around, keep the blindfold on, because then you won't see others, and the opportunity for conversation will not arise; and seeing you blindfolded, others will not try to harass you unnecessarily. So be blind. You have already heard about observing silence; now I ask you to be blind also.

To be silent is a kind of liberation, and to be blind is a greater and deeper liberation, because it is the eyes which make us run outside all day long. Closing your eyes, you will have much less scope for going outwards, and the energy will start circling within. So keep the blindfold on. While walking push it a little up, enough to see downwards, enough to see the road four feet ahead of you. Keep the blindfold on for the whole day. If you can sleep wearing it at night, do so. Only take it off if you find it uncomfortable. If you sleep with it on, there will be a difference in the soundness of your sleep. Keep it on during the rest of the time you are here. When we meet here for the morning meditation, the blindfold should remain on. Take it off for the afternoon meditation, but keep it on till you come to the meditation ground. At night also you have to come wearing the blindfold. Once here, remove it for the duration of the night meditation.

So, when I begin to talk in the morning, remove your blindfold, and for the afternoon and the night meditations. I am giving you these opportunities to use your eyes because having some chance to see the world outside may help your eyes to go within; otherwise keep your eyes closed. You will be surprised how much mental tension disappears when your eyes are kept closed. A lot of mental tension enters through the eyes, and it is eye tension which causes tension in the brain tissues. If the eyes remained undisturbed, calm and relaxed, ninety-nine percent of mental diseases would disappear. So make a conscientious and full use of the device.

There is no question of anyone being excused or exempted; if you try to avoid it, I am not the loser, you are. Bear in mind that you have to remain blind for most of the time. You have to give your eyes a one-week holiday; imagine that you have no eyes at all. After seven days you will realize how relaxed and calm your eyes can be. You would never have imagined that so much joy could flow from their relaxation. But if during these days you choose to deceive yourself, then I am not responsible. It all depends on you. No one is responsible for anyone else here. You can deceive yourself or not, as you wish.

As well as a blindfold, get cottonwool to put in your ears. We wish to give the ears a rest too. If eyes, ears and speech are shut down and rested, the result is a condition of sense deprivation. Put the cottonwool in your ears, then tie the blindfold over them. That way others, even if they want to, cannot disturb you in your silence. If your ears are open someone may be tempted to talk to you. There will be no temptation if your ears are closed. Keep your ears open only when I talk here in the morning, and at night when you go to sleep. Keep your eyes open and your ears closed during the afternoon and night meditations.

The fifth and last instruction is the most important and essential condition of all. It is this: only people who dance and laugh and are full of gladness and joy enter existence's temple. No weeping people have ever gained entrance there. So drop your melancholy and depression for these seven days. Be blissful! Laugh, dance and remain joyful. Let bliss be with you all the time. Remain cheerful and joyous even in your routines. Be blissful while sitting or walking – be drunk with music, mad with joy! When you are walking, do not walk as everyone walks ordinarily; walk as a seeker, as a *sadhu* would walk, with a dance in your step. Don't worry about what others may say. We have come here in order to be free of others' criticisms. At worst, others may take you for a maniac, a lunatic. So accept the situation right from the start; this is the worst that can happen. Try to create a blissful and joyous atmosphere for the entire camp.

Observe silence   a silence shimmering with joy and delight, a silence dancing in mirth and merriment; silence without, and the energy dancing within. In your delight, dance and laugh. If you feel to dance even during the afternoon silent meditation, you can do so. Be full of joy and happiness even during the morning meditation here. If you want, if you feel like it, even during the meditation dance and jump and laugh. If you weep, let that weeping be the outcome of your joy. Let your tears help your bliss to flow. Keep all this in mind. If you want to sway, then sway. If you want to dance during night meditation, then dance. If you want to swing to and fro, do it. If you want to laugh, then laugh. The vibe of joy should be always with you.

These five things are to be practiced from tomorrow morning. So make arrangements now to get a blindfold for your eyes and cottonwool for your ears. By sunrise tomorrow morning you will not be the same person who came here today. This is my expectation. Do what I have said, and if you fulfill my expectation, nothing can keep you from being able to say, *"Om. Shanti, shanti, shanti!* – peace, peace, peace!" when you depart from here. If, when you leave here, your heart can utter these words, then there is no difficulty for you.

# Neither Mine Nor Yours

2

*All the things of this world,*
*organic and inorganic,*
*are filled with God.*
*Enjoy them through renouncing them.*
*Be detached;*
*do not covet other people's riches.*

THE ESSENTIAL PROCLAMATION of the Ishavasya Upanishad, the very meaning of its title, Ishavasya, is: Everything is God's. All things belong to God. But our human mind tries to argue that it is all ours, and we live in this delusion throughout our lives. Something is mine. The idea is of ownership and possession – it is mine!

When everything is existence's, there is no place left for this 'I' of mine to stand. Remember, for its manifestation even ego needs a base. To endure, even 'I' needs the support of 'my'. If the support of 'my' were not there, it would be impossible to forge the 'I'. From a casual observation it appears that the 'I' comes first and 'mine' follows it. But the fact is quite the reverse. First, 'mine' has to be founded, and then the structure of 'I' is built onto it. If whatever you have which you call 'mine' is wrested entirely from your grasp, then your 'I' will not be spared. It will disappear. 'I' is nothing but the collection of 'mines'. 'I' is created from the fabric of 'mine' – my wealth, my building, my religion, my temple, my position, my name, my family, and so on.

As we go on throwing down each 'mine' the base of 'I' is simultaneously eroded away. If not a single 'mine' is saved, then there is no foundation on which the 'I' can stand. The 'I' needs a resting place, a shelter, a house of 'mine'. The 'I' requires a foundation stone of 'mine' otherwise the whole structure of 'I' will tumble down. The first proclamation of the Ishavasya intends to collapse the entire structure. The sage says, "Everything is of God." There is no place for 'mine'. There is no scope at all even for 'I' to say 'mine' for itself. If it can say 'I am', it is wrong. If it persists in saying 'I am', then it is a bewildered 'I'. It is necessary to understand this from two or three points of view.

The first is this: you are born, I am born. But nobody asks me whether I want to be born or not; no trouble is ever taken to find out my wishes. My birth is not dependent on my desire or on my acceptance. When I know myself, I know myself having been born. There is nothing like my being before my birth. Let us consider it in this way: you are constructing a building; you never ask the building whether or not it wishes to be built. The building has no will of its own. You are constructing it, and it is erected.

Have you ever thought that you also were never consulted before your birth? Existence causes you to be born, and you are born. Existence creates you, and you are created. If the building becomes conscious, it will say, 'I'. If it becomes conscious, it will refuse to consider its maker as its owner, as its master. The building will say, "The builder is my servant; he has constructed me. The materials are mine; he has served me. I was willing to be made, so he has made me."

But the building has no consciousness. Man has. And in fact who knows whether the building has consciousness or not? It is possible; it may be so. There are thousands of levels of consciousness. Man's consciousness is of one particular kind, it is not necessary for all things to have the same kind of consciousness. A building may have consciousness of a different kind, stone may have of yet another kind, plants another. It is possible that they, too, live in their own 'I'. When a gardener is watering a plant, maybe the plant is not thinking, "The gardener is giving me life," but rather, "I am showing favor to this gardener by accepting his service. Through my grace I accept his services." Nobody has ever approached the plant to inquire about its desire to be born.

It is absolutely absurd to call it *my* birth when it is caused without my desire. Where is the meaning in claiming as my birth, that about which I am never consulted before my birth? When death comes, it does not ask our permission. Death will not ask us,

"What do you want? Are you coming with me or not?" No, when it comes, it comes of its own accord, just as birth comes without our knowing about it. Death comes without knocking, without our permission, without instruction, without forewarning, and stands quietly before us; and it gives us no alternatives, no choice. It hesitates not even a second, whatever we may wish. It is sheer idiocy to claim as *my* death that for which I have no desire or willingness in the least.

That birth is not my birth in which there is no choice on my part. The death to which my willingness is irrelevant, is not my death. So how can the life which lies between these two ends be my life? How can the span between be mine, when both its inevitable ends – without which I cannot exist – are not mine? It is a deception – one which we go on strengthening, forgetting birth and death completely. But if we consult a psychologist in this matter, he will say, "You forget them purposely, because they are such sorrowful memories." When my birth is not mine, how poor and miserable I become. When my death is not mine, everything is snatched away from me; nothing is saved. My hands remain empty. Only the ashes remain.

We build a long bridge of life between these two ends, like a bridge spanning a river; but neither of the river banks is ours. Nor are the bridge's supports at either end ours. So think a little: How can the bridge spreading from one bank to the other across that river be ours whose foundation is not ours? Hence we strive to forget our birth and death – our foundations.

Man forgets many things intentionally. He tries not to remember, because remembering may smash all his ego and bring it all crashing down. "Then what will be mine?" So we refrain from thinking of birth and death, and this makes possible the great misconception that all we find in life is ours. But if we let ourselves explore and examine what we find, we discover with certainty that it is not ours.

You say, "I have fallen in love with somebody," without considering whether that love affair was your decision or not. Listen to what lovers say: "We do not know when it happened. We did not make it happen." Then how can that be ours which happened of its own accord? If it happens, it happens. If it does not happen, it does not.

We are so dependent, so regulated, as if somewhere everything is fixed and determined. Our condition is similar to that of an animal tied with a rope to a stake. The animal will go on circling round and round the stake on its rope and will live in the misconception that it is free because it is circling freely. It will forget the rope, because to remember it is painful; the rope tied to the stake gives us pain because it reminds us of our dependence. The truth is, that it tells us that we are not our true selves.

We are not fit to be even dependent, let alone consider the matter of becoming free. To *be* one's dependency – that is, to feel the rope's pinch – it is necessary to be aware of one's being; and that we are not. The animal roams around the fixed stake, sometimes to the left, sometimes to the right and thinks, "I am free," and when it thinks, "I am free," the 'I' is there. Then, by and by, it must begin to persuade itself that "It is also due to my willingness that I am tied to a stake. I can cut the rope whenever I desire, but I am thinking of my welfare."

We create so much delusion in our lives. We say, "I became angry, I made love, I disliked, I hated, I made friends, I became an enemy…" but none of these doings is our decision. Have you ever become angry *and* been the doer of that anger? You have never done so. When there is anger, *you* are not there. Have you ever made love which is made by you? If *you* can make love, then you can make love with anybody; but the fact is that you are able to love someone and you are unable to love someone else. You are able to make love with someone even when you don't want to, and you are unable to make love with someone even though you wish to do so.

All the feelings and emotions of life come from some unknown quarter – they come just as your birth comes. You unjustly intrude on this happening and become the master, the doer of it. Yet what have you done? What is there which is done by you? The feeling of hunger comes; sleep comes; in the morning waking comes; and in the evening your eyes begin to close again. Childhood comes. When does it pass away? How does it pass away? It does not ask us, it does not enter into consultation and discussion with us, and it does not delay its passing a moment, even if we ask it to do so. Then youth passes away, and old age enters. Where are *you*? – but you go on saying, "I am young, I am old," as if youth depends on you. Youth has its own flowers. Old age has its flowers too; and they bloom as flowers bloom on a tree. A rosebush cannot say, "I cause roses to bloom." It could only say so if it were able to make sunflowers bloom!

Don't take any credit for all these happenings. If there is innocence in childhood, it is there without any effort on your part. And when sex and other desires catch hold of you in youth, they do so just as innocence holds you in childhood. You are neither the master of your childhood innocence nor of the sexual desire of your youth, and don't consider it your achievement when your mind begins to incline towards celibacy in old age. It is just like this: sex takes hold of you in youth, and indifference takes hold of you in old age. Nor have those who were never slaves to sex any control over that fact. So don't pride yourself on the fact that you are not a slave to sex.

Examine every small atom of life and you will realize that there is no place for the I – the ego – to stand. Then why are we creating this illusion? How does it come about? From where does this deception come? It comes because we always feel that there is an alternative. For example, you insult me. Now I have two alternatives: I may insult you back; or I may ignore it, thinking the insult is not there at all. That is, I can choose to reciprocate if I wish, and if I don't wish, I can choose not to. But are there really any alternatives? Do you suppose that the person who returns an insult could have chosen not to, if he had wanted? You will say: If he had not wished to do so, he need not have returned the insult. But you will have to go a little deeper to understand this. Is that desiring there already in him, or does he bring it from somewhere? Is that desire to insult or not to insult under his control?

Those who seek within say that what the depths reveal is only that the happenings go beyond our control. A man thinks to insult, and he insults. Another man decides not to insult, and he does not insult. But from where does this idea of giving or not giving abuse come? Is the idea yours? No, it comes from the place from which birth comes. It comes from where love is. It comes from where consciousness is. It returns to where death is. It is absorbed where the breath goes.

It is easy to deceive ourselves by saying, "It is in my hands, it is under my control. Had I wished, I would not have abused." But who told you, who asked you, to abuse? People like Buddha and Mahavira would not give abuse. Do you think that they can simply choose to feel abusive? No; just as you experience a fixed and unavoidable situation in having to abuse, so Buddha and Mahavira experience an equally unalterable situation of not feeling abusive. They cannot choose, even if they wish, to feel abusive. That desire itself is not created.

A man came to a Zen master early in the morning and began to ask him why he was so calm and quiet, while he himself was so agitated and disturbed. The master replied, "I am calm and you are agitated, that's all. The matter is over there. There is nothing more to be said."

The man insisted, "No, I want to know how you became so calm."

The master replied, "I want to know from you how you became so agitated."

The man replied, "Agitation comes of its own accord."

The master said, "That has happened exactly with me. Calmness came to me of its own accord, and I do not take any credit for it. When agitation was coming, it was coming. I could not do anything to stop it, and now, when calm has come to me, I cannot do anything to bring agitation even if I wish to bring it, so much am I bound by the situation."

The man said, "No, please show me the way to be calm and quiet."

So the master said, "I know only one way, and that is this: give up your illusion that you are able to do anything about it. If you become agitated, remain agitated. Know that you are disturbed and that you can do nothing about it. It is out of your control. Don't make any effort to be calm. Even those people who make an effort to be calm become agitated and disturbed. They become agitated, and in their efforts to become calm they create fresh uneasiness in themselves."

But the man persisted, "Your advice does not settle my mind; I want to be calm."

The master said, "Then you are bound to remain agitated because you wish for something. You refuse to leave this matter to God, while the fact is that everything depends on him; nothing is within your control. I became calm from the day when I began to accept willingly whatever happened, whatever came to me. I could not be calm as long as I desired and tried to become something."

But the man would not accept what the master said. "I am jealous of your calm," he said. "I cannot remain satisfied with your explanation."

Then the master asked him to wait and to ask his question when there was nobody in his hut, because he had many visitors. The man agreed, and when there was nobody in the hut he again requested the master to show him some way. Then the master, putting his finger on his lips, said, "Be quiet."

The man was greatly perplexed. He said, "When there are people here and I ask you for a reply, you tell me to ask when there is no one here; and when there is no one here and I ask you for a reply you tell me to keep quiet. How will my problem ever be solved?"

Evening came, the sun had set, and all the people had left. The cottage was empty, and the man again sought a reply. The master asked him to come outside. The full moon was shining. The master asked, "Do you see these plants?" Small plants were growing in front of the cottage.

The man replied, "I see them."

Again the master asked, "Do you see those trees far off, reaching high into the sky?"

The man said, "I see them."

Then the master said, "Those trees are great and tall. These plants are small and low. There is no conflict between them. I have never heard any dispute between them on this matter. These small plants never ask the tall trees why they are tall; they are satisfied with their smallness. The tall trees also never ask the small plants why they are small. Tall trees have their own difficulties, as they discover when there is a storm. The small plants have their problems too, but they are content with their smallness, just as the tall trees are content with their tallness. I have never heard of a dispute between these two; I have always found them quiet. So please leave me. I am what I am, and you are what you are."

But how can that man be satisfied with this analogy? And how are we to be convinced? The mind always desires to be something. Why does it behave so? It is because we have always taken it for granted that we can do something. "No," says the Ishavasya, "you cannot do anything. You cannot be the doer." This was the secret of that great idea called fate. Fate does not mean that you should do nothing. That would be to sit quiet – and fate says that you cannot even sit at your own will. If fate seats you, only then can you sit. Fate makes "I shall do nothing" impossible for you. If fate wishes any nondoing, then nondoing will happen.

Please bear in mind, there is not a single fatalist among all those who seem to be fatalists. They say, "Everything is in the hands of fate. What can we do? So we do nothing." The very existence of the idea that we do nothing means that the feeling of doing is still present. The concept of total fatality means that we are not. There is no way to do anything. It is existence.

When we cannot do anything, when we cannot be doers, then what my-ness, what of mine, will there be? To whom shall we say, "It is mine"? Can we say, "This is my son"? It looks so, because it appears that, "I have given him birth." Such an illusion happens even though nobody has ever given birth to any son. Sons are born, they find their way through you. You begin to love a woman. That love does not come from you, love makes its way through you. The sexual desire, the love, the yearning of your bodies to meet each other – that yearning is not yours. It is hidden in every particle of your body, in the smallest hairs on your body. It is compressed into each particle and it presses you, it urges you. Eventually, a child is conceived, someone becomes its mother and someone becomes its father. It looks as though they have brought the child into being. Destiny laughs at you! It laughs uproariously at you. You have been made an instrument of birth: you have not given it. You have been just a passage. The mother is just a passage for someone's journey into life. Through her, fate gives birth. *You* have done nothing.

You construct a building and say, "It is mine." But do you observe birds also build nests for themselves? In this world even the smallest animal builds its place of abode. There are birds whose mothers fly away after laying their eggs. When the eggs are hatched, out come the young ones. They receive neither the mother's training nor the father's protection, they don't go off to school. And the miracle is that those birds make nests exactly like those their mothers made and their grandmothers before them. Nor is that nest an ordinary one; it involves great architectural skill. It is so beautiful that if man desired to build such a nest he would have to learn how to build it, and even after learning, it would be difficult for him to construct it so skillfully.

How is such a nest made? Scientists call it a built-in program. They say there is a built-in program in each small cell of the bird's body. The whole process of constructing the nest is hidden in its bones, flesh and tissues. That this bird can build her nest is a certainty. She will seek out precisely the kind of grass and leaves which her mother looked for. Nobody has taught her; the mother has not even seen her, and she has not been to school. Yet she will pick up those leaves and those straws of grass and build the selfsame nest made before by her mother and her grandmother. Man also constructs; all kinds of creatures construct. There is no cause to say, "It is mine" – absolutely no cause.

About what can we say, "It is mine"? Can we make such a claim about wealth? All animals accumulate: they do so in various ways, and man is certainly not the cleverest at it. There are animals far more skilled than man in the act of hoarding. In Siberia there are white bears: it snows for six months of the year, and man has difficulty surviving during those six months, but the bear protects itself. Its method of accumulating is wonderful. It does not collect things, it collects fat – enough to last it for six months. It just goes on hoarding more and more fat in its body. It stores so much fat in its body that it can live on it for those six months during which it sleeps under the snow.

Your treasure is not so deep within you. Thieves can steal it from you; and to be useful to you, your wealth is dependent on many circumstances. You may have wealth, but it will be of no use to you if the stock-market collapses. That white bear is cleverer than you. It hoards its food within itself, and because – lying under its heavy blanket of snow – it is inconvenient for the bear to chew and swallow and digest and form new flesh and tissues, it stores its food as fat that can be peacefully absorbed.

The whole world accumulates. Don't think that it is only you who does so. It is a natural process. When a mother breast feeds her child, the pride she feels is unfounded. No sooner is the child born than the mother's breasts become full of milk, her body begins to make milk. If the child refused to take milk, the mother would be in difficulty and feel very uneasy. It is a blessing that the child drinks the milk. The mother does not intentionally prepare milk. The birth of the child is a spontaneous process, and as a part of this process, milk is produced in the mother. As the infant grows older, the flow of milk begins to diminish, and when its need is over, the milk disappears.

All this happening is natural. The desire to accumulate is natural. That is why this sutra of the Ishavasya says, *"Prakriti"* – the

Ishavasya calls it God: everything is of God. Nature, destiny, prakriti, are all mechanical words; and he is so huge, so full of mystery, so full of life and consciousness, that he cannot be mechanical.

Science also maintains that nature does everything, but when we speak of God in the language of science, we become pitiable; we become worthless and mechanical. When the Ishavasya says, "God does everything," on the one hand our ego is ripped down, and on the other we become God. This is important; it is worth understanding. As science progresses, it emphasizes that man should give up the illusion that *I* am doing. Everything is happening. But the emphasis of science is on everything happening mechanically. Everything is happening as in a machine. The whole world behaves mechanically. And when everything is happening mechanically, man's position is pitiable. His ego is certainly smashed, but nothing is revealed that gives him any meaning or validity.

True, man's pride, his ego, is a very insignificant and petty phenomenon, like a flame burning from the oil in a small earthen lamp. It is extinguished by science, and there is deep darkness all around; but there is no rising sun to take its place. That is why the proclamation of the Ishavasya is more valuable than that of science. On the one hand it extinguishes your dimly burning light and snatches away your petty ego, saying, "Be extinguished! You are not, and your fear is unnecessary!" and on the other hand it gives birth to a super-sun. In one moment, from one side it says, "You are not," and immediately, from the other side, it establishes you in the position of God. From one side it snatches you away and wipes you out completely, and from the other side it bestows upon you the whole. It extinguishes the earthen lamp of ego, the dimly shining flame of smelly, smoky kerosene oil, but it gives you instead the bright, shining light of the sun. It wipes out I, the ego, but establishes us in the highest I – God!

This is the difference between the dimension of religion and of science. Science affirms those same facts which religion affirms, but the emphasis of science is on the machine. Religion, discussing the same things, puts its emphasis on consciousness, on wisdom, on the living; and this emphasis is important. If Western science succeeds, man will finally become a machine; and if the religion in the East succeeds, man will finally become God. Both demolish ego, but science degrades man in the process.

Some hundred and fifty or two hundred years ago, science began to declare for the first time that man is a helpless animal. When Darwin said to mankind, "Forget that you were created by God; you have evolved from animals, from beasts," then man's ego was smashed for the first time – with a bang! Man had believed that he was God's son, God's creation, though he had no proof of it. Then suddenly it turned out that the father was not God, but a chimpanzee! It must have been an immense shock. What a fall! One moment there was God, sitting on the highest throne, and we his sons, and the next moment we were proved the descendants of monkeys. This was very painful for man; it affected him greatly. So science declared for the first time that man should forget all about being a human being and consider himself as an animal, a beast. All man's efforts to nourish his ego were shattered.

But a journey once started, whatever the direction, does not end before it is completed; it searches for its end. It was difficult to stop at the level of the animal. First science declared that man is a kind of beast; then, after further investigations into the nature of animals, science found that animals are machines.

Watch a tortoise moving. You will see that when the heat increases, the tortoise moves into the shade. You will say it moved there because it felt too hot. Science rejects this. Science manufactured mechanical tortoises. They were kept in the sun, and there they stayed as long as the heat was not very great; but as the heat increased, they began to move. They moved into a bushy, shaded place. These tortoises were only mechanical things – what had happened to them? Science calls it the condition of homeostasis – the means by which notice is given of any significant change in the temperature. There is no consciousness at all involved. You see a moth flying towards the flame of a lamp. The poet describes it as a mad, blind lover of the flame, sacrificing its life to its love. The scientist will not accept this; for him there is nothing like madness in this happening. It is all mechanical. No sooner does the moth see the flame than its wings begin to incline towards the flame. They produced mechanical moths, and let them loose in darkness. Then they put on the light, and immediately the moths rushed towards it.

So science established that animals are machines; and its final conclusion was amazing. First scientists had established that man is descended from animals; then they established that animals are like machines: their final judgment is that man is a machine. Naturally, there is some truth in this argument. It is good that they smash man's ego, but having done so, they reduce man to the status of a machine – man degenerates into the mechanical. For man to think this way is dangerous, and has proved harmful. People like Stalin and Hitler could put millions to death because they looked upon man as a machine and so their hearts were unmoved by the slaughter.

Now consider this interesting situation. Krishna said in the Gita that man's soul is immortal, it does not die, so killing your enemies makes no difference. Stalin also could say that since man is a machine, without a soul, there is no harm in killing him. When Krishna said to Arjuna that the soul is immortal and will not die howsoever you try, the effect on Arjuna was that he became reconciled to killing his foes. But the results of these two actions are quite different. When the immortality of the soul is accepted, the question of death becomes meaningless. Stalin is pleased to put millions to death; but for him there is no such thing as soul at all, no wrong is done because man is only a machine.

There can be no objection to destroying a machine. If you strike a machine with a stick, even a nonviolent person cannot accuse you of committing violence. Outwardly, the results appear similar, but they are not, because the true significance of the results is very different and changes the entire meaning in each case. Science contends that nature does everything. Science not only smashes man's ego, but degrades man; when religion smashes man's ego it raises him to a higher level and sends him on an upward journey.

This sutra says your ego will disappear if you cease to call anything yours. Consider it all to be existence's. Don't entertain a desire for anybody's wealth. After all, why? When nothing can be mine, then neither can anything be yours. Be aware, because this sutra, "Don't covet; don't desire another's riches," has been greatly misinterpreted: so incorrectly has it been interpreted that one may become deeply puzzled.

Most of the commentators have explained it thus: "It is a sin to desire another's wealth, so don't entertain such a desire." But they appear to be stupid, because the first part of the sutra says that wealth belongs to nobody; it is existence's. The first part of the sutra says, "When it is not mine, how can it be yours?"

No. No, its true meaning is this – that you should not wish for another's wealth because the wealth which is not mine is also not yours. The scope for desire exists only when, since it can be yours, it can be mine also; otherwise the desire has no grounds on which to stand. The experts in the science of ethics have explained it as meaning that even to think of another's wealth is sinful; but since it cannot be mine, how can it be another's?

No expert of ethics can get at the real meaning of this sutra. It is subtle and deep. The moralist is anxious to see that no one steals another's property; no one should consider as his own what belongs to another. But his emphasis on another's property is just the converse side of his emphasis on what is his own. Remember, the person who says, "This is yours," is not free from the notion, "This is mine," because these two are different sides of the same coin. As long as the feeling persists, "The building is mine," its counterpart, "The building is yours," will continue: and when the feeling of 'my' building disappears, how can the corresponding feeling of 'your' building remain? Not to wish for another's wealth or property does not mean that the property belongs to another person, so to desire it is a sin; its real meaning is that property and wealth belong to none – wealth is existence's alone: it is because of this that desiring is a sin. Consider nothing as mine or yours, don't regard yourself as an owner, and don't try to steal from another – for that is to regard something as his. We can neither steal nor keep anything. It is all existence's, and what is existence's we can neither obtain nor hoard.

How hilarious this idea of ownership is! I put a board on a piece of land claiming it as mine. That piece of land was already there before I was even born. Looking at my action, that piece of land must be laughing heartily, because many before me have also put up such boards claiming it as 'mine' – and a piece of land buried them all. They were buried where you are now sitting! There are at least ten graves under the spot where each of us is sitting. There is hardly an inch of ground on this earth which might not contain the graves of ten people. So many people have been born and have died in the world that there might be at least ten people buried under each inch of ground. That piece of land knows full well that other claimants also erected such boards on it. But nothing stops man; as he is, he will still go on putting up his boards, and he does not want to see that he is adding his name to an old board, painted and polished over. He does not want to see that someone else will have to take the same trouble tomorrow. In fact, all this ado is about nothing. That piece of land must be laughing!

So don't wish for another's property, because it belongs to no one. I don't mean simply that it is sinful to seize another's property with a view to making it your own. It is a sin in the first place to consider it either his or yours. It is a sin to look upon it as anybody's. It is certainly a sin to pretend ownership is anyone's but existence's. If you can comprehend this interpretation, then and only then will you be able to grasp the deep and subtle meaning of the Ishavasya. Otherwise the apparent meaning of these sutras is that each should securely possess his own property and, to protect his own interests, should propagate on all sides that no one should wish for another's property.

This is why Marx and others of his way of thinking were not wrong when they felt that all religions have given protection to the affluent and rich, because interpretations of such sutras have been misleading and incorrect. From these interpretations it seems you should not try to grasp from another that of which he is the possessor. This clearly determines that the owner may get the help of the police to protect his property. So its intention is to maintain law and order, the status quo and the idea of ownership. But this sutra does not intend this; the very first proclamation of the Ishavasya is that everything belongs to existence. Existence alone is the master. Neither I nor you are the master, and our idea of ownership is an illusion. It alone is the master who never came to proclaim, "I am the master." Before whom would it proclaim? To whom would it say, "The land is mine"? To say so it is at least necessary to have the other – and all is existence's!

Remember this when you inscribe your name over a piece of land. You do so for the other, so that he may know that it is yours. You don't put up boards in a jungle. And suppose you were living alone on this earth, I don't think you would be so crazy as to go on erecting boards at various places. If you are the only person living on this earth, the whole land is yours. There remains no purpose at all in bothering to say so.

Existence makes no such announcement because it is the master. Bear this in mind too; it is yet another meaning contained in this sutra of the Ishavasya: those who make announcements cannot be masters. There is no need for the master to announce. The master is the master, though unannounced. Only servants make announcements. If a person makes a forceful claim about anything, it is likely to create an equally strong doubt in the minds of the listeners. When someone declares vehemently that the property is his, then take it for granted that it cannot be his. Why is the claim made so vigorously? We always lay claim to a thing loudly to prove that it is ours when in fact it is not.

Existence makes no announcement. For whom should it do so? Why should it announce? The proclamation would be meaningless. The proclamation, on the contrary, would prove that it is not its. All this belongs to it who has never laid claim to it. To none who have ever claimed it does it belong. Don't wish for the wealth of another, because it belongs to no one – it is all existence's. Don't consider it yours or another's, consider it as existence's: and be aware that this other, and you too, are all existence's – we are *all* its. So stealing and extorting is useless, meaningless and irrelevant. There is no skill or art in it. It is as good as labor lost. It is an effort like drawing a line on water.

There is still one more point: Enjoy them through renouncing them. It is said that if you renounce a thing, you can enjoy it. But no, that is not our belief. On the contrary, we believe that we can enjoy only that to which we hold fast. But this sage instructs us to do quite the opposite. He says that they alone can enjoy things who renounce them. The statement is very antithetical to our belief. They alone become real masters who refuse to be masters. Everything falls into the hands of those who have no desire to hold onto things.

A good analogy is the attempt to hold air in your hand. You can comprehend the real meaning of this sutra – renounce to enjoy – if you simply try to hold air in your hand. As soon as you tighten your grip the air escapes. The tighter you clench your fist, the less air you hold, until in the end there is no air left. Loose your grip and air will rush towards your open hand. There is always air in an open hand, but from the closed fist it flees. One who keeps his hand open has it always full of air; it is never empty, every moment the air is fresh. Have you ever observed this? An open hand is never empty, and a closed hand is always empty; and if a little air remains in the closed fist, it is stale and old and decayed. They alone are able to enjoy who renounce.

In this world, in this life, man gets as much as he is willing to give up and let go. This is paradoxical – but all the rules of life are paradoxical. They are not opposites; they are paradoxes. It only appears that they are opposites. The person who wishes for honor and respect in the world is sure to find dishonor and disrespect. A man desires to be rich, but when he begins to accumulate wealth, he becomes as poor and mean within as he appears rich without.

He who thinks or dreams of immortality is worried about the fear of death twenty-four hours a day. Death never visits the house of the person who is willing to welcome it: one who is willing to meet death tastes nectar, while one who is afraid of death dies every hour of the day. He dies all the time because he does not know at all what life is. One who says, "I will become the master," will soon become a slave; and one who says, "I am willing to be a slave," will have infinite mastery. But these are contradictory statements so it is very difficult to understand them, and when we try to interpret them we do so in such a way that we are saved from the paradox in them – and hence we miss the point.

Thus people have misinterpreted these sutras. "Enjoy through renunciation" has come to mean that if you give charity, you will be rewarded with heaven. Give a paisa to a beggar sitting on the bank of the Ganges and you will be rewarded a thousandfold. Nothing else in this world is as badly treated as are sutras such as these, and similarly, nobody is as unjustly treated as are the sages – because it is difficult to comprehend them in their true spirit. Instead, we interpret them from our own perspective. We think we understand the sutra: if you give away something in charity, you will go to heaven after death. But pay attention: the sutra says, "He who renounces, receives." It does not say, "He who gives up with a view to getting, will receive." In fact, he who gives up with a view to getting, does not give up, because he is just working out how to get the reward.

The person who gives charity here in this world so that he may get the reward in heaven is not renouncing at all. He is simply tightening his fist for the future. If rightly understood, his action is not only a tightening of his fist in this world, but a tightening of it also for the next world. He is telling others by his action, "This action is not very important here, it is quite ordinary, but it is very important there in the next world." If he is quite sure, if he is a hundred percent certain that he will be rewarded in the next world for his good actions in this world, then he is prepared to make some investment. He is prepared to risk some of his property if he is assured fully of his reward in the next world.

No, such a person has not grasped the meaning at all. That is not what this sutra is saying. It simply says, "He who renounces, receives." It does not say, "Renounce so that you may get in the future." A person whose eye is on the receiving end of something can never think in terms of giving up. When he apparently gives up, it is not renunciation but investment. He is simply shuffling his financial affairs to get more. If a person invests a million in a factory, can it be called charity? Certainly not. He is investing with a desire to earn a million and a half. Then he can invest a million and a half. Is that charity? Thus he goes on, investing more and more so that he can have a tighter grip on his property. He wants more and more. The man who practices charity with a view to what he will get in return does not understand the meaning of charity.

This sutra makes a straight, simple statement that he who renounces, enjoys. It does not say, "Give up if you desire to enjoy." It announces that if you can give up, then you can enjoy; but if you are nursing the idea of enjoyment, you can never renounce.

This is a wonderful sutra. It proclaimed in the beginning that everything is of existence: this includes renouncing. What is there left to own and hold on to for one who has realized that everything belongs to existence? Nothing is left to take possession of. Renunciation is complete – and the person who has realized this, who has renounced everything and whose ego has disappeared, is existence itself; and to become existence is to begin to enjoy. He is immersed in supreme enjoyment, absorbed in supreme bliss. He begins to experience that supreme enjoyment from moment to moment. Every minutest particle of his life begins to dance. What remains to be enjoyed by one who has become existence itself? He begins to enjoy all. Everything! The vast sky, the blooming flowers, the rising sun, the stars at night, a smile and laughter – all become his objects of bliss. That supreme enjoyment has now spread itself on all sides for him. He is the master and possessor of nothing now, but in all directions lie the expanses of enjoyment, and from all around he drinks the divine juice.

Religion is enjoyment. When I say this – that religion is enjoyment – many people become restless because their notion of religion is that it is renunciation. Bear in mind, one who thinks religion is renunciation will commit that mistake of investment. Yet the essence of life is renunciation. Life is renunciation. It is sheer stupidity to hold on to anything in life. The great mistake is to grasp tightly; in doing so one loses what one would have got. In claiming that , "It is mine," man loses what was his already.

Everything falls of its own accord from one who has realized that everything is existence's. Then there remains nothing for him to renounce. Remember, the act of renunciation is impossible for one who says, "It is mine." If a person says, "I am renouncing this," it contains the belief that the thing was his. The truth is that he who says so cannot renounce, because his notions about my and mine still persist. The only man who can renounce is the one who can say, "Nothing is mine; what can I renounce?"

Before renouncing something, a person must have possession of the thing. If I say, "I give you the sky," you will laugh at me and say, "Let it first be decided that the sky you are giving away is yours." Similarly I may say, "The planet Mars I give in charity to you." This is equally nonsensical; it must be mine before I can practice charity with it. This illusion of renunciation happens to one who is entertaining notions of my-ness. No, renunciation does not take place just by the act of giving something up. It takes place only in the realization of the truth that everything belongs to existence. Then renunciation happens – it is not to be practiced.

Renunciation is the experience, the realization of the fact that all is existence's. Now nothing remains to be renounced. Now even you yourself, who struggled to renounce, are not spared. Now there exists no claim for anything which could conceivably be given up. Total bliss comes to one whose renunciation is of this nature. All the essence, all the beauty, all the nectar of life is now his. Therefore the sutra says that he who renounces, attains to everything. He who empties himself, who surrenders even his I, becomes the master of infinite riches.

Enough on this sutra. We shall talk more tonight. Please take note of these few instructions about the morning meditation before we begin. The first point is this: Whatever I have been saying is all meditation. Keep your hand open and you will be filled with air. When you experience, when you recognize, that everything belongs to existence, you will be thrilled with the bliss within you.

This meditation will be of forty minutes. Keep your eyes and ears completely closed so that no light nor sound can enter. For the first ten minutes take deep breaths. Exert yourself to the full, so that all the energy of the kundalini may be roused. If your body begins to dance and spin and jump, let it do so. Don't worry about it at all. For the next ten minutes, with great joy within, relax your body completely. Your body will want to jump, dance, laugh, shout, cry, sing. Allow it to do whatever it wants; cooperate with it completely and fully. During the third ten minutes, continue co-operating with your body and at the same time keep asking your-self, "Who am I?" Keep asking, "Who am I?" as though you are chanting a mantra. Do this with pleasure, with joy. Then, during the fourth ten minutes, some of you will want to stand up, some will want to lie down, and others will want to roll around. Do whatsoever you like! Finally, during the last ten minutes, remain in silence, awaiting the entry of existence within. Keep yourself com-pletely relaxed and without any resistance so that it can enter you. You will have to wait for that.

Before we start our experiment, put your hands together, and before existence make a solemn vow. Close your eyes, put your hands together, think of existence as your witness, and repeat this vow three times: "In the presence of existence, I vow that I shall exert myself to the utmost in meditation."

# The
# Shape Of Water

3

*For a person like you,*
*who desires to live a hundred years*
*involved in his activities in the world*
*and believing that "I am the doer,"*
*there is no other path than this –*
*the path of living without being smeared*
*by your doing.*

THERE IS ONLY ONE PATH that can keep you unaffected while doing the things you must do in this world. The path which is discussed by the Ishavasya is this path: live by surrendering to existence, give it all away, leave everything at its feet. Surrender everything to it. Giving up the notion of yourself as the doer, you can live your life and remain unaffected by performing your worldly duties. This is the only path; there is no other.

It will be useful to understand two or three points in this connection. Number one: to live in this world without being affected by karma, by your doings, is a great alchemy, and a matter of great worth and wisdom. It is almost like imagining a person coming out of a coal-cellar without any trace of coal-dust on him. Moreover, this is not a matter of living in the coal-cellar for an hour or two. If we consider our whole life's duration, we are talking about a period of one hundred years; and if we consider many lives of the past, our journey will be through many thousands of years. Now, it will be a matter of great wisdom, or else of extraordinary luck, if a person living in such a coal-cellar, for one hundred years performing his daily routine – waking, sleeping, sitting, standing and so on – can yet remain untouched by the coal-dust in the cellar. It is quite obvious and natural that he will be smeared with soot. It is quite feasible to imagine that not only will the person come into contact with the coal-dust in the cellar, but may well actually turn into coal-dust. He will probably look like the incarnation of coal-dust! It seems difficult to believe – living in his cellar for a hundred years – that a man will not become coal-dust itself.

How can we pass through a thing without touching it? No sooner do we pass through it than we are joined with it. When we are angry, we become merged with our anger. When we love someone, we are united with him or her. Whenever we fight or run away or enjoy a thing, we are merged with our activity. Even when we make our renunciation, we are merged with it; and if we are joined with our renunciation, we tarnish our hands with soot. We are stained. The pride of having so much wealth arises in a man's mind when he is enjoying its fruits. Similarly, renunciation brings into his mind the pride of having renounced so much. That pride is coal-dust for us; that conceit is soot itself.

No matter how a person passes his life of a hundred years, he will do something, and if it is done with pride, it will blacken him. But this sutra of the Ishavasya tells us that there is a path which enables a person not to lose his purity, and where he is not affected by his actions, despite living in a coal-cellar. This seems impossible, but it is not impossible if we rightly understand the meaning of this sutra. A man can do anything, it says, but as long as he is the doer, he will be blackened. Only one alternative is available: to cease entirely to be the doer.

One cannot avoid actions. Actions will certainly be there as long as we live. It is a mistake to say, "Give up doing things so that there is no chance of being smeared by them." Actions will be there till death. To breathe in is an action. It is not only the man who runs his shop who is involved in action; the beggar also is doing. It is not only the housekeeper who is involved in doing; the man who leaves his house and runs to the jungle is doing too. Their actions may differ, but this does not mean that the one's is an action and the other's is nonaction: both are actions so there is no point in believing we can protect ourselves from the coal-dust, when leaving it all is as much an action as living it all. By thinking thus, we will get nowhere. Giving up actions one runs away, but then that running away becomes one's action. Action binds us fast.

There is only one way out of this predicament, and that is to find freedom from being the doer, even though we cannot free ourselves from doing. But how can we free ourselves from doing when the doing is going on? Shall I not become the doer when I am doing the action?

The Ishavasya tells us that even while doing, we can be free from being the doer. Ordinarily it appears to us that we can perhaps be free from becoming doers only if we give up actions. "I shall do nothing, hence I shall not become the doer." But the Ishavasya tells us quite definitely that this is impossible. On the contrary, what is possible is that you go on doing things, but you remain separate from becoming their doer.

Don't be doers! How can this be? We are acquainted a little with such action. To act on stage is to experience the possibility of doing without being the doer. Rama weeps aloud in the forest when Sita is lost. He runs from tree to tree, clinging to the trunks and crying, "Where is Sita?" Crying to the trees, the actor possibly wails more earnestly than Rama himself, and maybe more cleverly and skillfully too, because Rama had no opportunity for rehearsal. This actor has had plenty of practice. He performs the very same actions which Rama performed, but there is no doer behind them; there is only an actor.

Remember, actions can be of two kinds: one in which there is a doer, and the other in which there is an actor. If the actor replaces the doer, the action will continue on the surface, but there will be total transformation within. Acting does not bind you to the action, it does not affect you. It remains entirely outside, it does not enter within. It does not go deep within, it vibrates on the surface and then disappears. No matter how much the actor of Rama may weep and grieve, those tears do not come from his inner self. Usually he has to apply coal dust to make the tears fall, and if he does not use coal dust it is because he has learned to shed tears through practice. They do not come from the depth but from the surface. He shouts, he makes great noise, but it comes from his throat and not from his heart. The inner self remains absolutely untouched and unaffected. He passes through the coal-cellar, but not as a doer; he remains an actor.

Remember, it is the doer who gets covered in coal-dust, not the action. If it were the action that caught the coal-dust, then what the Ishavasaya says could not happen, what the Gita says could not happen. Then there would be no escape from action as long as one lived. Then one could be free from action only after death. Then it appears there would be no liberation as long as life persists. But how can one be free after death when one cannot be free while living? If one cannot be free while living, there is certainly no scope to find freedom after death.

If action itself can be smeared with the soot of life, then liberation is impossible. But those who search deep within say that the coal dust clings to the doer and not the doing. That is, it clings only when one says, "I am the doer," when the emphasis is on the action and when I and the action are identified with each other. Only when the tarnishing happens – when the I becomes one with the action, and says "I am the doer" – only in such a situation does the coal-dust cover the doer; and then life is filled with darkness and blackness.

If there is no one within saying, "I am the doer," and at the same time there is the knower who understands that the action is going on – that the actors have come together on the stage to enact the drama – then it makes no difference how great the stage is; let it be as wide as the whole world! It makes no difference that the curtain in the drama is raised only once at the time of birth, and is lowered only at the time of death. Nor does it matter that the drama is very long between the raising and lowering of the curtain. All this makes no difference; it does not affect you at all if you see it from within as a performance. If you carry this understanding within, then the whole world is a *leela* – a play, a drama, a stage for you – and life itself is like a story. Then we are actors, and nothing affects the actors.

This sutra of the Ishavasaya says there is only one way for a man not to be affected while performing his duties in life, and that is to transform life into acting. But we are extraordinary people. We transform acting into life, but we do not transform life into acting. We try many times over to present our acting as our real life, and our repetitive actions actually become the driving forces of our lives. If we consult psychologists, they say that man's obvious behavior is all cultivated action. It is all conditioning.

We call this man's nature, but the psychologists declare that there is nothing like man's nature. If there is anything like man's nature, it is endless fickleness. Man's nature is like water. If we pour water into a glass, it assumes the shape of the glass, and if it is poured into a cup, it assumes the cup's shape; if it is poured into a pitcher, it assumes the shape of the pitcher. Water always assumes the shape of the vessel into which it is poured. Then what is the natural shape of water? It has no natural shape. Its nature can be described as the capacity to assume endless shapes. Water is not obstinate, it is not stubborn. It does not assert, "I shall remain in this particular shape." It says, "I am willing to live in any shape, whatsoever it may be."

Man also has no nature of his own. The phenomenon which we call nature is just frequently practiced behavior patterns. It is actions performed in a cultural frame in often-repeated circumstances. So, a person born in the family of a nonvegetarian eats meat. It is not his nature that chooses it; if he had been brought up in the house of a vegetarian, he would have taken to vegetarian food. Then he might become nauseous or upset at the sight of meat. But this is no testimony to a virtuous nature, any more than eating meat signifies an evil nature. Characteristics such as these are no indicators of greatness.

The shape of an action is a practiced thing, which we are teaching to people from their very infancy. If we rightly understand what that training is, it is just a preparation for the performance a person will be expected to give in his life. Our educational institutions are rehearsal studios. They are the training studios where we prepare ourselves for the performances of our lives. We train a person to act in a particular fashion in our families, society, schools and universities. We train one as a Hindu, another as an American, another as a Chinese, and another as a Christian. When they are thus trained and their frame of mind becomes strong and firm, it looks as though that frame of mind is their nature. No, all these are just much repeated performances, so firmly fixed eventually in man's mind that it does not even occur to him that he is simply acting his part.

Have you ever thought what religion you belong to? Hinduism, Jainism, Islam, Christianity and other religions are all performances taught to you. If you had not been trained in them you would never have known about them. But when you say, "I am a Hindu," you become the doer. Then you can take a sword in your hand to defend your religion. Then lives can be sacrificed and killing can be done. Quarrels can be picked with anyone who says you are not a Hindu.

Psychologists used to say that habit is second nature. This was the view of past psychologists. But modern psychologists say, instead, that nature is the first habit. As more and more research is conducted into man's nature, it is more and more convincingly known that nature is the first habit – a deep-seated one that became so firmly fixed that man forgot that he was performing. If you can keep it in mind that you are performing, there will be no more killing one another. On the contrary, you will say, "What madness! I am playing the part of being a Hindu and you are playing the part of being a Mohammedan; why should there be any quarrel in that?" No, it is when this phenomenon is not looked upon as a play, as acting, that quarrels and fighting break out. People become serious then, and they cease to be playful.

Eric Berne has written a book called Games People Play. He does not deal merely with games like football, hockey, cards and chess, but with those of being Hindus, Mohammedans, and Christians. These are also games which people play, sometimes at great cost and with much harm. Chess players have been known to take up swords against each other over the issue of their victory or defeat, so it is hardly a matter of great concern that they kill one another over the matter of their religious differences.

It seems that when the games are taken seriously they become part and parcel of life; and whatever is taught is clung to. All over the world women have been taught that they are inferior to men, and they have believed it. But there are matriarchal societies also, where man is taught that he is inferior to woman; and the people in such a social order will cling to this belief. There are families where the woman has superiority over the man. The interesting thing about this situation is that in the case where woman is superior to man, the women have become more intelligent than the men. And where woman was taught her inferiority to man, the men became more intelligent.

We mold men like water in vessels. Then acting holds the ego so fast that it does not say, "I am acting"; it says, "I am!" Then being a Hindu is not a play: it is what I am. And the coal-dust begins to affect you as soon as you say, "I am." It could be considered less important if it only affected you: but a person smeared with coal-dust soon begins to throw it over others also. The coal-dust on our hands is passed on to others. We ourselves are blackened and we blacken others. We set about transforming the acting into a role performed by a doer.

When two small children celebrate the marriage of two dolls, we say they are playing. But have you ever recognized that the marriage of a man and a woman is, to some extent, nothing more than the marriage of dolls? In both the marriages, all forms, all considerations, all arrangements, all music, all show and all the other trappings are the same. The only difference is that the one is played by small children and the other is played by grown-up children. Small children forget the game quickly; they do not remember in the evening that the marriage was celebrated in the morning. But grown-up children go even to the lawcourts to fight for their marital rights. They do not forget the event, but cling to it fast.

Nobody is prepared to see their marriage as a play. It is difficult to do so, because if the marriage is considered as a play, then the family which is the result of marriage must inevitably be looked upon as a play. Then the community made up of these families is also a play. Thus the circle expands, until the whole human world encompassing this community becomes a play. That is why we have to cling firmly to every detail of our position and say, "No, the institution of marriage is not a play, it is a serious matter; it is a life-and-death issue." The family is not a play, the community is not a play. Then every step, every action, becomes as hard and intractable as stone.

The whole structure becomes more and more rigid; and we, the society, will destroy any person who regards this manmade arrangement as only a play, because such a person threatens to undermine all our serious arrangements. He refuses to obey the rules of our game, so we take revenge upon him. Our life is a long, continuous acting; but we have so structured the acting that we can say it is our doing – we are the doers.

The Ishavasya affirms the opposite. It says, "At least know acting as acting; there is nothing in this world of which you should be crazy enough to be its doer. If you become the doer, you are certainly insane. Let existence be the doer. Leave everything to it which always is, which was when you were unborn, will be when you have ceased to be. Leave all your doings to existence. Do not take the load of doing upon yourselves. That load will be far too much for you; it will be more than you can bear. To carry that load is beyond your capacity. You will be crushed under its weight and you will die. Nothing can save you from it."

But our ego finds it difficult to swallow this. On the contrary, it takes pleasure in the weight of the boulder on its chest. It says, "I am lifting such a heavy stone, and what you are lifting is nothing compared to my burden! I am carrying such a heavy load!" The president, the prime minister, are people who take pleasure in carrying heavy boulders. For lifting such boulders they receive thousands of insults and find themselves in thousands of difficulties. But they can say, "Look at the paltry little stone you carry on your back: you are no more than the president of your village – where is the comparison between you and me? I am the president of the whole state and you are the president of a village!" The desire to become village president is small scale; to become president of a country requires craziness on a larger scale. But the constant preoccupation of the village president is with the matter of when he will be able to carry bigger boulders. Throughout our lives we value the person in proportion to the weight of the stone – the greater the load on his back the greater he is.

The truth runs exactly contrary to this belief. Those who know look for the person with no load on his back; he carries no burden and is as light as a flower. But it is difficult to find such a person, because everyone clings on to some load or other; no matter how small, the load is there. If he is not the village president, he is at least the head of his family – and it is not always the case that only the father is the head of the home. If the father goes out for a while, his eldest child will assume the role of head over his younger brothers and sisters. He immediately begins to dominate them. He begins to play the role of his father. For instance, your eldest son is quarreling with his younger brother in your presence, but if you leave that place, you will, all of a sudden, find that the eldest begins to dominate. He begins to play the role which you were playing. Its scale may be small, its status may be small, but the drama is the same. You may be playing out this drama before two or three hundred people, while your son is enacting the same drama before two or three children. There is no difference in the drama, only the proportions differ. Small children will play small dramas, grown-up children will play big ones, and the elders will enact really great dramas.

Man is upset when he cannot show that he carries a big load on his back, so another interesting feature emerges: he generally boasts a bigger load than he actually has. There was a lady professor with me in the university where I was working. I was fed up hearing about her various illnesses. Can a person have so many illnesses? Whenever she met me she would complain about some great illness; she never suffered from small ones. Then I asked her husband about her suffering from so many illnesses, and added that, ordinarily, a wife is herself sufficient illness for a husband, "but in your case all these illnesses are added to it. How do you cope with it all?"

He replied, "Please don't believe in her stories. She never suffers from a petty illness. Even a little cold she will never talk of as anything less than TB!"

I was puzzled and began to wonder what secret lies behind the need to magnify one's illnesses. Here is the secret: if you have a serious illness, you have a heavy burden; you will be considered important. But if you suffer from a small illness you become a worthless person, because your illness is of a trifling nature. It does not carry much value, there is no need for others to worry about you. So serious illnesses are called royal diseases – TB was looked upon as a royal disease. Poor people did not suffer from it, only kings suffered from it!

Recently I was reading about a woman who approached a doctor and requested him to remove her appendix. The doctor asked, "Is your appendix troubling you?"

The woman said, "No, but that doesn't matter. All the women of the club where I am a member have been operated upon – some have their appendix removed, some have something else removed, but nothing has been removed from my body. I don't have anything to talk about!"

Man treasures the burden on his back, so it is difficult to discover a person as light as a flower who can say, "I carry no load." Only a man who has entrusted all his load to existence can say so, and the interesting thing about this is that the whole load is in any case existence's alone. We poke our noses in unnecessarily. Our condition is similar to that of a passenger who was traveling in a train with his load on his head. The other passengers persuaded him to put it on the floor, and then said, "Why do you burden yourself unnecessarily?"

He replied, "I only bought a ticket for myself." He was so simple and guileless. He said, "I haven't bought a ticket for my luggage. How can I keep this trunk and the bedding on the floor? It would be cheating the government. So I am keeping it on my head."

Now that simple man had no idea that keeping the load on his head would make no difference to the train's total load. The total load of this universe is borne by existence. The whole performance of managing the affairs of the universe is done by existence alone. But we are very strange passengers. We derive great happiness from keeping our luggage on our heads during our journey in existence's train. We even say to those who carry small burdens, "You have wasted your life. You should have increased your load." And why? So that by the time the man dies the load on him looks so great that everyone will remark on how much he has left behind! This is why, when someone dies, we gossip even about loads they were never carrying. We help make the load look greater.

I have heard: a man died, and the village priest, standing near his grave, began to talk about him while lowering his coffin into the grave. He praised his virtues, his good deeds, and his services to others. Hearing this, the dead man's wife became a little worried. She asked her son to bend a little to look into the coffin and to make sure that it contained his father's body, because she had never heard about all these good deeds he was said to have done. At night she went to the priest and asked him, "What were you saying about my husband? As far as I know, my husband never did any of the things you were talking about."

The priest replied, "Never mind. He may not have done any of those good deeds, but what will people say of your husband if no such activities are mentioned?"

Voltaire had a friend. He had insulted Voltaire throughout his life. He used to criticize him in every possible manner. He used to oppose Voltaire on every issue. He was not a good person. When he died, some people went to Voltaire and said, "Let there be peace between you now; after all, he was your friend. Granted that he insulted you a lot, called you names, criticized you bitterly, and tried to undermine you. But now that he is dead, please write a few words in praise of him." So Voltaire wrote, "He was a good man, and a great one – provided he is really dead." If a person is living we are unable to praise him. Once he is dead we have to praise him, and burdens which he never carried are ascribed to him.

But the Ishavasya is referring to a person about whom there remains nothing to praise after his death. It talks about one who has thrown all his authorship on existence. One who says, "I am not at all, it alone is there. If there is a doer, it is existence only. At the most, I am only a pawn in its game. I am willing to go wherever it directs; I am willing to be what it wishes, I am willing to do whatever it commands. If it wishes to defeat me I am willing to be defeated; if it makes me the winner, I am willing to win. Neither victory nor defeat is mine. Defeat is existence's, victory is existence's also."

The surrendering of such a person is total. He attributes everything to existence: "I too am – as all doings are – existence's." Such a man will do all that is necessary in life – living, breathing, walking, standing, sitting, doing his duties, eating his food and sleeping at night. All these activities will be there, but there will be no doer within.

This is the only path. Let me repeat, the sage of the Ishavasya is perfectly correct when he declares that this is the only path. And the people who have really lived unaffected in this world – untouched, always fresh and new, as innocent as when they were born – are those who never accumulated, never nourished any sort of ego during their journey through life; who lived in a state of egolessness. Ego means I am the doer, egolessness means surrendering – surrendering everything at the feet of existence.

# The
# True Desire

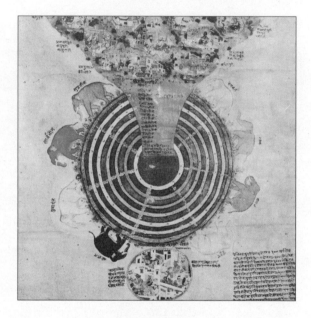

4

*The asuras –*
*the demons –*
*are those who are enveloped*
*in the darkness of self-ignorance.*
*Those who are killers of the self*
*go to the world of the Asuras*
*after death.*

THE UPANISHADS divide man into two categories. First, those who kill the *atman* – the self; they are suicidal because they kill their own selves. And there are those who know the self; they belong to the second category. The knowers of the self and the killers of the self. We have a word, *atmahatya*, meaning killing of the self, but we do not use it in its right sense. The Upanishad has used it in its true sense. When a person has destroyed his body, we say he has committed suicide – killed the atman. This is not right, because to kill the body does not mean to kill the atman. To kill your own body is certainly to commit suicide. It certainly means your own death, and yet, at the same time, it is not your own. It is merely a changing of the cover, of the body. It is the killing of the body, not of the self – not of the atman.

The Upanishad calls him the killer – the destroyer of the self who goes on living without knowing himself, who is covered in ignorance. Such a person is killing his atman. To live without knowing oneself is the real suicide. And we all live without knowing ourselves. We live but we do not know at all who we are, from where we are, why we are, for what purpose we are, where we move, what the meaning of life is. No, about all these questions we have not the faintest idea. We know nothing about ourselves. We may know about many other things, but we are utterly ignorant about one thing; we know nothing about ourselves.

The Upanishads will brand us as killers of the self, as *asuras* – as demons. Knowingly or unknowingly we mutilate ourselves till we can no longer know ourselves. First our ignorance troubles us, then it troubles others. Bear in mind, an ignorant person attacks himself first and attacks others afterwards. In fact as long as we have not already attacked ourselves first, it is not possible to attack others. It is impossible to give pain to others before we do so to ourselves. The man who has never cut his own legs on thorns does not scatter them across the paths of others. And one who has not given himself cause to weep can never plan to create trouble for others. The fact is, first of all we create trouble for ourselves, and when it has become solid and concentrated and begins to manifest through us, then we start distributing it. Only the miserable make others unhappy. This seems all right because we are sharing that which we have. But this giving is subsequent, secondary; first of all we give pain and misery to ourselves.

Are we not all tormenting ourselves? We are! We may strive to give joy and pleasure to others but in the end we give only suffering. The road to hell is paved with good intentions, and it is made with the efforts of good wishes that we entertain for ourselves. What our desires are is not the root problem. We all desire to give joy to ourselves, but no one can give himself joy without knowing himself. How can a person who does not know "Who am I?" have any idea of "What is my joy? I can know what my joy is only when I know my nature, my own being, my self."

As long as I do not know anything about the kind of roots deeply embedded in me, how can I have any sense of what flowers may blossom in me? What flowers can I hope for when I am so ignorant of the seeds that lie within me? What flower should I desire to be? If I have not the least idea about the seed itself, the result can only be unhappiness for me, whatever I may try to be, because I cannot be what I try to be, and in consequence I become miserable, afflicted, worried. I will die in tensions and worries. My whole life will be a mad race of cravings, but I will reach nowhere. Though the journey is very long, I will not find the destination, because it is hidden in my nature, in my self.

First of all I should know who I am. I should ascertain whether I am trying to discover what I am, or whether I am trying to discover what I am not. If I fail to discover what I am not, I shall certainly be miserable. Still more interesting is the fact that if I actually succeed in discovering what I am not, I shall still be miserable. Those who are unsuccessful in life certainly become miserable, but there is no end to the miseries of those who succeed either. That unsuccessful people become miserable can be understood. But the successful ones also become unhappy. Just go and find out from successful people.

Then it appears that life is a great joke, a mockery. In this world the unsuccessful become unhappy, which seems quite logical; it seems just and proper. But those who succeed in life also are unhappy. In such circumstances this world appears very crazy and un-balanced. When both the successful and the unsuccessful have to be unhappy, then there seems no way to be happy. So let us first of all ask the successful people why they are unhappy, as there is nothing surprising about the unsuccessful being unhappy. Let us ask people like Alexander the Great and Stalin; let us inquire of multimillionaires like Carnegie and Ford. Ask those who got what they wanted. Ask them, "Did you find happiness?" and you will be very puzzled to hear their replies. They say, "We have been successful, but successful in finding unhappiness." Those who are unsuccessful also say, "We failed to achieve happiness; we found unhappiness instead." Those who achieved success say, "We succeeded in becoming unhappy; we found only unhappiness in our hands."

Those who run fast in the race of life reach their destination only to arrive at unhappiness; and those who reach nowhere and wander here and there in the wilderness also wander in misery. When such is the case, what is the difference between the destination and the path? What is the difference between roaming about and reaching the destination? There appears to be no difference. The difference cannot be seen, because the person who does not know who he is will be made miserable even by his success. The day on which he becomes successful he will realize that the building which he constructed – his great achievement – has not fulfilled his need. It gives his nature no nourishment. The building has been constructed, he has accumulated wealth, he has found fame and fortune; but these achievements fail to nourish any part of his inner life, they fail to bring contentment. He should have sought to discover, "What is my true desire, what is my longing? What do I really wish for?" Without knowing your true desire you will simply go on and on desiring, jumping from one desire to another.

Some days before his death, Freud wrote in a letter to his friend: "After hearing about the miseries of thousands of people throughout my life, I have come to the conclusion that mankind is destined to remain unhappy always, the reason being that man does not know what he wants." When a man like Freud says such a thing, the matter is worth thinking about. He says, "I have arrived at the conclusion that man does not know what he wants, after studying the sufferings, worries, anxieties and mental conflicts of thousands of unhappy people."

Man will never know what he wants because, in the first place, he does not know who he is. Suppose I go out to get clothes made for myself. I do not know anything about my body, I do not know anything about my measurements, I do not know anything about my bodily requirements; in brief, I don't have any idea about myself and yet I go out to get clothes made. When they are ready I find that they do not fit me. There is something wrong somewhere; they are unfit for my use. By all means go and have your clothes made, but before going out find out who you are, find out for whom the clothes are to be prepared, for whom the building is to be constructed, for whom happiness is to be sought.

It is very interesting to observe that no sooner does a person know who he is than the journey, and all the arrangements and preparations of his entire life, are transformed. He no longer goes looking for the things which we seek. He shows no willingness to smile and look pleased because someone offers him at a throwaway price – or for nothing – the things for which we labor hard. If someone is willing to give him something free, he will turn away from that man in case the thing is thrust upon him. He is out to achieve something quite different, something unusual; and it is interesting to find that those who know themselves never fail. Up to now they have never been unsuccessful. They succeed as much as those who do not know themselves remain unsuccessful. The man who knows himself becomes successful because, on knowing the self, he opens for himself that secret and that door where bliss is. That bliss is hidden within the self.

So, the Upanishads declare there are two types of people: those who know themselves, and those who are ignorant of themselves. Those who do not know themselves pursue their way deep into ignorance, and everything they do is done in ignorance. They go on acquiring in ignorance, they make decisions in ignorance, and in their ignorance, their race becomes faster and faster. The normal view is: "I did not achieve what I wanted in my life because I did not run as fast as I should have. Let me run a little faster, and faster, and still faster, so that I may achieve my goal. Perhaps I did not get it because I did not stake all. If I stake all, I might get."

We never stop to consider whether what we are trying to achieve has any inner harmony with ourselves or not. Even if the thing is achieved, it will be of no use, and if it is not achieved it cannot be of any use; and the time spent in getting it or in being unable to get it is lost. To this extent we have become our own assassins. We have become asuras, demons, killers of the atman – the self. The word *asur* means those who live in darkness. It means those who live in a place where the light of the sun does not reach, a place where there is no illumination. They grope in darkness, they wander about in darkness, like germs of darkness. Those who do not know themselves are living in this darkness.

To know oneself is to become the sun. The journey of such an individual is into the world of light; but there are those whose inner light is not burning, is extinguished; they are deep in darkness. Those who keep on running, groping, hankering, following the blind, are like the blind following the blind. And there are some among them who are great talkers; such people have the following of those who talk less, and so the race goes on. The blind with a little courage gather around themselves the blind with less courage.

Kahlil Gibran has written that he was roaming from village to village, promising to show God to people if they followed him. Nobody ever followed him so no trouble ever arose. The villagers told him to come again as they were then very busy with other things. The crop was ripe and ready for harvesting, so he should come again after some time. When he visited them again, they said, "The crops are not good this year; there is scarcity and we are in difficulty. Please come next year." He continued to visit villages. He was not in a hurry to persuade anyone to follow him, but one impetuous man from a village decided to follow him. When Gibran said, "Follow me if you wish to see God," that man threw away his axe and said, "I am following you!"

Gibran became nervous. Then he thought, "How long will he follow me? In a week or two he will get tired and will leave me." But the villager continued to follow him.

One year passed. The man said, "I shall follow you wherever you lead me." Two years passed and Gibran became more nervous. He tried to avoid his follower, but the man always stood behind him, saying, "I am prepared to follow you wherever you lead me. I shall abide by whatever you ask me to do."

Six years passed in this way. Then one day the man took Gibran by the neck and said, "You have taken a long time, now show me God. Where do you wish to go now?"

The guru said, "Please pardon me; I have even lost my own way in your good company. I myself have lost my way since you followed me. Before you began to follow me, my road was quite clear for me. Everything was clearly visible. I was near the destination, God was in front of me. What a calamity that I let you join me! Now I too have lost my way. So, please leave me and go your own way."

That villager warned him, "Don't visit our village again!"

Gibran said, "Brother, I beg your pardon. I shall never visit your village, but I can go to other villages, because there are no such people as you in all these villages. They simply hear me and I go on my way alone."

Man, living himself in ignorance, is often given to telling others about the light of true knowledge; to do so comforts him and helps him forget his own darkness. It is important to be aware of such people. When you start to discourse on matters about which you know nothing it is difficult to estimate how much harm you do to others. But it is difficult to find a person who follows the rule of talking only about what he knows, and who keeps silent about that which he does not know. No, there is a great attraction to showing others, to telling others, if an opportunity arises. The attraction is tremendous. If we meet someone who appears a little weak on the subject of God and the soul, and who can be overwhelmed and awed by our talk, then we certainly thrust our knowledge upon him. Then we will show him the path to attain God and instruct him how to proceed.

This work of showing the path to others is delightful and gratifying because it creates a delusion in us that we already know the path: and in showing it to others over a long time, we forget, by and by, that we ourselves do not know the truth. There are very few people who really know, but there are lots of people who are always ready to advise others. It would benefit the world greatly if those who do not know but go on talking to others would remain silent on the subject of spiritual knowledge. But it is very difficult for them to keep quiet, and it is equally difficult for others to silence them. If you try to silence them they will begin to shout all the more, because in shouting aloud they can deceive themselves. Their own sound falling into their ears creates confidence in them: "It's all right, I know the truth!"

The Upanishads declare that there are two types of people. Weigh and consider carefully to which of the two types you belong, to which category you belong. It is necessary to make a decision faithfully and truly about yourself so that the next step can be taken correctly and in the right direction. Who are you? The self-killer or the self-knower?

If you are a self-knower then no question arises, the matter is over. Then there is no journey for you. If you are a self-killer then you have to make the journey. It has not yet begun, let alone the question of its being over. But it is easy to consider ourselves as knowers of the self, because all have read the Upanishads, the Gita, the Bible, the Koran and what Mahavira and Buddha have said. It is difficult to imagine how costly and harmful this has been for mankind. These 'religious' books are at the tip of everyone's tongue; they are all known completely. The fact is, nobody knows anything about them but all are in delusion that they know everything, because the whole book is memorized.

People write me letters, saying, "You said something about a certain matter, but it doesn't seem to be correct because there is something else written about it in such and such a book." Now, if you know what is right then it is not necessary for you to listen to what I say. And if you don't know what is right then how can you decide that what such and such a book has written is correct? This matter cannot be decided simply by thinking and pondering on it. One has to do something in this matter, simply thinking and pondering will not do.

Yesterday when I was leaving this place, a friend approached the car and said, "What you were saying in your lecture today is said in the Yogasara also." Now, this person has already read the Yogasara. So I said, "Take heed to do as I am telling you – because if you had acted upon what the Yogasara has to say, you would not have needed to come to me. You have shown the Yogasara great reverence; but you did nothing. Please don't honor me in the same way. And now you ask whether this has not been said already in the Yogasara. What difference does it make? You have read the Yogasara and now you have heard me. The question is: when will you put into practice what you have heard?"

The questioner was not a child, children never ask such foolish questions. He was an old man. If you want to gather very foolish stories, you should approach the old people, because their foolishness has been ripened and seasoned. They have experienced ignorance in all its strength and heaviness. They are familiar with all the scriptures. They know all that has been said. They have become 'knowers of the self.' There is no harm in having become so. It is very good, very praiseworthy. If someone becomes a knower of the self, it is cause for celebration. But then there is no need for him to come to me, and since he has come, I know that his reading of the Yogasara was useless and that whatever he has read up to now has been of no avail.

It is very likely that such people will make me as useless as they have made all their reading. They are so busy with this activity. If I say that what the Yogasara has said is right, then – I know it – the matter will be over. But if I say, "It is not said in this way in the Yogasara," they will seize the opportunity to start a debate. You can argue for the whole of your life.

I am not eager for any debates, I am not anxious for any isms. I am eager about this one small matter – that you may be able to decide clearly whether you are a killer of the self or a knower of the self. If you are a knower of the self, you are beyond consideration. Then I have no concern with you. The matter is over! If you are a killer of the self then something can be done, and I am telling you what can be done. Remember this: it is not my telling you that makes it right, nothing becomes right because of my saying so. You will not know it in any way until you have translated it into action. Know it after putting it into practice – after its execution.

Religion is experimentation, not thought. Religion is a method of acting, not of thinking. Religion is science, not philosophy. It is certainly a laboratory, but not a sophisticated one where we go and collect materials and instruments, and start performing experiments. You yourself are the laboratory. The whole experiment is conducted within yourself.

Enough for today. We shall talk on other sutras tomorrow. Now I shall say a few words on our experiment here and then we shall start doing it. I start with the belief that you are killers of the self. You may be offended by my words. It is good if you are offended.

It is good if you hurt a little. Sometimes I find people so emotionally dead that they are not even affected by such words. If you label them as killers of the self, they will say, "You are right, we accept your label." I tell you that you are living till now without knowing yourself. I want you to enter within your self, and to be able to say to your self, "I am living without knowing my self"; because the anguish of not knowing oneself is so acute that it will guide you in your experimenting. Otherwise it is not possible to do it.

Bear in mind, the experiment is such that you will know it only if you do it. You will not be able to know because your neighbor does it. In this afternoon's meditation I saw some ten absolutely childish people who were looking here and there to see what others were doing. What will they see? Someone is running, someone is dancing, someone else is shouting aloud. What are you looking at? Maybe you are thinking that these people are mad. I am telling you to think again – *you* are the mad ones! That person is doing something. Have you come to watch mad people? Why have you come all the way here? Just to watch someone dancing? Your labor in coming here was wasted. Such a long journey and worthless. If you wanted to see mad people you could have done so in your own town. It was not necessary for you to make such a long journey and to climb this mountain.

You will never be able to know what is happening within another's body. If he is laughing you will be able to hear the sound of laughing, but you will never know the dream which he is dreaming within himself. If he is weeping you will be able to see his tears, but you will never know the thing which has been excited within him and which flows out through his tears. If he is dancing you will see his hands going up and down, or you will see him jumping, but you will never know what sound began to play within him, what wires began to hum within him: you will not be able to hear that unknown sound of his inner flute, no matter how close you keep your ears to his chest. Therefore I tell you to forget the other completely, to leave aside all concern with others.

So I want to say that from tomorrow you wear blindfolds even during our afternoon meditations. Nobody should sit here without a blindfold on; and plug your ears with cottonwool. Leave aside your curiosity to hear and to see; you will get nowhere through such activities. You have to keep your eyes open during the night program; those who have kept their eyes shut to the maximum during the day will be able to go as deep as is possible. Those who have not done so today should bear this in mind and keep their eyes shut as far as possible. The night program will be with open eyes.

Remember this: when your eyes are open, your energy continues to flow out all the time. If you wish to do this experiment with your maximum energy, then keep your eyes shut as much as you can during the day so that energy may be accumulated. Your eyes can use this energy in the night program; otherwise it cannot be made use of. So be very careful about this tomorrow. Keep your eyes, ears and mouth shut to your utmost capacity. The morning program and the afternoon silence will be gone through blindfolded, and your eyes will remain open for forty minutes during the night program.

Now we will sit here for forty minutes and you keep on simply gazing at me; don't even blink. Keep the eyes wide open for forty minutes. You will begin to have many experiences, and those who have carried through the experiment in the daytime – and many friends have done it very conscientiously – will discover some very important results. Those who prefer to do it standing should move to the outer circumference on all sides and stand there, as they are likely to jump and dance vigorously. People sitting in the center around me on all sides in this corner should remain where they are. Now those who are standing should scatter in all directions. Those who have the least idea that standing will be a more appropriate position for them should move away now, so that they won't need to get up in the middle of the program, because once we start you will not be allowed to stand up and disturb those around you.

Keep complete silence – nobody should talk. I want to watch and see you for forty minutes. I shall be sitting in complete silence.

Then let whatever happens, happen to you. If you desire to take in deep breaths, do it; if you want to dance, then dance; but your attention should be on me, your eyes should gaze at me. If you have a mind to shout, or to dance, or to weep or to laugh, do that. Do whatever you want to do, but keep your eyes towards me.

I may give you a few instructions. When I feel that you are now well into your own tempo, I shall raise both my hands upwards. At that time exert yourself fully. That will be my signal that your kundalini within is rising – is awakening. Now put all your energy into your activity. And when I feel that you are so full of energy that godliness can descend upon you, I shall lower my hands. Then put all your energy, without keeping any remainder in reserve, in your activity – and much will happen!

# A Milestone
# Marked Zero

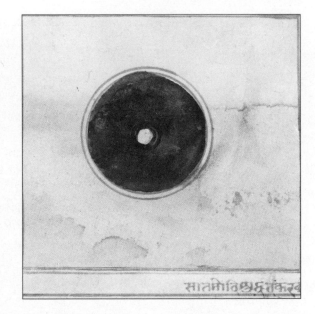

5

*That highest spiritual element,*
*the atman, is unalterable by nature,*
*and has a quicker motion than the mind.*
*The sense organs cannot*
*reach it, for it precedes them all.*
*In its stillness it surpasses all moving things.*
*Only in its presence does the air govern all the*
*activities of all living beings.*

 IN ITS STILLNESS, the *atman* – the highest spiritual element – is the fastest among the fast. It surpasses the motion of sense organs and the mind because it is prior to both. It is, before either was created. It is beyond both of them.

It is very necessary and useful for the seeker to understand this sutra. The first thing is that we are ignorant of this highest spiritual element; we don't have any knowledge about it. It is us, and yet we do not know it at all. It is the ultimate depth of our consciousness, from where our being is born and developed.

If you imagine yourself as a tree, understanding is made easy. The leaves on a tree spread out into the sky; behind the leaves branches lie hidden, and at the end of the branches is the top of the tree. The tree also has roots below, hidden in the interior of the earth. It is not too difficult for a tree to believe that it is leaves only, because the roots are invisible; they are hidden deep in the interior. So it is possible that the tree may think, "I am a cluster of leaves," forgetting that the roots are there also. But its forgetting them makes no difference. The roots will go on doing their duty in spite of that. Leaves cannot live long without their roots. It is interesting to notice that leaves cannot live without roots, but roots can live without leaves. Even if we cut down the whole tree, the roots will be doing their work and a new tree will sprout and blossom. But if we cut out all the roots, the leaves will simply wither, dry up and die. They cannot give birth to new leaves. The roots that are hidden deep below in darkness are the real life.

If we consider man as a tree, the things we call thoughts are nothing more than the leaves of the tree – and we look upon this sum total of thoughts as 'I am'. Roots lying in the depths are the real things, they are the highest spiritual element. But just as the roots of a tree are concealed deep underground and in darkness, so is our highest spiritual element, the atman, concealed in the primordial depth, in existence. From there we receive the essence of life, from there comes life itself. From there flow the streams of life-energy, and up into our leaves. If those roots are not there, our leaves cannot be there. So on the day on which those roots shrivel, our leaves wither, our branches dry up, people say of us, "The man died."

As long as those roots keep on drinking and sucking in the juice of life-energy, the highest spiritual element goes on expanding, and we feel we are living. Our thoughts are like our leaves, our desires are like our branches, and our ego is born out of the union of these leaves and branches. This is a very small part of our existence. Our most important part, our basic essence, is hidden underground; it is called atman by the Upanishad, meaning the highest spiritual element. It is that which we can forget, but without which we cannot live. It is that without which we cannot achieve anything. But it is so deep underground, in such a depth of existence, that we can afford to forget it. The highest spiritual element is forgotten; we lose sight of it.

It is interesting to observe that the thing without which we can still exist is not very deep, it is well above the surface, visible, and can be easily caught hold of, so when we try to catch hold of ourselves, it is our profusion of thoughts that we think of as 'I'. We think that the mind is 'I'. But mind – the mental element – is only our mass of leaves. The highest spiritual element is our roots. And bear in mind, one whose understanding does not reach to the very roots can never know that source from which the roots drink. Roots are the atman, and one who reaches to his roots will soon discover the earth that feeds the roots.

One who has come to know the highest spiritual element will also be able to know the supreme element – Paramatman – God.

But we live in leaves and think that mass of leaves is 'I'. So when a small leaf withers away and falls down, we think we are dead, we are gone, we are lost. And when all leaves wither away, we think life itself is extinguished. We do not know what life is. We live in the belief that the outer covering of life is 'I'.

The Upanishad says that one who lives in this outer covering is a killer of the self. He is the knower of the self who goes deep within the covering, down to the very roots, to where existence makes its original springhead; there he discovers the source of life. The knower of this is the knower of the self. Only he who knows this finds the light; he achieves life. He achieves the essence of life.

Three things are mentioned about this highest spiritual element. The first is that it is always still, while all around it a great network of transformation is going on. It is of great importance to know the secret of stillness at the center. Wherever transformation is happening, the center will be inevitably still, just as the axle remains stationary when the wheel of a carriage is moving. The wheel can move because the axle is still. The secret of the moving wheel is in the stillness of the axle. If the axle begins to move, the wheel will not move. Then the carriage will be overturned and destroyed. The revolving of the wheel depends upon the immobility of the axle.

How many miles has the axle traveled when the wheel has journeyed hundred of miles? The axle remains steady in its place. It is very interesting to see that the moving wheel needs the help of a motionless axle. The wheel of change moves on that which is unchangeable. So the first thing to remember is that everything in life changes; the leaves will be coming and going as long as transformation is there. They will sprout this spring and will fall next autumn. Nothing remains static even for a second. But there is some unknown element deep, deep somewhere within, which runs through the center of all things and carries the transformation around its own stillness.

Have you ever seen summer cyclones moving very fast through the atmosphere? Lifting a cloud of dust with it, the circular cyclone races up towards the sky. You will be very surprised to see the marks left by it in the dust on the ground. How fast it moves! At times it carries away fully grown people. You will marvel if you observe the marks made by it. There is a space the size of a pin, like the axle of a wheel, in the center of the cyclone. This space remains absolutely untouched. Even though the cyclone moves so violently there remains at its center a place which is untouched and undisturbed. An axis is produced there, and the entire cyclone revolves round that steady axis. As a matter of fact, nothing can revolve if there isn't a still center to it.

Life moves very fast; thoughts revolve very rapidly, desires hover about us in quick succession, and passions swirl with great force. Life is a fast-moving wheel. The Upanishads say there is a motionless element in its center. We have to seek it. A cyclone as powerful as life cannot run without the help of that element. This cyclone works around the support of that unmoving element. That steady element is the atman. It is always still, it is immovable. It has never gone anywhere. It has never changed. Remember that we have not known what life is until we have encountered that unaltered and unalterable element. At present we know only those changes that occur on the outer circumference; we are not yet introduced to that highest spiritual element. Up to now we are familiar only with the spokes of the wheel; we have not yet seen the hub on which everything depends.

What does this phrase 'in its stillness' mean? Whatever interpretation we may give it, there is a total possibility of making a mistake. Most of the commentators of the Upanishad have committed this mistake. The phrase does not mean stagnant; it does not mean that it is like a pond whose water does not flow. When we say the highest spiritual element is still, it does not mean it is stagnant. It is such a perfect element, it is so complete in all respects that there is no scope in it for any transformation. It is so overflowing, so great, so unconcerned, that there is absolutely no potential for any other change to take place in it.

That thing changes in which there is incompleteness – which is lacking in something. Transformation takes place where there is some scope for further adaptation, where there is some potential, some opportunity, to be something else. A child grows to be a young man, a young man grows to be an old man, because there is some room left for change; so change is continuously taking place. Leaves sprout, flowers bloom, they wither and fall, and new, fresh ones come again. The highest spiritual element is still. This means it is perfect, complete in all respects.

How can you change the perfect? In what part will the transformation of the perfect take place? There is no further room for transformation. There is no further scope for change. 'In its stillness' means it is fully blossomed. There is now no room for further blossoming. Bear in mind it is not like a stagnant pond, it is like a fully opened lotus. It has blossomed so much that there are no more buds to open. So here steadiness, stillness, means perfection. Where would the petals bloom, even if they wish to bloom? – because the highest spiritual element is perfect to the maximum, to the highest degree possible. It is so perfect that there is now no room for the petals to open more, even if they wish to do so. Here, stillness means that the total potential has become actual. Whatsoever was concealed in the seed is totally manifested – nothing invisible is left behind. So, stillness here does not imply inertia or stagnation; it means total perfection. So think of a fully opened flower and not of a pond, and then you will comprehend its meaning.

The next point which this sutra of the Ishavasya tells us is that the sense organs cannot reach the atman, 'for it precedes them all'. As you are in front of my eyes, I can naturally see you. But I cannot see myself with my eyes because the I is behind the eyes. I see you because you are in front of my eyes. I cannot see myself with my own eyes because I am behind the eyes. If I lose my eyes, if I become blind, then I shall not be able to see you at all; but it will make no difference to my capacity to see myself. If I lose my eyesight, I shall not be able to see with my eyes. But I had never seen myself with my eyes, so in spite of becoming blind I shall still have the capacity to see myself. In this matter, two points are to be properly grasped.

Sense organs become media to see, to know those objects which are in front of them. They do not become the means to see those objects which are behind them. The word 'behind' here also has two connotations. It does not mean only behind – at the back – it also means preceding. When a foetus takes root in the womb for the birth of a child, life comes first and sense organs follow it. It is quite proper because, if life does not precede, who will create the organs? So life precedes. The soul enters the womb first; the whole of the soul enters and then the sense organs begin to evolve one by one as the body begins to evolve. Sense organs develop slowly over seven months in the mother's womb, and they take their complete shape in nine months. But some things do not become complete even then. For example, the sex organs do not develop fully. It takes another fourteen years for their full development, even after emerging from the womb. There are some parts of the brain which develop by and by, and continue to develop throughout life. Even the dying person is still developing, even then. But life comes first, the sense organs follow it, and other features appear later.

The master comes first and the servants are called in afterwards. Who usually calls the servants? Who employs them? The master can know the servants but the servants, in return, cannot know the master. The soul can know the sense organs, but the sense organs, on their part, cannot know the soul, because it existed prior to them, before they came into being, and in depths to which sense organs have no access. They are on the surface. They too are coverings of life. So no one can know the soul with the help of sense organs, no matter how fast they run.

The mind is also a sense organ. How fast it runs! So, there is a contradictory statement in this sutra; even the mind which runs so fast is unable to reach the soul which is still. Such a fast-running mind fails to reach it. It is a very remarkable race. The competition is very puzzling: this racing mind cannot reach this unmoving soul! But this is what usually happens in life. The motionless things can only be had by remaining still, not by running after them.

You are walking along a road...there are flowers blooming by the side of road. They are still, rooted to one spot. The slower you walk, the more you will see of them, and if you stand still you will be able to see all there is to see of them. If you are in a car driving past them at ninety miles an hour, you will not catch even a glimpse of them, and if you are flying in an airplane over them you will know nothing about them. Just suppose, if a still faster vehicle is invented in the future, then you will never know whether flowers were there or not. An airplane flying at a speed of ten thousand miles an hour will miss the flowers growing on the side of the road. Although they are standing still, you will miss them because of your great speed.

The mind runs at a tremendous speed. Up to now we don't have airplanes or vehicles which can match the speed of the mind. Preserve us from such a vehicle, or from one which runs faster than the mind, so that our mind is left far behind as we race along! There would be great uneasiness, and great difficulty; man would find himself in great trouble. No, it will certainly not happen that an airplane can fly faster than our mind. By the time the plane had reached the moon our mind would have completed its journey to Mars. And when the airplane reached Mars, the mind by then would have entered another solar system. The mind races ahead of all airplanes, however fast their speed may be.

Yet the mind, with all its tremendous power of speed, can never reach that motionless atman. So what the Upanishads say is quite right. That which is absolutely still cannot be reached by running; it can be reached only by standing still. If the mind becomes totally quiet – absolutely still – then, and only then, will it be able to know that which is still. You also know this – that when the mind is absolutely quiet, it ceases to be. It is only there as long as it is running. Truly speaking, running is the other name of mind. To say the mind is running is a tautology. When we say the mind is running, we commit a slip of the tongue, just as we do when we say that lightning is flashing. In actual fact, that flashing *is* the lightning. It is not necessary to make two statements: "The lightning is flashing." Have you ever seen lightning which does not flash? Then why bother to say so? It is using words that creates the difficulty. We separate the lightning and the flashing when we express that phenomenon in words. Then we say, "Look, the lightning is flashing!" while the flashing and the lightning are really two names for one phenomenon.

We make the same mistake when we say the mind is running. In fact, that is called the mind which is always running. Running *is* the mind! Then a still mind has no meaning, just as nonflashing lightning has no meaning. If someone said, "The lightning is not flashing this time," you would say, "Then it is not there at all," because the statement, "The lightning is not flashing," has no meaning. When it flashes, it is there. If the mind is still, it ceases to be. A still mind becomes a no-mind.

Kabir calls this state of no-mind the state of tranquility. When it is still, it ceases to be. Mind is present only while it is running. This is why you will never be able to keep it still. If you become still, you will find that the mind is not. The mind can never know the soul, because the soul can never be known by running, and the mind is another word for running. Therefore the atman is known on that day on which there is no mind. We can know the whole world through the mind; only the highest spiritual element remains unknown. We are able to know that highest spiritual element only when the mind is not.

The mind has its own complete technology of restlessness. Because running without a purpose is not possible, the mind creates causes or purposes for its running. These are called desires. The mind says, "I desire that thing, so I will run after it." How can you run if you have no desire to achieve something in the future, or if there is no goal to reach? Therefore every day the mind decides to fulfill a particular goal in the future. Then the running begins, but by the time the goal is reached, it is found to be useless because it was all merely an excuse for the mind to run. The goal which is reached becomes worthless on fulfillment. Then mind seeks out another excuse, another goal to be achieved. After reaching that goal it will say, "There is no substance in this. Now I should try for *that* objective...." So it continues running, further and further.

This is why the mind is always in the future. It can never be in the present. One who wants to run will have to live in the future. Mind will always be ahead of you. It will not remain here where you are. To be here, where you *are*, the running will have to cease. The soul – the atman – is here where you are, and the mind is there where you are not – where you have never been. It is always ahead of you, and wherever the mind reaches it says, "This is useless, worthless. Go on!" It is like a milestone whose arrow always informs you to go on. But among these milestones we at times come across a stone with a zero marked on it, instead of an arrow.

Yesterday while going for a walk I saw a milestone with a zero mark on it. There was no arrow pointing this way or that way, because the zero means the destination. There is nowhere further to go; you have reached your destination. But the mind fabricates an arrow saying, "Go on." The stone with a zero mark is never seen on the mind's journey. And if at any time, any day, you come across such a stone, know that you have come to the place known as meditation. When you happen to see that stone on your journey, know that it is the realization of the atman. The soul is there where the zero is. So those who have known the ultimate have declared that you will not be able to know it through the mind; you will know it by the zero. Remember, what the realized beings call zero is no-mind.

I told you the mind creates excuses to chase things. When it begins to be fed up with all the worldly things, they are left aside. Mind says, "I acquired great wealth, I constructed many buildings, I bought many bodies for my enjoyment but got nothing substantial out of these things." Then it plays its last trick to keep it running: it begins to make arrows pointing to the next world, to heaven, salvation and God. Even then, it does not ask us to cease making arrows and to turn them into zero. No, it now says, "Try to achieve spiritual wealth. Worldly wealth I attained and found it useless, so let it go! Now let me try to achieve religion. I know I can do it. One way or another, I will make it!"

The urge to become persists. If the effort to get something continues, then the mind also will continue. Remember this: he is not a truly religious person who wishes to achieve something. The religious person is one who has realized the truth that all activity aimed at getting is just mind; he has given up trying to achieve anything. "Now I am not trying to get anything. Now, finally, I am ready for stillness. Now, even if God asks me to go to him, to take only two steps towards him, I shall remain still. Now I am standing on the stone marked zero. I have no journey to make now." Be aware, the one who stands still, in his stillness finds God. The man who runs after God never attains to him because the running is of the mind, and that highest spiritual element can never be obtained by the mind.

When you are fed up with the search after worldly objects by the mind, you will fabricate new excuses for the mind – the atman, God, enlightenment. Buddha goes as far as denying the existence of the atman, because otherwise you will put all your effort into trying to find it. The mind is so clever, it will say, "Okay, if there is nothing else, at least there is atman, so I will pursue that! I will devote my energy to attaining that!" If it does not run towards the home, it will run towards the temple. Run it must – if not towards a material object then towards God; in any case, mind must run.

But only those who stand still find it. This is the declaration of this sutra. It is behind the sense organs and beyond the mind. Neither can help you attain to the atman. Then what should we do? Since it is behind the sense organs, drop any notions that they can help you. Since it is beyond the reach of the mind, stop depending on your speed of mind.

I am telling you to put no faith in either the mind or the sense organs. When I ask you to close your eyes, it is, in fact, asking you to break your habit of depending upon a particular sense organ. I am telling you, you have seen more than enough with your eyes, and yet it was not seen. The eyes were active for many lives, but it could not be seen. Now let us see with eyes closed.

We tried hard to listen to its voice, but it could not be heard. We yearned passionately to hear its music, but our ears failed to catch it. Now, let us plug our ears. We thought and contemplated endlessly, but could never devise a sutra to get us there. We tried hard with the mind, we suffered many cares and anxieties, we did much reasoning and deliberating, and looked into many philosophies, many religions and many scriptures. We produced many books and established many theories and principles, but failed to find any trace of it. Now leave aside all these things. Let us give up thinking. Now let us enter the region of no-thinking. Perhaps here it may be found.

I use the word perhaps for you. It is *certainly* achieved here. But while it is still unattained, even genuine faith that in the region of no-mind it will surely be found is dangerous. So I use the word perhaps for you: often, keeping such beliefs becomes a hindrance to our progress. They persuade us that it is all right – that now we will get it, that now we have found the way for certain! So theories come to look like achievements. That is why I use the word perhaps, so that you may be induced to enter into the experiment.

It is certainly attainable, but the support of the sense organs has to be given up. The mind, running and racing, has to be discarded. Such is the nature of the highest spiritual element, which is already and always present within us, but which we continue to miss through our own devices and plans for life. It is never lost by us, it is simply forgotten. We simply forget it. But in forgetting it, our whole life becomes worthless, becomes a hell. In forgetting it, no flowers grow in life, only thorns. In forgetting it, life becomes a desert without rivers, with no flow of sweet water. All happiness disappears. Our life becomes a desert where, however much we seek, no stream of water can be found, and only the sands run through our hands. No matter how long we walk, no shade is seen, nowhere a shelter, nowhere a resting place.

Understand this: there is no shelter, there is no oasis in life, without that highest spiritual element, the atman. No ecstasy ever flowed without that highest spiritual element. It is all in all. It is the real essence. But those who are entangled among the leaves are not able to reach down to the roots. The leaves may owe their sprouting to the roots, but those who remain entangled among the leaves never discover the roots. Give up the leaves. Go deep down within, beyond feelings, beyond sense organs, beyond thoughts. Move within and behind them, slowly, slowly, until you come to the zero point. It is within everybody. Spinning around it, we wander here and there, but without it there could be no wandering. Without that zero within, without that still perfect element at the center, this whole process of transformation, this huge circular network, could not go on. This running of yours like a storm, this whirling like a cyclone, all these depend upon the presence of that zero.

Let me make one last thing clear in this matter. There are two ways of describing that one thing: as zero and as perfection. The Upanishads prefer the term perfection; they prefer to use the word perfect. When the Upanishads came into existence, when these sutras were first recited, man was only able to understand the meaning as perfect. This word expresses the meaning in positive language. To use the word zero is to express the meaning in a negative language. To understand the term perfect one must have the innocent heart of a child. The old are unable to understand this language, and man is moving further every day from the state of childhood.

Men, like children, understood the language of the perfect in the days when this sutra was composed. You will understand this situation if you have studied children, if you have followed their ways and behavior. Walking along the road a child asks all sorts of questions; all children do this. At times the questions are puzzling, but you give them simple easy answers to their questions, and they are pleased and become quiet.

Those questions are so difficult at times that older people have no answers to them. When a new baby is born in the house, the small child asks, "Where has the new baby come from?" The question is difficult. Now, the adults don't have the correct answer to the question; nor do those who know – the biologists – have the right answer. They say, "We are still investigating. We do not yet know definitely from where a new child comes. We can tell you as much as we have been able to find out, but life comes from far beyond that; we do not know anything definitely."

So even the researchers who have devoted their lives to the matter do not know. And those who give birth to children do not know anything at all about it, because it is not necessary to know anything about it in order to give birth to children. But the fallacious idea is created that the father of seven children ought to know where a child comes from, and since he also lives in this fallacy he will make a reply, he will find an answer. But observe minutely the reaction of the child. He asked such a difficult question – where do children come from? – that even science has not yet discovered the right answer; and as far as I see, science never will have it. But you at once reply that you have seen a stork bringing the child. The child believes you, and runs off to play. For him the matter is over.

He believed in you. His is a positive mind, unprotesting, undoubting up to now. He would not ask in protest, "How can a stork bring it? Where will it bring it from?" He is not raising any doubts now. Later on he will do so. A day will come when that answer, "The stork brings it," will not do. Then he will ask many questions and express many doubts. Then you will know that the negative mind has come into existence.

There was an age when the whole world, the whole of mankind, was as innocent as children; people believed in what they were told. So the older the scriptures, the greater will be your surprise and perplexity. You will be confused by the lack of logic, and by the absence of clever arguments. There are only direct statements. Somebody approaches a sage and tells him, "I am very uneasy and worried. What should I do to attain peace of mind?" The sage says, "Repeat the name of Rama." The questioner is satisfied and says, "All right, I will do it," and goes away. He does not even question what will happen or ask how he can be helped by repeating the name of Rama. He does not ask any questions. Bear in mind, nothing will happen by repeating Rama's name, but the condition of the man's mind is such that even if the sage had asked him to repeat "Stone, stone!" he would have been benefited.

Nothing happens by repeating either the word Rama or the word stone. But it is the positive condition of the mind, the innocent mood of acceptance, knowing no denial or disobedience, giving birth to no doubts, that makes it fruitful. That is why they used to say, "Go and repeat the name of Rama and everything will be all right." The man goes home, repeats Rama's name, and everything *is* all right. Remember, nothing happens by repeating Rama's name. It happens because of the positive attitude of the mind. If that sage had said, "Take this amulet," or if he had given him some water and had him drink it, the man would certainly have drunk the charmed water and it would have been fruitful. Anything would be effective. It makes no difference whether the remedy is this or that. The important thing is the positive mind behind the whole affair. If that is there, the result is a sure success.

But now that positive attitude of the mind has disappeared. It had completely disappeared even by the times of Mahavira and Buddha. So both Mahavira and Buddha had to make use of negative language. Mahavira used it a little and declared, "There is no God!" – not because there was no God, but because now there was no man who would dance with joy on being told that there is a God. Such a man would not have asked, "Where is he?" He would simply have danced his way into ecstasy. He would have said, "If God is, I shall come to him, and the doors of heaven will be opened for me." And remember, there is no door which will not open for such a trusting and innocent mind.

No such people sat with Mahavira. When he told somebody, "God is," that person at once confronted Mahavira with numerous questions on the subject. Then Mahavira said, "There is no God." In fact, his first answer is true, but when someone starts to raise doubts the whole situation becomes absurd and worthless. There is no meaning in the answer if doubts are raised by it. That was the answer of the ancient sages. But people in Mahavira's times began to ask, "Who is God? Where is he? How many heads has he? How many hands has he? How was he born? Where did he come from? Where can we see him?" So Mahavira said, "He is not there at all."

The old answer was no longer any use. The answer from which questions begin to crop up is of no value. The purpose of an answer is to have the question concentrated in it. That is an answer which includes the question, so that the question drops. "God is!" was the greatest answer, but Mahavira was obliged to give it up. And Buddha had to go a step further.

Mahavira accepted the existence of the soul, the atman, for his mission. This distinction in the viewpoints of Mahavira and Buddha arose so quickly. There was not a great difference between the ages of Mahavira and Buddha, only thirty years in fact. Yet Buddha was obliged to say, "There is no such thing as soul." Mahavira had said, "There is no God, the soul is." Buddha had to say, "There is not even soul," because in Buddha's times people began to ask, "What does the atman mean?"

There was no answer to it. Buddha said, "It is zero; it is nothing." Remember, questions cannot be raised with regard to zero, because it means that which is not. What questions can be raised about it? Questions cannot be raised regarding the zero. And if you raise any questions at all, it means you have not understood. The meaning of zero is that which is not. Now, what more questions can you ask about it? We ourselves say, "It is not." Buddha said, "Zero. Nothing!" and instructed people to become united with it. The whole language is changed. But I tell you that the zero and the perfect are one and the same thing. The word perfect is the answer of a positive mind, and the word zero is that of a negative mind.

It is interesting to observe that we, in this world, have no experience of the perfect, other than that of zero. That is why the circle is made and accepted by us as a symbol of zero. It is the most perfect figure drawn by man. No other figure is perfect. It is also interesting to know that, among all the countries of the world, the figure of zero was first invented in India; and it was not invented for mathematical reasons but for Vedantic ones, for purposes of understanding.

The numbers one to nine were also formulated in India, but it is very interesting that all these numbers from one to nine are imperfect. Something can be added to them. To the number one, another one can be added, and that to which something can be added is not perfect, because its value increases by the addition. Something can be taken, deducted from it also, and that from which something can be deducted, thus lessening it, is not perfect. You can neither add anything to zero nor deduct anything from it. It is perfect. You cannot deduct anything from zero – how can you deduct from nothing? – nor can you add anything to zero. How can you?

Zero is the symbol, the image, of the perfect. It is a geometrical image of the perfect. We carry this zero, this image of the perfect, within us. If you can come to understand God through the perfect, that is fine. And if you can't understand through the perfect, then arrive through zero. It will make no difference to the final result.

Through our changing mental attitudes two paths have come into being, leading to the same destination. If your mind is positive and you feel you will not realize it through the zero, you should take the path of dancing, singing and being in ecstasy. And if you feel your mind is negative and doubting, then remain in silence, be quiet, be in zero, and get lost in zero. If you think your mind has a negative approach, then become united with zero. The final result will be the same.

That dancing, that ecstasy, will come through zero also, but it will come by *being* zero, and zero will come through dancing, by your becoming one with the dancing. One whose mental condition is for the perfect will dance, sing and chant prayers in the beginning and so disappear into the zero. When the dancing becomes fast and wild, then only his dancing remains, and when it becomes as frenzied as a cyclone, he begins to experience the zero within. He will feel someone is standing behind. The body will continue dancing and the zero, the atman, will stand, will be awakened within. The still point will begin to appear along with the revolving wheel.

Bear in mind that if the wheel is motionless, it will be difficult to know the still point because both will be still. It will be difficult to distinguish which is the axle and which is the wheel if the wheel is motionless. If the wheel is in motion, it will be easy to know the axle because it will not move when the wheel is moving. Immersed in ecstasy by becoming one with the perfect, some Chaitanya or some Meera is dancing. As the dancing goes on, the wheel spins faster and faster, and the centerpoint appears as separate in its stillness.

If you begin with the zero you begin to feel the void within. When everything within becomes void, the wheel outside begins to be seen revolving; thoughts are coming and going, *samsara*, the world, is going on.

The journey to the ultimate can begin from the axle or from the wheel. Both will bring us to the end of the journey. The highest spiritual element can be known either by becoming the perfect or by becoming the zero; but the sense organs cannot take us either to the perfect or to the zero – likewise neither can the mind take us.

# Truth
# Is Absurd

6

*The highest spiritual element*
*is moving*
*and is also not moving.*
*It is far away and yet is near.*
*It is concealed in everything*
*and is outside of everything also.*

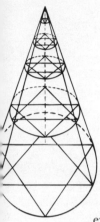

THE HIGHEST SPIRITUAL ELEMENT, the atman, is not moving and yet it is moving. It is the nearest thing to us and yet it is far off. The highest spiritual element is within us. It is the inner soul, and yet is visible outside. This is one of the greatest sutras ever uttered in the history of mankind. It is very easy and at the same time very deep and profound also. There are no truths more deep and profound than all the simple truths of life. They appear so unambiguous, but they contain the mysteries, and paradoxical words have to be used to unfold them. If a logician were to study them, he would say they are entirely incorrect.

Arthur Koestler, a great thinker of the West, has made much fun of the Eastern way of looking at things. He has condemned it as absurd. What could be a more absurd statement than this – that the highest spiritual element is nearer than the near and farther than the far? Are you in your senses? Whatever is near must be near; how can it be far away? This highest spiritual element is motionless and is also moving! What nonsense do you talk? There is no sense at all in what you say. It is deep within and pervades the outer too? If it is so, then what difference is there between within and without? If it is within, how can it be without? Or if it is without, how can it be within? If it is far away please say so, don't say it is near. And if you say it is near, then please stop saying it is far away.

This is how Koestler argues. If you are true to your own attitudes you will enjoy Koestler's opinions. He is a very honest person, and I prefer his honesty to the alternatives, because ways can be found for such a person. Koestler says, "I consider such statements illogical. They come only from lunatics, but a lunatic, if he talks like this, can be pardoned." But Koestler does not know that even science has arrived at this position during the last years, and has begun to make similar statements. Even Einstein talks in such language.

Leave them alone! The sages may well be crazy people. They certainly do not claim that they are not insane, because no one in this world, except the madman, claims that he is not insane. The sages are so intelligent that they are quite prepared to be mad. Those who achieve the highest wisdom are content to be considered foolish.

Yesterday I was telling somebody that to claim wisdom is the only stupidity. Nobody but the stupid have ever claimed to be wise and intelligent. All the wise people born into this world have said, "We are great fools, we know nothing. We know this much: that we know nothing. As we began to know, we also began to realize that we are deeply ignorant."

Even Koestler cannot say that Einstein is crazy. But a difficulty has arisen in the last ten years – a difficulty such as the Upanishads had to face. Such a difficulty arises when some thought, some search, touches the highest mystery. When the sage of the Upanishads arrived at this highest mystery – the ultimate atman – he had to make use of paradoxical language. He said in the same breath that it is far away and it is also near; and he followed the one so quickly and immediately on the other that you cannot think it is far away. He said it is near, and immediately followed it by saying that it is also far away, so that you may not make the mistake of thinking that it is near. What was first said was immediately taken back in the next statement. Now the discoveries of science are approaching very close to that highest spiritual element.

Scientists were greatly puzzled when the electron was discovered. They had no word to describe it. Man has words for all things, but the scientists were confused as to which word they should use for it. Should they call it an atom or a wave? The atom and the wave are separate and contrary things. The atom cannot be a wave. The atom means a particle which is stationary. The wave means a thing which is moving. If it stops moving, it ceases to be a wave. Wave means a thing which is floating, which is flowing, is continually becoming, is continually changing its shape – a process. The wave is a process.

And the electron, what is its status? Two scientists are studying it; one of them says, "It appears to be a wave to me." The other says, "It looks like an atom to me." Both say so at the same time. Another scientist says, "It looks like an atom at one moment and the very next moment it looks like a wave. It is both at the same time." So there was great difficulty in naming it. There was no word in any language of the world which meant an atom and a wave at the same time – which could mean both simultaneously. So they coined a new word, quantum, for it. Quantum means both the wave and the atom.

Koestler would call Einstein, Planck and others like them madmen. He would consider them crazy. Somebody asked Einstein, "What do you say to this? How can it be both an atom and a wave?"

He replied, "How can I decide that it is possible or not possible? I can only say, it is so."

The questioner said, "This statement of yours refutes all our laws and principles of logic. All the logical theory propounded by Aristotle is overturned."

Then Einstein replied, "How can I help it? If logic is to be refuted when confronted by a fact then it must be refuted. The fact cannot be discarded. You change your logical reasoning."

The fact is so. Aristotle is incorrect. The electron is simply not prepared to prove Aristotle right. You will have to change your way of reasoning, because the fact is as it is. Let Aristotle be in the wrong. The electron is not about to become an atom just to oblige Aristotle; nor is it prepared to be simply a wave to prove Aristotle right. It is both. It doesn't worry about Aristotle. His logic says opposite things cannot coexist as one. What he says is right. How can a person be living and dead at the same time? But those who know the deep secret of life say that life and death are the two legs, left and right, of one and the same person. When you are living, you are at the same time also dying. You do not die on one day; you are dying from the day on which you were born. At one end life is going on, and from the other end death is approaching. And you reach the end in seventy years.

This is interesting to ponder over: can a dead person die? To die, a living person is required. That is to say, it is absolutely necessary, unavoidable, to be living in order to die. This condition cannot be disputed. If one is not living, he cannot die. Now this becomes a totally contrary statement. It is an unavoidable condition to be living in order to die. Then this means that it is an unavoidable condition to be dying in order to live. The person who is not dying this moment, is also not living. Death and life are names of the same process. We are dying and living at the same time. We are being effaced and are becoming, simultaneously.

Aristotle says darkness is darkness and light is light; they cannot be united as one. Ordinarily, this seems correct. There is darkness where there is no light, and there is light where there is no darkness. But science tells us insufficient light is called darkness, and insufficient darkness is called light. The difference is of degree. Similarly, heat and cold are not two separate things.

This sutra of the Upanishad will be very easily understood if you perform this experiment. Warm one of your hands a little by a fire and keep a piece of ice in the other hand for some time. Then dip both the hands in a bucket full of water, and ask yourself whether the water is cold or warm. One hand will tell you it is cold and the other hand will tell you it is warm. Then you will have to say it is cold *and* warm if you do not want to make a false statement; you will have to give contrary statements. According to Koestler this would be absurd. But the water is neither cold nor warm. There is simply a difference of degrees between the water and your hands, as you find when they make contact with it.

The Upanishad says the atman is near and far off also. It says so because no matter how far the leaves may spread, they are always near the roots. They are linked with the roots, or else they cannot exist. The juice comes from the roots. If we see rightly, leaves are nothing but the extended hands of the roots. It is extension – the roots extended and turned into leaves. There is no discontinuity anywhere in between. There is no place in between where you can say that here the roots are discontinued and from here the leaves begin to appear. The whole tree is united together. The leaves are on that extremity and the roots are on this extremity. Nor are the toes of your feet and the hair on your head discontinuous with each other. They are joined, they are one. They are the two ends of the same thing.

See how very close the roots are to the leaves! They give them all their juice, all their life force. How can they be far away? And yet they *are* far away, very far away, and if the leaves want to know the roots, they will have to take a long journey.

Why do I say the roots are far away? They are far away in the sense that the leaves do not know even that the roots exist. The sun also appears to be near the leaves, although it is very far away, tens of millions of miles. But the leaves might feel the sun to be very near. They begin to dance in the morning when the sun rises. They are aware of the sun's presence every day, but they are always ignorant of the roots which are hidden under them and are a part and parcel of them. In this sense, the sun is very near, while the roots are very far away.

The highest spiritual element – the atman – is very near to us because we cannot exist without it, and it is very far away also because we are utterly unaware of it despite our search for it through innumerable lives. It is said that it is absolutely still, and yet all the movement of life is dependent on it. The axle does not move; the wheel moves, yet the axle also makes the same journey that the wheel makes.

Suppose you start on a journey in a carriage. Its axle will not move an inch; only the wheel will move. But when you stop after driving ten miles, the axle has also made the ten miles' journey, without moving an inch. Koestler will call this statement a foolish one. But the event – the journey – has happened. How can one dispute the fact? If Aristotle is proved wrong, let him be wrong; the fact cannot be wrong. The axle has not moved at all and yet a tenmile journey was made.

The atman never walked, even for a moment, and never moved; and yet it has made a journey through innumerable births, stopping at innumerable camps and resting places, and traveling so far. That is why the sage of the Upanishad says it does not move and yet is moving also. He says it is within and at the same time is without. In fact, within and without are temporary distinctions. When you inhale you say breath is going in, but before you complete your sentence it is going out.

Have you ever thought of this? You say, "Breath is going in – it is within." Before you can complete your statement, before you can get time to say so, it is already out; and when you say it is out, you immediately see that it has started to go in again. What is the difference between within and without in this case? It is merely that of direction, there is no other difference.

Is there an iota of difference between the sky which is outside your house and the one which is within your house? There is none at all. You constructed walls and thus encircled a portion of the sky. It is a part of that sky which is spread outside the house. The inner one is the same as the outer one, and yet there is some difference. When the sun is hot, we know the outer sky is different from the inner one. There is comfort inside while there is discomfort outside. The outer and the inner sky are one and the same, and yet they are different, separate. When we sleep under the inner sky at night we feel more at ease, more comfortable than if we sleep out.

Therefore, the Upanishads say, the same one is within as is without. And yet you will have to begin from within if you wish to know it. Only after knowing it within can you say that it is the same without. Before knowing this, it cannot be said that it is without also, because if you do not know your within, you will have no idea of what is without.

How can those who have not known even the small sky of their

own homes, know that huge, limitless sky without? Get acquainted
first with this small one and then you will be acquainted with that
limitless one without. Those who wish to know it will have to start
from within. And those who reach the final stage of knowing,
complete their journey without. The first step, self-knowing, takes
place within and the final step, knowing the ultimate, takes place
without. The journey begins with the atman and ends with the
supreme spirit – with Paramatman.

This apparently very absurd, absolutely illogical and irrelevant
statement is very profound – a great truth and full of reality. But
those who stop at logical reasoning can never arrive at the fact.
Only those who are brave enough to give up even reasoning are
able to arrive at the fact, because the truth – the fact – does not
respect your reasoning. All reasoning is man-made, and the facts
never worry about that. Your reasoning may argue in any way it
likes, but the facts, unperturbed, will continue to proceed in their
own fashion.

Facts go on speaking for themselves, without the least anxiety
about your reasoning. That is why reasoning has to be smashed to
pieces when there is a dispute between facts and reasoning. That is
why, when the wise men of the East arrived at life's truths, they
gave up logical reasoning. They declared, "Reasoning cannot be of
any use." That is why those who have become very proficient in
reasoning find it difficult to know the truth. They stick to their
reasoning. They go on saying, "How can water be hot and cold at
the same time? Cold is one quality, heat is another and opposite
quality!" But they are one and the same. They go on saying, "How
can birth and death be one?" But they *are!*

The seeker of truth has to be daring enough to give up reasoning, even though it is the greatest daring. This sutra is beyond logic
and hence it is great. As I told you, it is one of the greatest sutras
uttered in the history of mankind. Now let us enter that great truth
which is beyond logic. Don't try to reason out how dancing or
shouting or weeping or laughing are going to help us. Don't think.
Leave logic aside and take a jump!

# Become
# A Mirror

7

*He who sees the entire world*
*of animate and inanimate objects*
*in himself*
*and also sees himself*
*in all animate and inanimate objects,*
*because of this,*
*does not hate anyone.*

DISLIKE OR HATRED of another is the basis of deep-seated complications for mankind. It can be said that the poison of hatred becomes manifest in all his poisonous displays. The word hatred means the desire to destroy the other. Love means being willing to sacrifice oneself for another, if necessary. Hatred means being willing to destroy another for oneself even if it is not necessary. In the way we all live there is an abundance of hatred and no music of love.

The feeling which we call love is, in fact, a form of hatred. In making love we make another our means for happiness; and no sooner does one make another a means than hatred begins. In making love we live for our own self. We want to serve our own selfish end. At times we appear to do something for another, but it is simply because we are out to get something from him in return. We do something for another only when we have some hope of getting something from him – we desire the fruit; otherwise we do nothing. That is why our love may turn into hatred at any moment. It happens: the love shown to somebody a few minutes before may turn into contempt for him soon after. If a small obstruction crops up that gets in the way of the fulfillment of our desire, our love will be changed into hatred. Love which can be turned into hatred and contempt is only concealed hatred. There is only hatred within, and the outer covering is just a semblance of love.

The Ishavasya presents here a very important sutra which makes love possible; otherwise not. Without understanding and acting upon this sutra, there is no possibility for the flower of love to open. This sutra says that hatred will come to an end only when a person begins to see himself in all animate and inanimate objects, and begins to see all animate and inanimate objects – the whole existence – in himself. Remember, the Ishavasya does not say that love will be born then but says, "Then hatred will come to an end."

There is a very well thought out reason for saying so. There is no other obstruction in the way of love except the presence of hatred. If there is no hatred, love blooms of its own accord – spontaneously, naturally. Nothing else is to be done for it to blossom. It is like removing a stone blocking a small stream: once removed, the stream flows on of its own accord. In the same way the stone of hatred weighs on us. Because of the stone of hatred we are unable to see our faces reflected in the mirrors of all animate and inanimate objects; nor can we become mirrors reflecting all those objects in ourselves.

Both these phenomena happen simultaneously: the person who can see himself in all animate and inanimate objects – all the animals, the whole existence – will inevitably be able to see all in himself. The person for whom the whole world becomes a mirror, himself becomes a mirror for the whole world. They happen simultaneously. They are the two sides of one and the same occurrence. The Upanishad says that when this happens, hatred disappears.

What is born then? The Upanishad hasn't said that love is born then, because love is eternal, it is our nature. Neither is it born, nor does it die. For instance, when the rainy season has set in and the sky is covered with clouds, the sun is obscured. Now, can we say that the sun will be born when the clouds disappear? No, we can only say that the sun, which was always there, will be visible. When the clouds came the sun was not destroyed, it was just obscured. It was no longer visible, concealed behind the clouds. Clouds will disappear and the sun will shine again. Clouds are born and clouds die, but the sun is always there.

Love is the nature of life, so it has neither birth nor death. Clouds of hatred are born and die. Love is covered when those clouds are born; it manifests itself when they disappear, when they are no more. But love is eternal, so the Upanishad does not talk of the birth of love, it says this much only: hatred dies and disappears.

But how? The sutra is not as easy as it appears. Many a time it happens that the things which look difficult are not so, and similarly, those which appear easy are not easy. Mostly, there is great depth and intricacy hidden within easy matters. This sutra seems to be straightforward and easy. The whole statement is completed in two lines only. It says, the person who sees himself in all objects – animate and inanimate – and begins to see all objects in himself, will have his hatred destroyed. But to make all his mirror, or to be a mirror for all, is the greatest alchemy and art. There is no greater art.

I have heard: A Chinese man once went to the court of the emperor of Iran and said, "I have come from China, and I am a very great artist. I can make paintings such as you have never seen before."

The emperor said, "Then make them here. But remember, there is no shortage of painters in our court and I have seen very wonderful pictures."

The Chinese painter said, "I am ready to meet any challenge."

The best among the court painters was selected to compete. Then the emperor warned his painter, "Use all your talent, do your very best. This is now a question of the prestige of the empire. See that you are not defeated by this foreigner."

They were given six months to complete their work. The Iranian painter began his work very seriously. With the help of ten to twenty co-workers he covered his whole wall with beautiful pictures. News of his paintings reached distant regions, and people came from afar to see his work. But a greater miracle than this was happening. The Chinese artist said, "I need no implements or materials for my work, nor any paints either. I insist on one condition only – that the curtain covering my wall not be removed till the picture is finished."

Each morning he would go behind his curtain, and reappear in the evening quite exhausted, with drops of perspiration on his forehead. But it was a matter of great perplexity, mystery and wonder that he did not carry any brush or paints with him when he disappeared behind the curtain. Neither were there ever any traces of color on his hands, nor any spots of paint on his clothes, and he carried no brush in his hands. The emperor began to wonder whether he was crazy. How could there be any competition under such circumstances? But it was necessary to wait for six months to fulfill the condition.

With great impatience everyone waited for the six months to pass. The news about the pictures of the Iranian painter reached far and wide, and along with this news, the word also spread about his crazy competitor who had entered the competition without any paints. You can't imagine how eagerly the people waited for those six months to pass.

After six months the emperor went to see the pictures. He was spellbound on seeing the pictures of the Iranian painter. He had seen many paintings in his life, but he had never seen paintings of such unsparing skill. Then he requested the Chinese painter to show his work. He removed the curtain covering his wall. On seeing it the emperor was very much puzzled. It was the same picture. The Chinese painter had created the same picture as the Iranian, but with one additional feature: it was not painted on the wall, but emerged from twenty feet deep inside the wall. The emperor asked, "How have you done this? What is this magic?"

He replied, "I have done no magic. But I am an expert in making mirrors, so I turned the wall into a mirror by rubbing it continuously for six months. The picture which you are looking at is that of the Iranian painter's on the opposite wall. I simply turned the wall into a mirror."

He won the competition, because shimmering in the mirror the Iranian painting became infinitely more profound than its original. The Iranian painting acquired great depth when seen in the mirror. It became a three-dimensional picture. The Iranian one was two-dimensional; it had no depth. The Chinese painter's picture gained a three-dimensional depth. The emperor asked him, "Why did you not tell us in the beginning that you only know how to make mirrors?"

The Chinese painter replied, "I am not a painter, I am a *sadhu*, a monk."

The emperor said, "This becomes more and more interesting. First you didn't tell us that you make mirrors, and now you tell us you are a sadhu. Why should a sadhu make mirrors?"

The Chinese painter replied, "I have been making only mirrors since I made myself a mirror and saw the world in it. Just as I turned this wall into a clean mirror by continuously rubbing and cleaning it, so I made myself a mirror, pure as crystal, by keeping constant watch on myself. And such a beautiful image of this world as I have seen within was never seen without. The day on which I saw and realized the world within me, I became like a mirror. All the animate and inanimate objects of the world have penetrated within me."

We will be able to see God on the day on which our heart becomes like a mirror. Then all the world enters into us, and the whole world becomes a mirror for us also. Then we are able to see ourself every moment, everywhere. But the whole world cannot be turned into a mirror; only our own self can be turned into a mirror. That is why the seeker after truth begins by making a mirror of himself.

To know the alchemy and art of making ourself a mirror, three points are to be understood. First, perhaps it is not correct to talk of making a mirror of the self, because we are all mirrors already, but covered with dust. Our work is to clean and polish our mirror and make it bright and clear. A mirror is not a mirror if dust is allowed to settle on it; then it does not reflect anything. Its capacity to reflect is destroyed when it is covered with dust. We are such mirrors – the dust has accumulated on us. Just as dust collects on a mirror carried along a busy road, so it collects as we pass through countless lives. It is gathered in many many ways from our desires, our innumerable actions, and from our becoming constantly the doer. No one knows what a heap of dust is collected – the dust of actions, of becoming doers of actions, of ego, of thoughts, of desires and feelings. So there is a very deep layer of dust on us.

The important matter is to remove it. If it is swept away, we are mirrors again. And everything is like a mirror for one who is himself a mirror. Why? – because whatever we are is seen by us on all sides. To understand this, keep this important sutra in mind: "We see only what we are, we never see anything else but this." Whatever is seen by us is always our projection. Always we are that. It is only our face we see. If no good is seen by us in the world outside, then it is because the seed of such a view is within us. If only ugliness is seen in the world outside, we should know that ugliness has taken a firm root within us. If faithlessness is seen everywhere outside, we should know that faithlessness is within us. The projector is within, only the screen is without, and we go on projecting onto it. We go on expanding whatever is within us onto the screen.

If God is not seen in the world outside it means simply that we do not experience the divine within us. He who realizes God within begins to see God instantly in all objects. Then there is no other way. Then he will see God even in a stone. But at the moment only stone is seen in God. For me there is no other meaning to the word materialist but this: he is a materialist whose spiritual heart has turned to stone. One whose heart within is like a stone sees stones everywhere. For me, he is a spiritualist whose spiritual heart is not like a stone but throbbing, living, pulsating, vibrant.

The scientist would say that there is nothing spiritual in the throbbing of our heart. It is a kind of system, nothing more. The scientist would say that any heart about which we talk can be seen by dissecting it; and what we will find is a pump which circulates blood, by the pressure of air, throughout the body. There is nothing more to it than that. And if this is how the scientist sees his own heart and source of life, then he can have no experience of life, and no consciousness of the world outside. If heart means for a man only a machine to push blood around within, then he will see only a mechanical expanse in the outside world: then the whole system is complete. The world is merely a mechanical thing. The world outside is only stones.

No, there are other ways to go within. It would have meant great difficulty if the way of science was the only way to go within.

Then the scientist would have won. But he cannot win, his defeat is sure. It is possible there will be some delay in finding ways to go within, because there are many possibilities. For example, someone wants to learn to play a *veena*. Now, it is possible to find out what a veena is by breaking it open and looking into it. One could tear off all its strings, smash it into pieces, examine the pieces, and finally declare, "There is no music at all in it. Who said this was a musical instrument? Here it is in front of me separated into parts, and there is no music in it at all."

If this is the only way to know what a veena is then the musician is already defeated. But there is also another way to find out what the veena is. Certainly it is a hard way; it is easy to destroy it, but to know what it really is, is very arduous. Only by playing it can one know what is hidden in the heart of the veena. It is so subtle that it is difficult to grasp, certainly, and if you are deaf you will not grasp it at all. If you are only intellectually efficient, but deficient in sensitivity, deficient in sentiment, then you will not understand even if you hear it. When one listens to music one hears only sounds – a profusion of sounds. But music means something more than just hearing. In hearing it, something else is added. We have to pour out heart into it; then and then only, the sounds turn into music. Otherwise there are only confused sounds, there is only noise.

If there was only one way of knowing the heart – that of the surgeon who dissects it on his operating table – it would have been no good; but there is one more way also. A spiritual person knows it, a saint knows it. He has come to know it by playing upon the heart, not by taking it apart. He has known it by producing music in the heart. So he asks, "Which heart within are you talking of? You are as mad and idiotic as a person who breaks an electric bulb, takes the pieces of glass home and says, 'This is light.'" It is true that light was produced through it, but the glass pieces which you carried home are not and were not light. That the light vanished when the bulb was broken is a fact. So the logical reasoning behind this happening seems correct – that when the bulb was broken the light went away, so the bulb was the light; otherwise the light should not have gone out when the bulb was broken. The pieces we have brought home make up the total light. This is true, that when a bulb is broken the light disappears; it is not lost or destroyed, it simply disappears, becomes invisible. The medium that makes it visible is broken.

If we demolish the heart, the medium for the spirit to manifest is broken. The bulb is broken. Then the spiritual heart cannot shine out, just as the light cannot shine on breaking the bulb. The spirit is then concealed. The heart only helps the spirit to manifest. But there are very few people among us who have known the spiritual heart. We know only the physical heart, through which the blood is circulated and life is mobilized. We have known only this mechanical arrangement, so we see it magnified in the outside world also.

The day on which we come to know the supreme consciousness within us, then the outside world also will appear to us like the expanse of the supreme consciousness. The whole will be a mirror to us when we become a mirror within. If we stand near a stone, then we will be able to see ourself even in the stone. Then we will not look at the stone with that hardness with which we look at man now. Then we shall touch a stone as if we are touching our beloved, because the stone is not stone then, it is God. Then we shall tread on the ground with great care, sensitivity and awareness, because there also life is hidden, there also is the expansion of existence, and there also life is throbbing; there also someone is dancing. Existence is dancing in various dimensions, in various forms, and in various ways. We are not the only masters of life. Endless are its forms, and we are one of them. Ours is a very small way. And yet we have no knowledge of our way within.

How can we become a mirror? To become a mirror we will have to brush away the dust settled on us. Not only do we have to remove it but also we have to stop gathering new dust. If we go on brushing aside the dust at this end and at the same time we continue the way of life that collects it, then there is no possibility of becoming a mirror. We have to make a twofold attack. The old dust, the accumulated dust, will have to be removed and at the same time we have to stop gathering new dust. The old dust is accumulated in the form of memories and the new dust is collected through desires. The old dust is hoarded in memories and the new dust comes through desires.

Both efforts have to be made simultaneously. We will have to free ourselves from memories and from desires. We have to tell our desires that we don't wish to get anything now, there is now no further journey, and we have to tell our memories that what happened in the past is only a dream now. There is no need to go on carrying this load uselessly. But all of us are carrying our load of memories. We forget nothing; on the contrary, we nurture old memories and hold onto them. We collect this refuse and keep it on our shoulders. From birth to death we collect our refuse. So we have to dispense with memories. We have to say, "What has happened has happened, I am not that old self now." We have to tear ourselves away from yesterday. We have to free ourselves from the past and from the future too. When we are free from these two, then our mind will become a mirror.

For me, a sannyasin is one who says, "I tear myself from the past. I am not now what I was yesterday – I end that identity." That is why names are changed. The changing of names is symbo-lic. It means: "I will not be that old I which was linked with the old name. Now I free myself from that. Now I bury those old memories, that old mess of things of the past, along with my old name. Now I am a new person and begin my journey from the start." In the steady determination to be new from today, from now, is found the real sannyas.

Remember this: freedom from the past is possible; but if we continue our old habits then our past will remain as our past. How long will the effect of the change of name last? It will not remain new even for a moment. After breaking off with the past, if we continue old habits, then we will be collecting old memories around the new name, and the same old burden will be there, and the mirror will remain concealed.

So sannyas is a twofold resolution. Tearing away from the past – that is, "I am not now what I was yesterday; I break the continuity. I am aware. I am a new person now. That old name is no longer mine. He is not my father, that is not my family. No, that past has nothing to do with me. I am reborn from today."

A man called Nicodemus once approached Jesus, and asked, "What shall I do to achieve that ecstasy which you are talking about?"

Jesus said, "You will have to be born again."

The man asked, "How is that possible? What are you talking about? How is that possible? I have already been born, I have already been an infant. Now how can I be born again?"

Jesus said, "You have not understood me. You have never taken birth, so I tell you, you will have to be born again. You will have to be born a new person. You will have to be born free from your past mess of memories and relationships."

We used to call such a person twice-born in our country. Twice-born does not mean that one has gone through the brahmin initiation ritual of putting on the sacred thread. It means one whose second birth has taken place. Nobody can be twice-born before becoming a sannyasin. Nobody can be twice-born just by putting on the sacred thread. Nobody can be twice-born by being born in a brahmin family. The word *dwija* means one who took a second birth. The first birth is given by the parents and the second is the result of one's own endeavor.

It is a twofold process. "I am breaking myself off from the past and also from the old pattern of living through which I was becoming more and more attached to the past. Now I am born anew every day. Now there will be no dust settling on my mirror. Now this name will remain fresh forever. Now there will be no memory linked with it. Now I shall never say I did this and I did not do that. I shall now never declare that I am the doer. I shall now never say that the building is mine, or the wealth is mine, or the property is mine."

Remember this: a sannyasin is not one who leaves his home and begins to say, "The ashram is mine." The sannyasin is one who stops using the word 'my'. It does not matter where he lives. He may sit and run a shop, provided the shop does not become 'mine'. Then the whole matter ends. But we have a habit of leaving the shop, of quitting it, and then reasserting our old habit by entering an ashram and beginning to talk of *my* ashram. It makes no difference then whether we live in the house or live in an ashram. Then changing the name is of no use. It is as useless as the elephant's practice of bathing in a river or pond, and then coming out and throwing dust over its body. The bath has served no purpose. The whole labor is wasted.

This sutra of the Upanishad is asking us to be a mirror. A right mind is a mirror. One who can say, "I have neither past nor future, I am living in the here and now; this very moment is all," becomes a mirror immediately.

How can there be any hatred in a heart which reflects all animate and inanimate objects in its own mirror? And how can there be any feeling of hatred when his own reflection is seen in all animate and inanimate objects? The feeling of hatred goes away; its smoke vanishes. The clouds of smoke disappear, and what becomes visible is the sun, the sun of love. Remember, as long as there is still hatred in your heart, the love you make and go on making can only be a form of hatred. When hatred dissolves at its very roots – that is, when it has utterly and finally disappeared – the thing that is born is love.

Only a sannyasin can make love. It is only from the self – the soul – that love's stream flows. Nothing but hatred will flow from the body and the mind. Only hatred will flow from selfish ideas – ideas of mine and thine. The seeker must correctly understand the art of becoming a mirror himself. As soon as he can he has to learn to make the present moment his existence, and begin to live from moment to moment. He has to separate himself from the past as well as the future. He has to find freedom from memories and from desires. Then the accumulated dust will fade away and there will be no possibility for new dust to settle.

# The Shadow Of The Ego

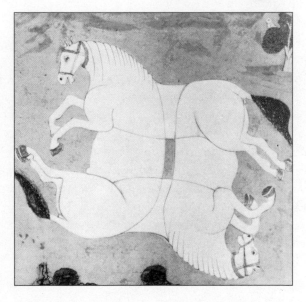

8

*What grief or attachment*
*can there be for a realized soul –*
*a man of wisdom –*
*when all the animate and inanimate*
*objects of the world*
*have become his self,*
*when he sees oneness everywhere?*

WHAT SORROW or what attachment can there be for that realized person – that wise man – who has known himself in all animate and inanimate objects, or known all animate and inanimate objects in himself? There are three or four important points to be understood in this sutra. Number one, whom do the Upanishads call a man of wisdom? The root word from which this word comes is *ved*. The word ved means to know. The meaning of the words 'man of wisdom' is one who knows. What does he know? Someone knows mathematics, someone knows chemistry, somebody knows physics. There are thousands of things to know. Someone knows the scriptures. Some know all those matters of deep mystery told by the saints. But the Upanishads do not consider them wise.

This is a very strange and interesting thing. The accumulation of information is not knowledge according to the Upanishads. They call him a wise man who knows only that one great element – truth: that is, who knows himself, because one who knows himself, knows all. When he knows himself he becomes a mirror in which reflected images of all begin to appear. But the fact that he knows all does not mean he must be a great mathematician or a famous chemist or a great scientist. No, that is not the meaning. The only meaning of this sentence – "By knowing himself he knows all" – is that through knowing himself he comes to know that supreme, that purest, that occult element which is hidden within all. He knows the formula, the essence, whose play is all this. He knows that supreme law whose authority abides everywhere. He knows that supreme lord who is in everybody. He knows that supreme showman who holds in his hands the strings on which dance all the puppets!

He is not an expert – he is not at all an expert. If you ask him about a particular thing he may not know the answer. He knows the essential which is hidden in the entire universe. He does not know each leaf, but he holds the root in his hand. He knows that deep and mysterious great life-force; and no sooner does he know that than he becomes free from grief and attachment.

This is the characteristic of the wise man, and it is a strange one. It is not his capacity to reply to your questions, it is not that he will be able to solve your problems. It is that he becomes free from the effects of grief and attachment. A mathematician, however great an expert he may be, will not be free from grief and attachment. Let him be a great psychologist like Freud – and there have been very few psychologists like Freud in this world – his mind will still be that of an ordinary man, even after learning a great deal about the mind. It makes no difference, there is not the least transformation in his mind. He still becomes anxious, afraid, burning with anger and jealousy, and is as grieving and attached as any ordinary person. And the paradoxical thing is that he has more theoretical knowledge about fear, about jealousy, than perhaps any other person in the world. He has a fund of knowledge about sexuality, but even in old age it agitates his mind as much as it does anybody else's mind.

The Upanishads do not consider such a person learned. They do not even consider his knowledge as true knowledge. They call it a fund of information. Such a person is an expert. Whatever is known about fear is known by him. He knows about the fear, but not the fear itself. If he had really known the fear he would be free from it. An expert in religious scriptures knows everything *about* religion, but does not know religion. He knows what the Vedas say, what the Upanishads say, what the Gita says, what the Koran says, what the Bible says – he knows all this. He knows what is said, but he does not know the one for whom it is said, in what way it is said, with what experience it is said.

The difference is like this – that a person knows everything about swimming but does not know how to swim. It is not difficult to know theoretically about swimming; a book on swimming can be studied. All the literature on swimming can be memorized. A person can be an expert on swimming and can answer any question asked about swimming. And yet, don't push such a person by mistake into a river, because to know swimming is altogether a different matter.

Nor is it necessary for a person who knows swimming to know all about swimming. It is possible that he knows only swimming but is ignorant of any theoretical knowledge. But the entire theoretical knowledge of a person will not be of any use to him if his boat is sinking and his life is in danger. At such a time, the person who knows nothing about swimming but who knows swimming itself, will be able to swim and save his life. This is why the sage of the Upanishad correctly points out the fundamental characteristics of the truly learned person. He says they are the learned, the wise, who see all the animate and inanimate objects in themselves and see themselves in all animate and inanimate objects. Such people become free from grief and attachment.

Why has he grouped these two – grief and attachment – together? They are grouped together because these two are one; they are unavoidable, concomitant parts of the same mental condition. Of the two, one is never alone. So understand them correctly. The mind which is attached will have sorrow and grief also; and where there is no attachment, grief cannot be there. In fact, grief comes when the object of attachment is destroyed. There is no other cause for sorrow. Suppose I have an attachment to somebody: if he dies I am immersed in sorrow. Sorrow is like a shadow that follows attachment. If I have no attachment to anybody it is impossible to be sad, even if I wish to be.

There is a house to which I am attached. If it catches on fire I feel grief. There is grief immediately attachment is frustrated or fragmented – wherever it meets with some difficulty, wherever it is broken, wherever it is opposed. And remember, when grief comes you will have to create a new attachment to save yourself from the grief. When grief comes you will have to find a new object for your attachment, to save yourself from the grief, to get away from it. If a person whom you love dies, you are not able to forget him until you find a substitute to love. It is difficult to forget the old attachment until you throw it away and replace it by showing your love to the new substitute.

So grief comes when attachment is broken, and to run away from that grief we have to create new objects for our attachment. Thus this vicious circle goes on. Every attachment brings sorrow and every sorrow is suppressed by new objects of attachment. Sickness comes; medicine has to be given, and it causes other types of sickness. Then new medicines are given for the new sickness and those new ones give rise to new sicknesses. Thus the circle goes on. So it was a wise decision to group these two together.

This is why it is said that one who knows becomes free from grief and attachment. How can ideas of mine and thine come to one who sees himself in all animate and inanimate objects and sees all of them in himself? How is attachment then created? It is created only when you bind yourself to somebody, and say, "This is mine, the rest are not," or when you say, "This building is mine, the rest are not mine."

When I was coming here, a certain woman came to see me. She said, "Because of your great grace my son's shop was saved from catching fire. The adjoining building had caught fire, and it had got up to our shop. But our shop was saved." She had brought sweets to offer to me. She was delighted that her son's shop was saved. No, she was not at all grieved for the buildings that were destroyed in the fire, because she had no attachment to them. On the contrary, she was pleased because the building to which she was attached was saved.

Attachment is always exclusive; it clings to one and leaves out the rest. It says, "This is my wife, this is my husband, this is my son, this is my house, this is my shop" – there is I in all these – "and I am not concerned with the rest!" It will not affect you in any way, it will make no difference to you, if anything happens to the rest. You are pleased that your own is saved.

The degree of attachment decreases as the field of attachment spreads. The greatest attachment is for oneself, because nothing appears more 'mine' than oneself. So if, for example, it appears that a boat is sinking, and a husband and a wife are in it, and the situation is such that only one of the two can be saved, then both will wish to be saved. If fire breaks out in a house, the owner will jump out first and then inquire about other members of his family. No sooner does a person know about the fire than he himself runs out. So, attachment is concentrated mostly around I; it is strongest linked to I. Then it gradually decreases as the field of 'mine' goes on expanding. It will be less towards the family, still less towards the town, still less towards the country, and even less towards the whole of humanity. And if people are living on some other planets, there will be no attachment towards them.

Scientists declare that there is life on at least fifty thousand other planets. We show no attachment in relation to them. Even towards humanity it seems minimal. We remain unconcerned and unaffected when seven hundred thousand people die in Pakistan. If one person dies in our family we are more grief-stricken than when so many die in Pakistan, and if one of our fingers is cut we experience more pain than we felt when those seven hundred thousand died. As we approach the 'I', attachment becomes more concentrated, and as we go further away from 'mine', its shadow becomes thinner and rarer.

Attachment is the shadow of the ego. Attachments are immediately created wherever you see 'I am'. But as I said, attachment is exclusive; to make attachment possible, something or somebody must be left out. Therefore, the sage says, one who has seen all animate and inanimate objects in himself, becomes nonexclusive; the feeling in him now is, "All are mine." He becomes all-inclusive. Then attachment does not happen, because there is now no foundation for it.

When all are 'mine', there is no purpose in calling anyone mine. There was a purpose to saying 'mine' as long as there was a purpose to saying 'thine' – there was someone who was not 'mine'. So you made boundaries, you drew lines to show the limits of what was 'mine'. You created a wall, a boundary. Beyond this limit, another world began with which you had no concern at all. "Whether it dies or is destroyed is no concern of mine." On this side of the boundary is your world, for which you desire that there be no misery, no distress, no affliction, because you are grieved when it is in trouble.

The Upanishad says a man's attachment vanishes when he sees himself not only in all animals, not only in all living things, but in all animate and inanimate objects, even in a grain of sand – that is to say, in whatever exists in the world. Then no attachment is left. Attachment is there while the boundary is there. Attachment cannot be limitless. Remember, limitless attachment is an impossibility. It lives within limits. As the boundary widens, the attachment weakens; and as the limits are narrowed, the attachment grows stronger. In limitlessness, attachment disappears.

And then, how can grief be possible when attachment has disappeared? It does not exist without attachment. If there is no attachment, there is no grief. So the Upanishads call him a wise man who stands beyond both attachment and grief. And how does he stand beyond? He stands beyond by seeing himself in the whole of existence, which is there spread all around us but invisible to us because we are also there in it.

The following event happened in the life of Rabindranath Tagore. It is worth noting. He wrote prayers about God in the Gitanjali, for which he received the Nobel prize and became famous the world over. But there lived an old man near his house who began to harass him constantly. Wherever he met Rabindranath, he would hold on to him and ask, "Please tell me truly: have you known God?"

The old man was obstinate and Rabindranath, being an honest person, could not tell a lie. The old man looked so straight and deep into the eyes of Rabindranath that his hands and legs used to tremble. Here was the winner of the Nobel prize. Wherever he went he was much honored by the people. People used to say, "Here is a living example of one whom the Upanishads call a Maharishi." Yet here he was, being troubled by an old man from his neighborhood. And the harassment was not for just one day or one morning or evening, but continued every day, because the old man, having nothing to do, spent all his time sitting on a chair near the door of his house so Rabindranath found it difficult to avoid him.

Rabindranath has written in his diary that he found it very difficult to leave the house: "Before going out, I would inquire whether the old man was sitting there or not. Otherwise he would grab hold of me and ask, 'Have you seen God? Have you known him?' I used to tremble on hearing these questions because I know nothing about him. On hearing my answer the old man would laugh loudly and heartily. His laughing in that way spoiled my sleep, it began to haunt me; I began to be afraid of that old man. Once I thought, 'I really created trouble for myself writing this Gitanjali.' I thought, 'That old man must have had some glimpse of God, otherwise he could not haunt me so.'" From his eyes it appeared he knew something, because Rabindranath could not get away with it by staring at him and repeating one or two lines of the Gitanjali in answer to his question.

Thus years passed, and the old man continued his haunting. Rabindranath has said: "A great load was removed from my mind on the day on which I could tell him, 'I have known God.'" It was the beginning of the rainy season, and the first downpours were leaving puddles everywhere. Reservoirs and small pits on the roadsides filled with water. Frogs were croaking. It was morning and Rabindranath was tempted out by these changes in nature – the croaking of the frogs, the confused din of the falling rain, the new fragrance of the earth. He saw the old man was not on his usual seat. Perhaps he was not up yet.

Rabindranath ran out of his house. The sun was rising over the sea. He stopped at the seashore. The sun was shimmering on the water. He looked at the sun and its reflection, and then began to return to his home. The sun was reflected in each puddle, in each small pond, in every dirty ditch on the roadside. It was shining all around – in dirty puddles, on the sea, in clean small streams, on every side. Seeing all this, some music, some unknown, indefinable sound within began to play in Rabindranath's heart.

As he returned, he was dancing. He was dancing because he saw that the reflection of the sun was never tarnished. He was dancing because he saw that the sun's reflection was as fresh and clean in the dirty, muddy water as it was in the cleanest water. Reflection can never be dirty. How can it be dirty? Only water can be muddy and dirty. But the sun that looks into it, whose reflection appears in it, is not dirty. It is absolutely fresh and clean. No water can spoil it. This was a tremendous, a revolutionary experience for him. It meant that God, who is even within the worst of men, cannot be made dirty. The reflection of God in the most sinful person is as pure as it is in the most pious person. So he was returning dancing. A door had opened within.

That old man was sitting near his door. This was the first time he was not afraid of the old man, and for the first time the old man said, "It is all right, it seems you have known him." And the old man approached Rabindranath and embraced him and said, "Your ecstasy, your dancing today, tells me that you have known him. Now I can honor you!"

Then for three days Rabindranath remained in a state of ecstasy – in a state of madness. The members of the family were afraid to see this. Only the old man often used to come and tell them, "Be glad! Be joyful!" and began to inform the neighbors that he knew God. But the people in the house were very much afraid because Rabindranath was behaving in a very strange way. If he saw a pillar he would embrace it. If a cow passed by on the road he would embrace her, too. If he saw a tree he would embrace it. The people in the house thought he had lost his mind: "He has gone mad!" But the old man continued to say, "Don't worry. He was mad until now, and now he is fine. Now he has begun to see, in all existence, that without which the song he was singing all this time was useless. It was only rhyme, a poor excuse for poetry. Only now, real music is born in his life."

Rabindranath has written: "I could, by and by, control myself

and bring my ecstasy under control, with great effort. Otherwise I
yearned to embrace everybody and everything I met. Until now
I was yearning and praying, 'Oh God, where is your door?' Now
God was my door, and now wherever I looked I saw his door. Up
until now I was searching for him and asking, 'Where are you hid-
ing?' But now I was amazed because he was there already in me;
there was nothing else but him."

He who sees his presence in all existence or sees the entire existence in himself is truly a wise man; and such a person is beyond
attachment and grief. Remember, there is neither happiness nor
unhappiness in his life, there is only ecstasy. The purity of existence dances in his life. He is life itself, dancing and singing the
praise of existence. His life itself is music; and all that brings grief,
all that binds, all that becomes attachment, all that seems to bring
happiness today but is the cause of unhappiness tomorrow – all
these have no place in his life. He is now a mirror.

When you stand before a mirror you are seen reflected in it, and
when you go away from it, it at once leaves you. It does not hold on
to you. No sooner are you gone from it than it becomes empty,
without reflection. The mirror carries no attachment to you. That is
why, when you stand aside, instead of in front of it, it is not broken
into pieces out of sorrow for you. Its heart does not break into
pieces. It does not say, "How can I now live without you?" Instead
it says, "When you stood before me you were very beautiful, very
good, and you showed me great favor; and when you leave me I feel
no displeasure." Nothing changes. The mirror is as joyful when it is
empty and unreflecting as it was when it was filled with reflection.

Thus lives a learned man, like a mirror in the world. He is pleased
with whatever comes before him. He is happy if he sees a flower and
becomes its reflection, throws its reflection back, sees godliness in it.
If there is no one in front of him – when all is empty – he sees godliness in emptiness. The very emptiness is godliness. Then he dances
in that emptiness, and is in ecstasy even in emptiness.

Enough for today. Now let us try to become mirrors ourselves.

# Beyond Science

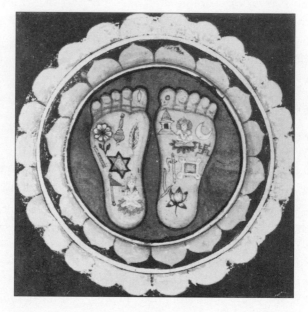

9

*It is all-pervading,*
*it is the purest,*
*it is bodiless, it is indestructible,*
*it is without sinews, it is spotless,*
*it is sinless, it is all-seeing,*
*it is all-knowing,*
*it is the best among the best,*
*and it is self-created.*

THIS SUTRA GIVES US some indications about the nature of the *atman* – above all, that it is created of itself. Atman, existence, alone is self-created. The word *swayambhoo* means self-originated. It means that which is not created by any other thing, that which is self-created. Its existence is from itself. Its existence is in no one else's hands; it depends upon itself.

So this first point, that the atman is self-originated, should be comprehended fully. Everything we see can be produced. Whatever is produced, whatever can be made, will not be the atman. We construct a building; it is not self-originating, it is made. We manufacture a machine; it is not self-created, it is manufactured by us. Seek that element, that essence, that is manufactured by no one. This uncreated essence is the atman. In our effort to seek into the existence of the universe, if we reach there, if we can grasp that supreme substance of the universe which is not created by anyone, which is eternal, unoriginated, the self itself, then we shall attain to godliness.

The atman and the supreme atman are not two; they are the names of the same thing seen from two viewpoints. If you find it within yourself, then that unmanufactured, unborn, self-created element is called the atman. And if you seek and find it in another, then that element is called the great, the supreme atman. The atman is simply the supreme atman known from within. The supreme atman is simply the atman known from without.

If you examine yourself you will see that this body is a created thing. It could not have been produced without the cooperation of your parents. Even if, in the future, it is made in a test-tube, it remains a manufactured thing. The scientists and biologists of the West may be able, if not today then in the future, to fulfill their claim of producing a child in a test-tube. They will succeed in manufacturing a body in a test-tube, and hope thereby to finally defeat religion. But they are mistaken in their view, because the spiritual man never saw this body as the atman.

The spiritual man says, "That which is unborn, uncreated, is the atman." By manufacturing a body in a test-tube, scientists will simply prove that the body is not the soul – the atman. It seems that the body will be manufactured in the future; I do not see any reason why it should not be so. Many spiritualists are apprehensive about this: "What will happen to the atman when the body is created in a test-tube in a laboratory? It will prove that the atman does not exist if we are able to produce a child without the parents' cooperation and with the help of chemicals." But such spiritualists do not know that the body is not the atman. It is precisely if the scientist succeeds in his experiment that this sutra of the Upanishad will be proved true – that this body is not the atman. Only this much, and nothing more, will be proved.

Even now we know that the body is not the soul. This fact is proved by the physical sciences. In the future the body will be created by artificial and chemical processes. At present, when the chemical substances of the parents combine and create that cell which is the first cell of the body, then the soul enters it. If in the future that cell is produced in the laboratory, and if that genetic situation is created which is being created by parents up to now, then the soul will enter there also.

But that cell, the cell which is the first cell of the body, is not the atman. It is a manufactured thing, it is not selfborn. It is made by somebody. Its existence, its birth, depends upon something, so those who know the atman are not prepared to call it the atman. It is not the atman. To know that, we shall have to work our way back and back; we shall have to go down deeper and deeper.

So I myself am pleased and hope that science succeeds in making a test-tube baby as soon as possible, because then we will be helped by scientific investigations to break our identity with the body. Then we will know for sure that the body is a kind of machine, and that to believe in it as the self is foolish. It is foolishness even now, but at present we are unwilling to recognize that the body *is* a machine. It is a machine even so. It is produced by natural forces, so by understanding the secrets of nature we will be able to produce it, and then we will have the cooperation of natural forces to break our identification with the body.

Entering deep within ourselves, we have to reach that place, that essence, which cannot be created; and as long as manufacturing it is possible, know that it cannot be the atman. So by going deeper and deeper into manufacturing, science helps religion, because whatsoever science can create, that is not the atman. The atman is further than that. The atman is always beyond that which can be made.

So we are greatly obliged to science that it goes on making one thing after another, extending the limits of what can be manufactured and thereby defining what the atman is not; because we call that element the atman which is self-originated, which is unborn, which cannot be created. It means the original.

There has to be, without doubt, an ultimate, a fundamental element for this universe to be created, and this ultimate element must be uncreated. If a basis is required for the creation of everything, then creation is impossible. If you say, "God is required to create the world," then you will have to say another superior God is necessary to create God. There is no end to this sort of logic. Then we shall never reach that place where we can say, "Okay, here is the place for whose creation no other creator is necessary."

It will be better and more scientific if we understand it thus: that which is self-originated is the atman. This is more scientific than saying that the atman is self-originated. It is more scientific if we say, "We call him the supreme atman – God – who is uncreated, who is not created by anyone," than to say, "Nobody has created God."

Science also experiences this. In their investigations, scientists reach certain limits and then they feel that there is something beyond the limits, which is beyond creation. As it happened, science was always making investigations about elements, and the ancient scientists declared that there were five elements. This was not said by the ancient spiritualists – the religious people – because they had no concern with such elements. They were concerned with only one, the self-originated element.

The old scientific thinking of nearly four to five thousand years ago maintained that everything is created from five elements. Now the mistake happened because there did not exist separate books of science; every subject was included in religious books. The religious books were the collections of all the knowledge of those days, and so the belief that everything was created from five elements was available in religious books. But this matter relates to science and not to religion. Religion seeks only one element – the self-originated element.

Science continued its investigations, and it found that the principle of five elements was incorrect. When this was found out the foolish so-called religious people were very worried. They thought everything was now in confusion, because they had come to believe in five elements. But science went on steadily with its research. Now scientists have discovered one hundred and eight elements. But I want to make it clear that the new researches of science disprove only the old science.

No discovery of science can disprove religion, because the directions of religion and science are quite separate. Someone may compose a very fine poem, but that cannot disprove a principle of mathematics. There is no relation between poetry and mathematics. Similarly someone may develop a deep and difficult mathematical theory, but that will not disqualify a good poem, because their directions are separate; they don't cancel each other. They don't even touch each other. These directions run parallel like railway lines. If they seem to meet each other somewhere, it is our illusion. If you go to the meeting point you will find that they run parallel. Only an illusion of their meeting each other can arise, as it does in the case of railway lines.

When science disproves something it disproves the old fact or belief. The whole Christian world became very nervous when science declared that the earth is not flat but round, because it is mentioned in the Bible that the earth is flat. But what is written in the Bible about the earth's shape is the affirmation of scientists of those days; it is not a religious affirmation. So when science found out that the earth is round it disproved the old belief. But this new discovery showed that the ancient science was wrong. Science can never make religion incorrect, nor can religion ever make science wrong. They have no relation at all to each other, there is no interconnection between them. There is not even communication between them; their dimensions are different from each other. Their directions are absolutely separate.

Starting with five elements science found many other elements and their number is one hundred and eight today, thus proving that the ancient five elements were incorrectly known as elements. They were certainly not elements. In fact, those which were known as elements in the beginning were not elements; they were compounds. As for example, earth. Now there are many substances in earth – there is not just one substance alone in any sort of earth. Another example is water. Science says there are two substances, hydrogen and oxygen, in water. Water is not a single element, it is a mixture of two substances. A combination is not an element; according to science, it is called a compound. So water cannot be considered an element. Oxygen and hydrogen are elements.

So science discovered one hundred and eight elements. But as science went deeper and deeper into its researches, scientists by and by began to realize that all these one hundred and eight elements have a common intermediary. It may be hydrogen or it may be oxygen, but both of them are created by electric particles. So it appears that hydrogen and oxygen are also not elements. Electricity has now become the element. The union of some electric particles makes hydrogen and the union of some electric particles makes oxygen, and these one hundred and eight elements are simply the combinations of electric particles. If three particles are there, they make one element; if there are two particles, another element is produced. If there are four, another element is created. But whether they are three or four or two, they are all particles of electricity.

Hence science had a new experience – that there is only one element, and that is electricity. All the one hundred and eight so-called elements are, in the final analysis, compounds. They are combinations. They are not elements, they are not basic substances.

The position of science at present is that it is prepared to believe that electricity is uncreated, that it is self-originated, and that all this vast growth, this expansion, is that of the only element – electricity. Electricity, says science, is not a compound produced by the combination of two substances, it is uncreated. Science calls that substance an element which is self-originated. So now science calls electricity a self-originated element. It cannot be created, because only that substance which can be produced by a combination can be made. If you combine two things, a third thing will be produced. If you combine three things, the result will be the making of a fourth. But how can you create the original element which is without any combination? You can neither make it nor destroy it. If we wish to destroy water, we can do so by separating hydrogen and oxygen, because water is made by combination. If we wish to destroy hydrogen, we can do so. If we separate its electric particles – which we call atomic energy – then hydrogen will no longer be there. Only the electric energy will remain. Only the energy will remain. But we cannot destroy that energy because there is no combination of two substances which we can separate. We can simply do this much – we can either combine or separate things. We cannot create. That which is uncreated is element.

At present science calls electricity, electrical energy, a self-originated element. But religion calls the atman a self-originated element. It will become possible, if not now then in future, for scientific investigation to break, to separate electricity also; and then we will be able to see that even electricity is not self-originated. Some years back we knew water as an element; then we were able to analyze it and found that oxygen and hydrogen are elements, water is not. Then we analyzed hydrogen and could see that it is also not an element; electricity is the element.

There are two possibilities: either it may be established that electricity and the atman are one and the same, or it may be that electricity will also be broken down and we will discover that it is also not an element. As far as I understand, electricity also can be broken down, and when it is broken we will find that only consciousness remains.

Now, it is interesting to consider that no one regards stone as energy. It is a substance – a matter. Our old distinctions divide things into matter and energy. Stone is matter. But when stone was analyzed, and in the final analysis the atom was found, then matter was lost and energy remained; and science had to abandon its old notion of duality – duality of matter and energy. On matter being analyzed further and further, it was found that it did not exist; there was only energy. Matter is energy. Now there is no substance like matter; the latest position of science is that there is nothing like matter. Now the materialists have to be very careful in saying anything in support of matter because nothing like matter exists; there is only energy.

As long as we had not arrived at the final analysis of matter, two substances were accepted by scientists – matter and energy. You will definitely see the distinction if you hold a stone in one hand and touch an electric wire with the other. You will know that a stone is a stone and what is passing through the wire is energy. There is a great difference between the two. But now science says if you go on breaking and analyzing a stone, you will end up with energy which can pass through an electric wire. By further breaking it, we killed one hundred thousand people in Hiroshima. That was an electric shock! By breaking matter, by the explosion of a small atom, so much energy was produced that we could kill one hundred thousand people in Hiroshima and one hundred and twenty thousand in Nagasaki. So many people would not die by touching even the most powerful current.

A small atom produces a tremendous amount of electricity, and by transforming it into electricity the atom was destroyed – it was no more. So science now says that its old notion of duality – matter and energy – is gone. Now only energy remains. But I tell you, there still exists one more distinction, and that is the distinction of energy and consciousness.

When we touch electricity we know it is energy, but when we talk with a person we don't feel that he is simply energy, we feel his consciousness also. If the electric current is on, this tape recorder here will work, it will speak. But it will only repeat what I am saying. So when it speaks, it is only energy. But when I speak it is not only energy; there is consciousness also. The tape recorder cannot make any changes, it will report what I have said; but even if I want I cannot repeat tomorrow what I am saying today, because I am not a machine. I myself do not know what sentence will follow this sentence. When you listen to it, I am also listening to it.

The distinction between consciousness and energy still exists. It should be said that the old world was not a duality, it was a threefold world of matter, energy and consciousness. Out of these three, matter has been dropped. Now there are two – energy and consciousness. Deep investigations into matter proved it to be nonexistent; it disappeared because we knew that it was energy. And I tell you energy will also disappear in further and deeper investigations, and we shall see that there is only consciousness. That consciousness is the atman. Then there will be no matter, and no energy; everything will disappear and only consciousness will remain.

That is why we have named that supreme element *satchitanand*. To convey the true meaning of the word 'atman', three words are used. The word *sat* means existence – what is, which is always existing, which was never nonexistent. Sat means that which is there always. It is never in that state of which you can say 'It is'. Everything changes and goes on changing; yet it is there, unchanged.

The word *chit* means consciousness. It is not that it is simply existing, but it knows that 'I am'. It knows its presence. A thing can exist; for example, a stone is lying on the ground, but it is mere existence. If that stone knows that it exists, then and then only, it is consciousness also.

The third word is *anand* – bliss. It is not enough that it is the atman, it is not enough that it is consciousness, it is not enough that it exists and is aware of its existence. Just as it is aware of its existence, it also knows that 'I am anand' – the highest ecstasy!

The atman is said in this sutra to be self-originated because it can neither be created nor destroyed by anyone. Remember, as it is self-originated it is indestructible, it is immortal. The thing that can be made will die; that which can be manufactured will be destroyed. No production can be everlasting, no structure can be of a permanent nature. All constructions are produced at the appropriate time and disappear at their destined time. In fact, the thing that is born will die. However strong it may be made, it is sure to die though it may last a little longer. Palaces, whether made of paper or granite, are sure to fall down. Millions of wind blasts eventually fell the stone walls of palaces. If they are made of steel they will take a little longer, but in the end they are sure to fall. A palace of playing-cards will fall down even with one light puff of wind. It is a difference of degree only.

The difference between the falling of a house made of playing-cards and that made of stone is simply a matter of difference in wind velocity. There is no basic difference in the houses; the palace of cards is a constructed thing, so it must fall, and the stone palace is also a constructed thing, so it too must fall. Where there is making at one end, there will certainly be destruction at the other end. Because it is self-originated, the atman is indestructible. As it has never been made at one end, it will never be destroyed at the other end.

The self-originated has two characteristics: it is uncreated and it is indestructible. Let me tell you also that science supports this view, that whatever is made by the combination of two things will die; while the element which is made of one thing cannot be destroyed, cannot die. There is no way for it either to be destroyed or to be created. To create something other things have to be combined, and to destroy a thing, those things have to be separated. To make is to join, and to destroy is to separate. But the element which is single, which has no other element in it, cannot be destroyed. How can it be destroyed? It cannot be broken. If it were made of two things it could have been broken. But as it is single, it will be always. The element which has its origin in itself is indestructible, and that element is called the atman by the Upanishads.

Some of its other features, its unavoidable characteristics, are also described. It is said that the self-created atman is all-knowing. What does all-knowing mean? It can have two meanings, and the wrong one of the two is fashionable. It usually happens that the fashionable thing is wrong. True knowledge is so deep and mysterious that it can never be the fashion. A matter without much depth can be understood by all and is likely to be fashionable.

One meaning of the term all-knowing is having knowledge about everything; this is the fashionable meaning. For example, the Jainas call Mahavira all-knowing, because when a person knows the atman he becomes omniscient, all-seeing; such is the nature of the atman. Mahavira himself has said that he who knows the one, knows all. In this sense it is correct to say that Mahavira knew all. Then what usually happens is that the follower interprets this as meaning that Mahavira knows how to repair a bicycle puncture! But Mahavira did not know what a bicycle was. Or that Mahavira must know how an airplane is built…. If the term all-knowing is understood in this way, it gives rise to great delusion and difficulty; and the Jainas were in great difficulty when they began to consider Mahavira all-knowing in this sense.

Buddha frequently ridiculed this belief of the Jainas. What he was really laughing at was the absurdity of Mahavira's followers interpreting his enlightenment in this way, because they actually began to claim that Mahavira knew everything. So Buddha on many occasions joked, "I have heard some people claim that a certain individual is all-knowing, but I have seen that individual begging in front of a house in which there was nobody. After some time he realized that the house was unoccupied. I have seen him walking in the pale morning light; did he know of the dog lying in his path when he trod on its tail?"

So Buddha laughed at the foolish interpretations of that term all-knowing. He would say, "I have heard about this all-knowing individual standing on the outskirts of a town asking people the way to that town." But this fun is not directed at Mahavira. Mahavira never made such claims. The claimants are his followers. They say, "Mahavira is all-knowing; he knows which road leads to what place."

All-knowing has another meaning – a negative meaning. This positive meaning of 'he knows all' is incorrect. The negative meaning is that now there is nothing left to know; there is nothing left worth knowing. Is it worth knowing where a particular road leads to, or whether there is anyone in the house? What does it matter if such matters are not known? Is it worth knowing whether a dog is sleeping or not sleeping on the road? Where is the harm if it is not known?

As I see it, the word all-knowing means that after knowing the atman, nothing is left unknown which is worth knowing. All that is worth knowing is known. In this humdrum world many things seem to be worth knowing, but what difference does it make to know them? So to me its meaning is that nothing is left out which is worth knowing. Not the slightest thing is omitted from our knowing that might bring about even the tiniest diminution in our life's ecstasy. Nothing is left out whose omission might cause a hindrance in our becoming satchitanand.

If a particular road goes to the left it will lead one to a certain place and if it goes to the right it will lead one to another place, but this makes no difference in the quality of satchitanand. If Mahavira misses his way and reaches the wrong destination it will make no difference to him, because what difference does it make for a person who has attained his goal, who has reached the final destination, to miss his way during his wanderings in this world? What difference does it make for a person who, having reached his destination, wanders here and there? What does it do to us who have not reached our destination to find the right village? And what difference does it make to us if we know all our roads as accurately as if we are geographical maps?

Because of the mistaken interpretation of the term all-knowing by his followers, Mahavira was unnecessarily subjected to a lot of ridicule, because the claims they made were foolish; and now, yet again, these claimants are greatly puzzled. For instance, they were in difficulty recently when the astronauts landed on the moon for the first time, because the astronauts' description of the moon did not correspond with the moon as it is described in their scriptures: and it is stated in their scriptures that the facts declared by 'the all-knowing' cannot be wrong. So the Jaina devotees have gone to the extent of saying that the space travelers were under an illusion that they had landed on the moon. They had not landed on the moon, but had traveled to the far side of the moon where the vehicles – chariots of the gods – remain in waiting. There they had landed and from there had returned! They had certainly not landed on the moon.

One Jaina follower even began fund raising, and managed to collect hundreds of thousands of rupees from simple, foolish people to prove in a laboratory that the astronauts had not landed on the moon, but in some god's vehicle. "And if they ever reach the moon, they will find the moon as described in our scriptures, because whatever is said in those scriptures is the testimony of an all-knowing person."

To use one's scripture to cling to such foolish arguments leaves the scripture worthless. When it is mentioned in your scripture that the moon is so and so, and the statement is later proved incorrect, remember that the statement in the scripture is that of a scientist of those days, not of one who knows the atman. What concern has the knower of the atman with describing what kind of stones are and are not found on the moon? And if such a statement is made by him, it is not made in his capacity as a knower of the atman.

Such a position creates great difficulty. Let us consider the case of a great thinker like Einstein – a great mathematician. Being a great mathematician does not define all other features of his personality; there are many other things in his life. He is not a mathematician when he plays cards. And what concern would he have with mathematics when he falls in love with a woman? He is not making a mathematical statement at all when he says to her that there is no other woman more beautiful than her. But if somebody claims in the future that such a great mathematician as Einstein must have said so only after measuring and comparing the beauty of all women in the world, the claim is certainly childish. No, such statements are made by anybody and everybody in this world. Every woman meets some man who will tell her so. It is not necessary to be a mathematician to say so. Such a statement is made, not in the capacity of a mathematician, but of a lover.

So the word all-knowing means that there is now nothing left worth knowing, nothing which would enhance this man's ecstasy. His ecstasy is *entire*. And there is nothing left which might be a hindrance to it. All his ignorance, all his folly, is destroyed. His anger, his attachment, his greed, are all gone, all destroyed. He is in a state of supreme ecstasy. All-knowing means one is living in supreme ecstasy. He knows that true knowledge which puts him in ecstasy and removes any possibility of unhappiness.

The atman is all-knowing in this sense, and not in the sense of the knower of the three tenses – the past, the present and the future. He does not know what will happen tomorrow or the day after tomorrow. He does not know who will win the election or lose it; and there is no reason or necessity to know such things. All the events happening within limits of time are to him like lines drawn on water. He keeps no account of them, he does not worry about them. Who wins or who loses is the substance of dreams to him; such matters belong to a children's world, he is too mature for them. He is not concerned with such things.

In knowing the supreme element he becomes all-knowing – that is, his ignorance falls away. The avarice, attachment and anger produced in ignorance fall away. In their place comes ecstasy, born out of true knowing. The light of knowing begins to shine, and to live in its illumination is to live in supreme ecstasy – ceaseless and eternal.

The third characteristic of this atman is purity – always immaculate, always holy, and always innocent. When we become impure it does not become impure. Our whole impurity is our delusion. As I was saying last night, the sun's reflection is as pure in a dirty pool as in a crystal lake. There is not the least difference in its purity. Its purity is not an accidental characteristic; it is intrinsic, inborn. So this matter will be easily understood if you understand the difference between the accidental and the inborn.

The accidental characteristic is foreign; it is linked to you but does not come from within you. For instance, a man is dishonest; his dishonesty is accidental, not inherent. It has been practiced, it has been acquired. This is why no person can remain dishonest twenty-four hours a day. Even the most dishonest person cannot be so every hour of the day, because what is acquired is a burden which has to be put aside sometimes. The person needs to be relieved of it some of the time. It is not his nature, so he has to be honest with someone in his dealings. And sometimes it happens that dishonest people are honest among themselves to a degree that even honest people are not. The reason is that what we call honesty is also an acquired thing from which we sometimes have to seek relief.

You cannot live incessantly with a thing which is acquired, which is accidental. You will have to take a break from it at times. You will have to do so, otherwise the tension will increase and the burden will become great. Hence the serious-minded person has to seek out some entertainment at intervals, otherwise his seriousness becomes a burden for him. Mahavira and Buddha had no need for entertainment because they were not carrying any load of seriousness. Keep this in mind. We tend to think it is because they were so serious-minded that they would not go to see a film or a play. If they were serious they would have to go to see a play. No, they were certainly not serious-minded.

This does not mean either that they are nonserious. Seriousness and nonseriousness, both are false. Mahavira, Buddha are themselves; they are in their intrinsic selves. They acquire nothing from without, so there is nothing from which they need to take a break. If a person practices saintliness and makes it a habit, then he will have to take a holiday from it occasionally. For three or four days every month or fortnight he will have to take a holiday. And he will not be able to maintain his saintly role during the day if he has not gone into the nonsaintly world for an hour or two during that time. It will be difficult for him.

Accidental attributes are those which we learn, which we acquire. They come to us from without, they do not come from within. They are all learned by us. For example, language is an accidental, acquired attribute. Anyone can learn Hindi or Marathi or English or German. There are thousands of languages and there could be many more also, without difficulty. All the languages that we could devise would be accidental.

But what about silence? It is not accidental. So while there will be a difference if two people are talking, if they observe complete silence there will be no difference in that silence. There can be a discussion in speech: there cannot be any discussion in silence.

There will be no distinction in the inner attribute of two people when they are in complete silence. What difference will there be in two silences? But there will be a difference if silence is assumed from without, because speech will be going on within. There will be a difference if two people observe silence for show only. I am sitting silent, you are sitting silent beside me. I continue my thinking, you continue your thinking. So though the lips are closed, the act of thinking goes on, and there will be vast differences between us in such a condition. We will be thousands of miles away within. Nobody can say where you will be and where I will be.

But if silence is really achieved, not assumed from without but blossoming from within, unfolding from within, then and then only are we really in complete silence. Then what difference will there be between you and me, when words vanish from within, when speech has dissolved from within? There will be no difference at all. We will be standing at the same place. We will be as if we are one. By and by, as silence progresses, our two flames will be fused into one flame. They cannot remain as two separate things, because the boundary line marking the distinction between the two has disappeared. Distinction creates a boundary; in its absence, the boundary disappears.

So silence – abiding silence, inner silence – is natural, while speech is accidental; and whatever is accidental is not everlasting. This is why you cannot maintain anger for twenty-four hours, although you can live in forgiveness for twenty-four hours. Think about this. You cannot live in anger for the whole day. You will be angry, and after some time you will be without it. There will be a sort of coming and going away of anger. But there will be no obstacle to living in forgiveness for twenty-four hours. You can remain forgiving for the whole day. Similarly, if you wish to live in hatred twenty-four hours a day it is not possible; you will create a hell for yourself. Whereas if you want to live perpetually in love, it is possible.

But it is not possible to remain in that feeling which we presently call love, because it is not real love, it is an occasional thing. You can be full of love for maybe ten minutes out of twenty-four hours; for the rest of the time it is not possible. And if someone makes an effort to be in love for a longer period, it will be difficult for him to be in love even for ten minutes. Why? – because we can only be forever in that which is our nature, and we cannot be forever in that which is foreign to us and which has been imported from without. That will have to be removed, that load will have to be cast away.

The atman is pure, spotless. It does not get spoiled, it does not become impure sometimes and then need us to rectify it, to make it pure again. If the atman can be impure, we will not be able to make it pure. Then who will make it pure? He who could have made it pure is himself impure now. Whatever that impure atman does will now be impure.

No, it is not the case that the atman becomes impure and we are required to make it pure. It is already pure. It is only we who accumulate impure and unholy attributes on all sides of us, just as we hang a black curtain on all sides of a lamp. The shining light does not change into darkness because of it. The light is burning in its own brightness even then, but the surrounding black curtain prevents its light from shining out in all directions. And if the light is as mad as we are, and forgets that "I am the light," then it will face the same difficulties which we are experiencing.

Our relationship with the nature of our self is completely broken and we are identified with the web made up of our body, mind, thoughts, feelings, passions and desires, surrounding us on all sides. We begin to say, "This is me!" That one which is within us identifies itself with anything and begins to say, "This is me!" And that element within is so pure, so spotless and clear that whatever is reflected in it is reflected in full; we catch hold of that reflection and begin to say, "This is me!"

The mistake is like this. Suppose the mirror in front of which you are standing becomes conscious and looks within itself and sees your image standing in front of it, and then says, "This is me!" Such an unfortunate happening only takes place because of the mirror's purity. The atman is pure and spotless, and because of its crystal clear purity, whatever approaches it is reflected in it as in a mirror – whatever the thing may be. If the body goes to it, it is reflected as in a mirror and the atman says, "I am the body."

You have no idea of the continual changes in your body and of how you identify yourself with them. If the first cell created in your mother's womb were taken out and put before you and then you were told, "You were once this," you would at once deny it and say, "How can this be me? It is impossible." If five to ten photos of you are taken every day of your life there will be a long series of your photos. Every photo was once claimed by you to be yourself. But what a difference there is between the photo of your childhood and that of your old age! What a vast difference there is between the new-born child and the corpse going into the grave. In all these changes you are there. Whatever is reflected in your mirror, you have said, "This is me."

Have you ever found any similarity between your infant photo and the photo of your adulthood. Is there any affinity? Are you that baby? No, once you had owned it, and the claim was fixed in your memory; and only the claim is still there today – that this was you. The body changes every day.

Scientists tell us that every cell of the body is completely altered over a period of seven years; not a single old cell remains. But our identity continues. Identification goes on. In seven years' time our bones, our flesh, our blood and all other cells are altered. If a person lives up to seventy years, the body has changed totally ten times. The whole body has undergone change ten times.

The body changes every moment, but there is a spotless mirror within. Whatever reflection is made in it, whatever picture is made in it tells us, "This is me." If this identity is broken, if this ignorance is removed, if we stop saying, "This is me," then we shall be able to say, "I am the knower of all these changes, I am the witness of all this. I knew my childhood, and I was not that; I knew my youth and it was not me. I shall know my old age also, but it will not be me. I knew birth; this is not me. I shall know death also, and neither am I that. I am that which knew all these different phases. I am that which knew this long series, this long caravan of films. I am the knower, I am not that which is known. I am not that which is reflected. I am that in which reflections are made." Then the atman is pure and spotless, a clean mirror, a dirtless pool, where no ripple of impurity ever was.

When the Upanishads say it is pure, they speak of a total purity. Not the least impurity has ever entered the atman. So the Upanishads affirm, by breaking this identity we also become the purity. In fact nobody has ever become impure; it cannot be, it is impossible. The impurity is in the identifying. Identity makes one a sinner or a saint. Remember, the saint is also impure because he is identified with his holiness. The sinner has an iron chain, the saint a golden one. But what difference does it make? The market value of iron and gold may differ, but identification, bondage, continues.

Someone says, "I am a sinner," somebody else says, "I am virtuous." As long as we continue to say, "This is me," we are unnecessarily making ourselves impure. Though we are not intrinsically impure, we go on adopting impurity. The day on which you are able to say, "I am not this, I am not that," you will be able to say, "I am that in which everything is reflected. I am that mirror in which all shadows come and go. I am that void in which everything glitters and vanishes."

No one knows how many births, how many bodies, how many forms and shapes, how many accidental attributes, how much worthiness, how many positions and how many variations have glittered in it. Endless are the journeys but the lake is one; and it is always clean and spotless. Travelers go on traveling on its banks and the lake goes on supposing, "This is me, this is me." At times a thief is passing on that road and the lake says, "I am a thief"; sometimes a sadhu passes on that way and the lake says, "I am a sadhu." Sometimes a saint passes that way and the lake says, "I am a saint," and sometimes a sinner passes on that road and the lake says, "I am a sinner."

Thus the lake goes on proclaiming as caravans of reflections pass along that road. And they pass on so quickly that no sooner does one reflection vanish than another appears in it. We do not take even that moment – that interval between the two happenings – so that we can look at the lake in which there is no reflection at all.

Meditation is the practice which focuses on that interval. In that moment when nothing is reflecting, we can glimpse the lake itself; we can know, "I am the lake, I am not that caravan which is passing on the bank. I am not these reflections which form on me. I am that on which all shapes are made and yet which is itself unmade. I remain unmade, uncreated."

Keep in mind these three things. All the other things included in the Ishavasya Upanishad are only different aspects of these three.

# Ignorance Will Show You The Way

**10**

*Those who follow
the path of ignorance
enter darkness;
and those who are absorbed
in knowledge
enter a greater darkness.*

THIS SUTRA MAKES a profound proclamation of the truth – a very bold proclamation. Such an announcement can be made only by a sage. It is declared that those who tread on the path of ignorance lose their way and wander here and there in this world; but those who walk on the path of knowledge – that is, the path of "I know" – lose themselves in greater darkness. It is difficult to find another statement as bold as this in the whole history of mankind – to find a parallel to a statement that dares to say that the ignorant grope about in darkness, but those who claim, "I know," grope about in greater darkness. Whoever said this arrived at it through very deep thought.

That the ignorant wander in darkness is easily understood by us, there is no difficulty in it. The statement is straightforward and clear. The ignorant do get themselves lost. But the sage says they lose themselves in darkness – not in deep and great darkness. The ignorant wander in darkness only. Then why do the so-called learned wander in greater darkness? And where is the remedy to be free from darkness when the ignorant wander in darkness and the so-called learned wander in greater darkness?

The ignorant wander in darkness only, not very deep, because however much wandering ignorance may cause, it cannot be very deep. The thing that leads into greater darkness is not ignorance but ego. Mistakes may occur through ignorance, but ignorance is always prepared to correct the mistakes, so there is little likelihood of straying far. Ignorance is always likely to make mistakes, but it is also always ready to correct them. Ignorance has its own humility. This is why children can learn quickly and the old cannot. Children are ignorant and ready to improve. When a mistake is shown to them they will correct it; but when old people are shown their mistakes they are displeased and refuse to correct them. On the contrary, they will first try to prove that it is not a mistake at all. When children are shown mistakes they are ready to admit them and will soon correct them; hence they learn so quickly.

The old cannot learn in years what children are able to learn in days. Their capacity to learn decreases. What is the cause? The capacity of the old to learn should increase, but no, it does not. The old are in a delusion that they know. The child is only in darkness, the old man has fallen into a deeper and greater darkness. The delusion is established in him that he knows something. The child knows he does not know anything, so he is willing to learn. He is happy to learn whatever you teach him. Thus children can wander in darkness, while the old wander in greater darkness.

The ignorant man, if he becomes conscious of his ignorance, becomes very humble. If we remember our ignorance, if we can remember, "I do not know, I am ignorant," then there are no grounds on which the ego can stand. Where can ego build its structure when it has no foundation? It is interesting to see that if the ignorant man becomes conscious of his ignorance, then his wandering loses momentum, he finds himself still, and his mistakes cease to happen; he begins to travel on the right path. And the learned person who is sure in his belief that he is a learned person has begun his journey into greater darkness. When the ignorant becomes conscious of the fact that "I am ignorant," then his journey towards wisdom begins. Consciousness of one's ignorance leads to humility, whereas the delusion of knowledge, the claim to knowledge, leads one to ego – and the real hindrance is ego.

Ignorance is not deep darkness, it is like evening. There is no sun now, there is no light of understanding now, but at the same time neither is there the dark night of ego. It is just evening. Ignorance stands on the threshold from where it is also possible to go towards the light. But as the boast of the learned becomes stronger and stronger and his notion, "I know, I know, I know," becomes firmer and firmer, his night becomes darker, his evening disappears, and he sinks deep into the darkness. And as his boast grows from strength to strength, his night will become as dark as a moonless night.

Ego leads man into great darkness, and an interesting paradox emerges in man's world; the wise see themselves as ignorant – not knowing – and the ignorant assert their claim, "We know!" Then where should we go for true knowledge? What should we do? Which is the way?

Two things are to be remembered. We need always to go on enhancing our awareness of our ignorance. Remembrance of ignorance is the destruction of ignorance. To become aware of our ignorance is to dissolve our ignorance. This awareness that "I am ignorant" is like a person who has lighted a lamp and has taken it into a room to look for darkness there. That person had said, "Let me light a lamp so that I can see where the darkness is," and he begins to search for it with a lighted lamp in his hand. Of course, wherever he looks he finds no darkness. When there is an awareness within to know where ignorance is, a desire to go where ignorance lies and a desire to know it, then the knowing, the understanding, can happen. Wherever you go with this lamp of awareness, ignorance will vanish from there.

So the first thing is the remembrance of ignorance – that "I am ignorant." If you wish to enter the world of light, of wisdom, of true knowledge, you must be fully aware of your ignorance and remain constantly in search of where your ignorance lies. Wherever you find it, admit it at once, don't linger even for a moment. And bow down at the feet of anyone who shows you your ignorance – he is your teacher, your master. And don't try to prove that your ignorance is knowledge, as your mind will goad you to do. Your ego will say, "Don't believe in him." Your ego will coax you to say, "What are you talking about? I an ignorant person? Impossible!" This is how we are all perpetuating our ignorance.

We all persist in protecting our own opinions and attitudes.

Those who know nothing at all make great claims that they are right. Those who do not know anything even about a stone lying on a roadside, go on making claims about God and assert that their God is the only true God. There is no end to the claims of those who know nothing at all. Ignorance is a great supporter of its claims and it goes on claiming. Save yourself from such claims. If you want to make any claim at all, then make only the claim of being ignorant. Say boldly, "I do not know." Whatever occasions arise, whatever chances you get, and whatever conditions you meet with where your ignorance is exposed, stop, and know that, "I am ignorant." Acknowledge as your master anyone who points out to you your ignorance, who draws your attention to your ignorance.

But in fact we make a teacher of the man who boosts our ego. We go to him, pick up some stray pieces of wisdom, and return home full of vanity and hypocrisy – and then say that we also know. He who inflates our boast of knowledge we call our master. But he is the real guru, the real master, in whose contact we come to know that there is none as ignorant as we. He is the real master who takes away our knowledge, who destroys our boast of knowledge, who smashes our structure of ego to the ground, who throws us to the ground and says, "You are nothing at all, you are nowhere, you have known nothing!" Such a person is the master; not the one from whom we get knowledge, but the one through whom we are reminded of our ignorance.

Remember that remembrance of ignorance leads one to understanding and the accumulation of knowledge leads one into great darkness. So the first thing is to be mentally alert to ignorance, to be fully conscious, to know ignorance and to look into it. Know yourself as a deeply ignorant person.

The other thing to remember is that whenever you think, "I know," stop a while, and reconsider your thought; ask yourself, "Do I know it really?" It will be enough if you reconsider once. Be honest in your attempt. Be fully aware and reconsider your thought before you say, "I know." Be mentally alert to the discovery of your ignorance, as well as to knowledge; and when you start to check yourself you will know that you know words, you know principles, you know scriptures, but you have no idea at all of the truth. Those so-called pundits whose minds have been stuffed with scriptures and words, who have been burdened with words and who make false claims of knowledge, have become figures of fun for the sage, who says such people grope about in great darkness.

I have heard: a Christian priest used to give sermons in the evenings in his church every Sunday. He was by repute a learned person. One day, he left his spectacles at home. Half of his knowledge was at risk because the sermon was written and now he could not read it. But he thought it improper to tell the congregation that he had forgotten his glasses – they were eager to listen to him – so he decided to make do without the glasses and started speaking, glancing at his paper. Functioning as he did from memory, mistakes were bound to occur, because he had left his memory aid behind. Nothing he said was the imparting of true knowledge; wisdom can speak without the help of eyes, without need of spectacles. All he ever said was drawn from his crammed memory. But today the means to look into his memory was left at home.

Talking about one of Jesus' miracles he made a mistake. Jesus was in a forest with four thousand followers, and had with him only seven loaves of bread. With these he not only fed all, but the seven loaves were not eaten. There were four thousand followers but the priest made a slip and recounted that there were seven followers and four thousand loaves, and that after Jesus had fed all, the bread still remained. This, he said, was the miracle.

As usually happens in a temple or a church, most of the people were dozing and paid no attention to the error; only those who were awake heard it. Even so, having left their reasoning faculties at home, as people do who go to church, they were unresponsive. They merely heard the words. Only one person became alert and thought, "What kind of miracle is this? – only seven people and four thousand loaves?" He got up and asked, "Sir, is this a miracle? Anybody can do that!"

On hearing this, the priest was enraged. He had no idea that he had made a mistake, so he was all anger and exasperation. He asked, "What do you mean, anybody can do it? You are blaspheming against Jesus."

The man replied, "Why, I myself can do it!"

The priest was puzzled and asked the congregation about what he had said. Someone replied, "You made a mistake. You said the opposite of what you meant; you said there were four thousand loaves and seven followers. This feat can be accomplished by anybody, there is no miracle in it."

The priest was very troubled by this incident. He was by repute a wise man, so he was much agitated and resolved to put his challenger in his place. The next Sunday he came fully prepared. During his sermon he raised the matter of the miracle again. "Once Jesus went to a forest," he said. "Listen properly! He had four thousand followers and only seven loaves of bread with him, and he fed everybody. All were fed to their hearts' content and yet the bread was not consumed." Then he looked at the man who had put him into difficulty the Sunday before, and asked him, "Dear friend, can you now perform such a miracle?"

The man stood up and replied, "Yes, I can."

The priest was very nervous and asked, "How can you do it?"

The man replied, "I can do it from the stock that was left over from last time!"

Shifting of words here and there, punning of words, memorizing words – the scriptures are all a great joke. There is not much meaning in such things. It is a great folly to try to correct others, and it is sheer vanity to try never to admit our mistakes. That poor priest could not even say, "There was an error in my statement." It was a trifle, and he could have simply asked their pardon. But our ego never lets us admit our mistakes, though we are eager and pleased to get others to admit their mistakes.

So the other point to remember is this: reconsider whether you know a little or not. Ask yourself whether you really know, or whether all this is a jungle of mere words, scriptures, principles and memory. Ask yourself, "Have I known anything? Have I lived it? Have I practiced something of it? Have I tasted it from my life's experience? Have I danced in that supreme experience of godliness? Have I experienced that vibration? Or have I merely burned the midnight oil to commit to memory the words of the scriptures?" The nauseating smell of kerosene oil emanates from those who have crammed the scriptures into their memories. Kerosene oil burns with thick smoke. It is very difficult to find people more ignorant than the learned.

Hence, says this sutra, the ignorant grope about, but the learned grope about in thick darkness. It is better to be an ignorant person than to be a learned one. Ignorance will show you the way. Do not try to enter the great darkness; to remain in simple darkness is far better. From this darkness it is easy to enter light, but the journey from the great darkness will be long and arduous.

Enough for today. Now let us go into meditation. Let us take a few steps from darkness towards the light.

# I Too
# Am Listening

*One result, they say,
is obtained by vidya,
and another result, they say,
is obtained by avidya;
thus we have heard
from the wise ones
who explained it to us.*

11

THE TRULY LEARNED, the wise ones, tell us that the fruit of true knowledge, wisdom, understanding – what the Upanishads call *vidya* – is quite distinct from the fruit of material, informational, acquired knowledge; this the Upanishads call *avidya*.

Avidya also means ignorance – absence of vidya. Its intended meaning in the Upanishads is material knowledge – physical, scientific knowledge which looks like real knowledge but which leaves the person ignorant. Through avidya we may know all the subjects of learning but remain ignorant of who we are. Such learning, which creates the illusion of knowledge, is called avidya, ignorance, by the Upanishads. It can be interpreted to mean science, though this interpretation may appear very strange. The word avidya, then, means knowledge about physical science, knowledge of other things; and the word vidya – literally knowledge, learning – means the knowing of the self.

Mere knowledge is not implied by the word vidya. The word vidya implies transformation. The Upanishads will not call that vidya which does not transform one's being. If I know something and yet I remain as I was before knowing, then such a knowing is not vidya according to the Upanishads. That learning will be called vidya which transforms you immediately upon knowing it. No sooner do I know than I am transformed. I become another person on knowing it.

If I remain as I was before knowing, then knowing is avidya –

ignorance; and if I am transformed it is vidya – true knowledge. Such learning is not merely an addition to your fund of information but is transforming. Through it you change, you become quite a different person. That which is called vidya, knowledge, by the Upanishads, gives you a new birth.

Socrates has given us a very short sutra similar in meaning to this interpretation of the Upanishads. He said, "Knowledge is virtue." This was discussed and debated for hundreds of years in Greece, because the relationship between knowledge and virtue is not obvious. A person knows anger is bad, yet anger does not vanish. Another person knows stealing is bad, but he continues to steal. Another person knows that greed is bad, and yet his greed does not stop. But Socrates is saying that your greed goes away once you know that it is bad.

If a person knows that greed is bad and yet remains greedy, then his knowing is avidya. It is merely an illusion of knowing, it is false knowledge. The test of true knowledge is that it immediately becomes a part of your behavior; it does not even require practice. If someone thinks, "Let me know it first and then I shall put it into practice," then that knowing of his is not knowledge but ignorance.

Suppose a drink is set in front of you and just as you are about to drink you discover that there is poison in the cup; then your hand, extending to pick up the cup, will immediately refrain from doing so. That is, no sooner did you know that it was poisonous than the cup remained untouched. Hence, when knowing becomes action it is called true knowledge. And if you have to make an effort to change your behavior after knowing, then that behavior is imposed, it is thrust upon you. It cannot be called the result of the knowledge.

Knowledge which has been imposed to produce a certain action, which does not become action of its own accord, is called avidya – ignorance – by the Upanishads. It is vidya – true knowledge – which changes one's life effortlessly, as if without knowing that any change has happened. On one side ignorance is burnt, and on the other darkness vanishes. Both happen simultaneously. Is it possible to create a lamp which, when turned on, does not remove darkness? And will it be necessary for us to make a special effort to remove darkness after putting the light on? If it were so then the lamp would be a symbol of avidya – of darkness. But darkness does not exist when the lamp is lit. Lighting the lamp means the extinguishing of darkness. Such a lamp is vidya.

There are two points to be remembered in this connection. Why does it happen that, even after our knowing, transformation does not take place? A lot of people come to me and say, "We know anger is bad; it is poison, it burns, it is fire, it is hell, and yet we are not free from it."

Then I tell them, "It is a mistake on your part to think that you know it. You think you already know and yet you ask yourself, 'What should be done so that anger goes away?' This is your mistake. In fact you do not know that anger is hell."

Is it ever possible that a person would not leap out of anger once he knows it is hell?

Buddha has said this somewhere. A person whose life was full of troubles and anguish had approached him for advice, for a way out of his miseries. There was nothing but sorrow and affliction in his life. Buddha told him to give up those cares and miseries, to come out of them immediately: "I will show you the way to be out of them," he said.

The man said, "Show me the way now, and then I will try, by and by, to follow your way."

Then Buddha said, "You are like a man whose house has caught fire and who says, 'Thank you very much for your advice; now I will gradually try to get myself out of the house.'" Buddha went on to say that it would have been better if the person had said, "You are telling a lie – I do not see any fire." But the man does not say so; he says, "I believe you, I believe there is a fire, and by and by I will try to get out."

Does anybody leave by and by, when the fire alarm sounds? He gets out immediately. He won't stop even if the informant remains behind. One who knows there is fire jumps first and thinks after-wards, when he is out of the house. So Buddha said, "You believe the fire is there, but you refuse to see it so you suffer unnecessarily. A person like you should not even trouble yourself to find out. You should not even try to test my advice. You have not even opened your eyes to see that there is fire all around you. You have admitted you are in difficulty and now you think, 'Fire is there, now I will get out of it, by and by – and you ask me to show you a way to get out!"

When somebody tells me, "I know anger is bad and yet I cannot be free from it," I say, "It would be good if you could say, 'I do not know that anger is bad.' What you really know is: 'Anger is good, and I am doing what is good. But I have heard from other people that anger is bad.' It is what you have *heard* that you consider to be knowledge."

Then what is true knowledge? You will have to know within yourself that anger is bad. So you will have to pass through it, you will have to endure the difficulty of the fire of anger, you will have to bear the anguish and pain caused by anger. When all your limits have been burnt by the flames of anger and when your life has become a great turmoil full of smoke, then it will not be necessary to go to anyone to ask whether anger is bad or not. Then it will not be necessary to seek out any method, any ritual, any remedy to escape from your anger. On knowing that anger is fire, you will be at once free from it. Such a knowing is vidya – true knowledge.

That knowing which is called true knowledge by the Upanishads carries freedom within itself and liberates the knower at once; and that knowing which lacks this attribute is not true knowledge. We all have a lot of information, we all know many things. If we were to refer to the Upanishads about the quality of our learning they would declare it to be avidya – ignorance – because our knowing does not even touch us, it does not transform us; though our knowledge increases we remain where we are. Knowledge becomes a storehouse of information, and we stand far away from it. Our treasury goes on growing bigger, but it is mere accumulation though we claim it as knowledge. And whoever considers this as knowledge will soon be wandering in a hopeless condition. This is ignorance.

Accept as true knowledge not that which is an addition to you but that which transforms you. That is true knowledge which does not require any memorizing but which becomes your life itself; that is true knowledge which does not turn into memory but which is absorbed into your life itself. It is not a matter of knowing intellectually that anger is bad, but of your behavior reflecting your discovery that anger is bad. It is not that you hang up signs saying, "Greed is sin!" on the walls of your house, but that your eyes, your hands and your face reflect your understanding that greed is sin. It becomes true knowledge only when your total personality demonstrates that greed is sin.

The Upanishads have praised vidya greatly. It has been highly valued. It is considered the alchemy to transform life. What we understand as knowledge is simply an arrangement to earn our livelihood. One person is a doctor, another is an engineer, another is a shopkeeper. We all have our own knowledge, but it does not transform life, it simply helps us carry on with our lives. These various branches of specialized knowledge do not give a new turn to life, they simply make life secure. No new flowers open because of them, they simply prevent the roots of life from drying up. No ecstacy enters life because of them, only protection, planning and arrangements to avoid hardships and inconveniences in life. What we call knowledge is simply a means to earn our livelihood in an efficient and convenient manner. The Upanishads call this avidya.

That is vidya, according to the Upanishads, which does not simply drag life a little further on, but which raises life to a higher level. Remember, avidya is horizontal. Vidya is vertical – it moves towards the sky. Avidya is like a bullock-cart trundling along the ground. There is no take-off in it, as there is in an airplane. It cannot take off and fly high in the sky. In its journey from birth through to death it never leaves ground level, and we die at the very level at which we were born. Generally, the cradle is the grave.

There is hardly any difference between the levels of birth and death. Continuously walking horizontally we all eventually find our graves because they are not very far from the cradles: and even if they are far, the level remains the same.

Vidya is vertical, going up. The level is changed. You are not what you were before. No sooner do you achieve true knowledge than you are another person. Buddha or Mahavira or Krishna are standing quite near to us, in our neighborhood, touching our shoulders, and yet they are not with us – they are nowhere near us. They are way up on some peak. Their bodies seem to be near to us, but their spirit is not with us. They have passed through vidya. They are learned in the true sense of the word.

This sutra of the Upanishad tells us that avidya has its own value just as vidya has its qualities. Avidya has its own usefulness. The Upanishad does not say, "Kill avidya"; it only says, "Do not consider avidya as vidya." It does not mean that you should not live with your feet on the ground in this world but should only float higher and higher into the sky. Really, the man who wants to rise up towards the sky has to keep his feet firmly on the ground.

Nietzsche has said somewhere that the tree that wants to touch the sky has to send its roots deep into the ground below. A tree goes as far down as it climbs high. A tree that reaches for the stars in the sky has its roots deep into the earth. The tree can only go as high as its roots go deep.

The Upanishads are not opposed to avidya. The belief that they are, has given rise to a great delusion. I will explain it to you, because nobody can tell how much misery and affliction the East has suffered because of this mistaken belief. The Upanishads have not been correctly understood. We make the mistake of thinking avidya to be vidya. The Upanishads are opposed to this. They tell us avidya is not vidya and the distinction should be properly understood. Then we make another mistake. The simple truth is that we stubbornly insist on being mistaken, because we make either one mistake or the other.

According to the Upanishads, our present-day universities

should be called centers of avidya, because they have no concern with, and no relation to vidya whatsoever. Our universities are the centers of avidya, and their chancellors are the chancellors of avidya. Only avidya spreads from these centers. But the Upanishads are not against avidya. They simply say, "Do not think of this avidya as vidya; don't make this mistake."

Understand the distinction between them clearly. Avidya has its own utility. It is not that doctors are not necessary, it is not that life would be better without shopkeepers. No, the shopkeepers, doctors, engineers, the sweepers and laborers – all of them are required, they are useful to society. But the mistake is to consider this education for livelihood as an education for life. Such a person will only earn his bread and die.

Jesus says, "You cannot live by bread alone." This does not mean you can live without bread; but can bread alone be life? Bread is a necessity of life, but it is not life itself. No one can survive or make progress without bread, and yet it is not life. We fill in the foundations of a building with stones, and the building cannot be constructed without them, but remember, those stones in the foundations are not the building. Don't live in the delusion that the building is constructed when the foundation is filled in. Not that the building can be constructed if the foundation is not laid. The foundation has to be laid: it is a necessary evil. The Upanishads say avidya has its own utility – namely that it provides the means for livelihood. It is an outward attribute for life; it concerns physical life, it is an arrangement to maintain life. But don't see it as everything. It is necessary but not enough. Everything will not be fulfilled by it alone.

The countries of the East, and especially India, committed the second mistake. They said, "When the sages of the Upanishads – who are wise and learned – say something is avidya, we should be indifferent towards it. We should stick only to vidya." So science could not make any headway in the East. We ignored whatsoever we considered avidya. Therefore the East became helpless, poor and enslaved. Had we been keen to pursue avidya we would have become soulless, but we became so eager to ignore it that we became helpless and poor in physical life.

The Upanishads say both are useful. Both are useful in different dimensions. Avidya has its place. It is not to be given up. The only thing to remember is that it is not everything. It is not the ultimate. Vidya has its place too.

The sage has said one more thing in this sutra: "We have heard this from those who knew." It is necessary to go into this statement a little in order to understand it. It is said: *Thus we have heard from the wise ones who explained it to us.* Did this sage who said this not know it himself? Is he telling us that which he has heard? Does he himself not know it? Is he repeating to us second-hand knowledge? No, this point needs to be understood correctly, because much confusion has been created by it. It is necessary to understand the form of expression in those far-off days when the Upanishads were written.

No one ever said, "I know." There were reasons for it. The reason was not that he did not know. The reason was that ego – the I – disappears after knowing. If the sage of the Upanishad had said, "I say this after knowing," the people of those days would have laughed and said, "Then don't say so! You cannot know, because your 'I' is still there." Therefore remember this: the sage knows it well, but says, "I have heard it from those who knew." The interesting thing is that the persons from whom he has heard have also said, "We have heard this from those who knew." There is some secret behind this. There is no individual claim, no egoistic claim behind it, because where is that 'I' of the knower to be found? Therefore they say, "We have heard from those who explained it to us." And I want to tell you another interesting thing about this: that individual himself is also included in the 'we' who have heard." This statement is a little hard to grasp.

As I told you this morning, when I say something to you, I hear it as you hear it. We hear it simultaneously. That speaker knows nothing who is not the listener to that which he speaks. Truths are not ready-made; they are not made beforehand. They are created, manifested, they are born naturally, they are spontaneous. They appear as flowers appear – blossoming out of the plant and full of fragrance. When I want to say something to you it can be done in two ways. The first is to think it over and then prepare to deliver it to you. What you eventually receive will be stale and old; it will not be fresh and alive, it will be dead. But when I begin to utter what comes from within me, then I hear it, as you do, for the first time. Then I too am a listener. You are not the only listeners; I am also.

So, the sage says, "We have heard from those who explained it to us." He has heard, he says, from those who knew; but it is from himself he is hearing it – he too listens to the explaining coming from himself. Hence the sage calls himself a listener.

There is another reason also. When a person attains to the highest truth, it does not appear to him as if he has achieved it. It appears as if it has descended on him. The supreme truth does not appear as if it is my creation, my achievement; it appears as a revelation before me, as an unfolding, as an inspiration. If someone were to ask Mohammed, "Have you written the Koran?", Mohammed would reply, "Please don't say such sinful things to me. I have heard the Koran, I have seen the Koran, and having heard it I have put it in writing. I have not written it – I am not its author."

This is why Mohammed is God's messenger – one who has delivered the message given to him. Truth was revealed before him, and he came before you and said such is the truth. That truth is not his creation. This is why we call the sages 'seers' – and not authors or creators. We do not say they created the truth, but that they saw the truth. That is why we call what they have seen *darshan* – the vision, the thing seen. We can call it whatever we like to call it, whether darshan or *shruti* – the thing heard. This sage is in fact telling us that truth is quite detached and separate from us. We do not create it. We only hear it, know it, see it. We are simply witnesses. You may call him a witness, a seer or a listener – but remember the idea of passivity behind it.

The sage says, "We are passive, not active." When you construct something you are active. When an artist is drawing a flower, he is an active agent. But when he is standing near a roseflower and is looking at it, he is a passive agent. At that time he is doing nothing, he is only receptive. He has simply opened the doors and windows of his being. He invites the flower, he offers it his heart, he welcomes it, and stands still. He is receptive. Then the flower enters his heart and touches it with its petals. Its fragrance reverberates in his whole being; and because he has allowed it within himself as a witness, as a receptive agent, it will bloom in all the corners of his being. But the receiver himself is passive, he simply receives.

This sage of the Upanishad says, "I have heard thus." In saying so, he wants to tell us that only the passive man attains to truth. Passivity is the door.

The sun is shining in the sky. We cannot bring its light into the house, but we have only to open our doors and the sun's light will enter. Its rays will gradually dance into all the corners of the house. But we cannot say that we brought the sun into our house. It is too much to say, "We brought it." It is boastful. We can say this much only, that we did not put up any obstacles to prevent the sun coming in. We kept the doors open. It is not necessary for the rising of the sun that we have our doors open, but it is a fact that the sun will never be able to enter our house if the doors are closed. And if the doors are open and if the sun does not rise, we can do nothing, we are helpless.

Have you understood what I mean? The sun is not obliged to come because your door is open. It is his freedom to come or not. But it is quite definite that he cannot enter if the door is closed. Even if he wants to come, he cannot. This means that if we wish we can remain blind towards truth, then the truth cannot do anything. If we wish we can be wide awake towards truth; but then we are not creating truth, we are simply open to its revelation.

Whatever is valuable, whatever is beautiful, whatever is best, whatever is true, whatever is auspicious in life, is found only by a receptive mind. He who keeps the door open finds it. Therefore the sage does not say, "I have it," but says, "I have heard it from those who knew. I have heard it, I have received it from where there is wisdom." In this statement there is a keen desire to rub out the 'I'. That is why no Upanishad bears the signature of its author on it. We don't know who speaks this, who tells this, whose words these are. Somebody proclaimed such invaluable truths without disclosing their authorship.

In fact, great truths have to be declared without claiming authorship, because the author dies before the birth of the great truth. These sages remove themselves completely from the claim of authorship. Nobody knows who is speaking these sentences, nor is it known whether these are the writings of one or more people. In the Upanishads it is probable that different sutras are the revelations of different sages, and yet there is an interesting observation to be made. These may be the words of different people, but there is one harmony, one music in them. There may be a number of people, there may be a different author for each sutra, but they must have been absolutely like one person somewhere deep down within themselves.

If you ever go to a Jaina temple you will see twenty-four idols of the *tirthankaras* – the enlightened masters of Jainism. There is no distinction among these statues, except for a very small mark at the foot which is different in each of them. These have been kept for our recognition, otherwise it would be difficult to know which is Mahavira, which is Parshvanath, which is Neminath. If those marks are erased all the statues will look alike. Even their faces are identical. This cannot be an historical fact. Mahavira's face cannot be the same as Parshvanath's. It is difficult to believe that all the twenty-four tirthankaras had identical forms and features. Even two people identical in form and feature cannot be found. Imagine the difficulty of finding twenty-four such people!

Is it possible that those who made these statues had no idea that someday someone would laugh at seeing all these identical images and would say, "This cannot be an historical fact"? No, they carved with wisdom. Disregarding the outer identity, they created images of the inner form. There is an absence of difference within. There must have been many physical differences between Mahavira and Parshvanath, but there comes a stage in life where the 'I' vanishes. Then there is no distinction within; then comes a kind of facelessness. One is freed from the outer face, the personality. Then the outer faces have no value. Therefore we did not make idols of outer bodies.

Those idols manifest the similarity that is within, the likeness that is within. That is why they are all alike. These sutras of the Upanishads are composed by different people, and it would not be a matter of wonder to find that one line of a couplet is composed by one sage and the other by another. Such a thing has happened.

Forty thousand incomplete poems were found in the house of Coleridge, the great English poet, after his death. Before his death his friends often asked him why such wonderful poems were left incomplete. They urged him to complete them. They said, "There will not be a greater poet than you in this world. You have kept forty thousand poems incomplete. Think, and complete them. Some poems have three lines, the fourth is not there. Some have seven lines, the eighth is not there. Some have eleven lines, the twelfth is not there. They are incomplete by only one line. Why don't you complete them?"

Coleridge replied, "Eleven lines have come, and I am waiting for the twelfth. Ten years have passed, yet it has not come. How can I complete it then? If someone finds the line, he can complete it. It has not yet come to me. If I want I can compose a line, but then it will be like a fabrication. It would be like a wooden leg. It would be like a wooden leg on an otherwise physically perfect man. These eleven lines are living: they have descended on me, they are not composed by me. They have come to me in a receptive moment, in a receptive mood, and I wrote them down. The twelfth has not yet descended. So I am waiting for it. If it comes during my life I shall add it; otherwise I shall leave the poem incomplete. The lines can come in someone else's life. It is possible someone else may become the door for the twelfth line, then he will complete the poem."

It is not essential that the couplets of the Upanishad should be by one individual. They are the poetries of those people who have not themselves composed them, but have noted down what descended on them. So the statement by the sages that they have heard it from those who knew is simply an admission of their egolessness. It is an announcement that I am not, I am only the door.

# *I Am Not The Body*

**12**

*One who knows
both vidya and avidya together
overcomes death through avidya
and experiences immortality
through vidya.*

ONE WHO KNOWS both avidya and vidya, having overcome death, will know the immortal. This is a very rare couplet. I told you that the Upanishads are not opposed to avidya. They favor vidya but are not at all opposed to avidya. It is said, "He who knows avidya will overcome death." The whole conflict of avidya is against death. The doctor is fighting against death, the engineer is fighting against death. Science's entire endeavor, all its activities, are directed against death – against sickness, against insecurity, against future dangers. To see that life does not end, to see that it is preserved, is the total effort of avidya – of scientific knowledge. The whole avidya is in a constant fight with death. So he who is proficient in avidya succeeds in holding death at bay. That is, he lives comfortably. In this sense, through avidya he overcomes death – but he cannot reach the immortal. He simply controls death quite comfortably.

With the help of avidya we can exist, but we cannot taste the substance of life. We can merely exist. This should be called vegetating. We will run the course of life. Everything – food, a house, medicine, and so on – will be available to us. We will get it all, and life will pass nicely, comfortably. But the immortal will be unavailable to us. And even if avidya succeeds altogether in preventing death, the immortal will still not be available.

Modern science is busily searching for ways and means to conquer death. The entire effort of science is really to save man from death. That is why science is so keen to find out how death can be avoided, how it can be avoided forever. The situation may arise in the distant future when we are able, if we wish, to avoid death forever. If we rightly understand the progress of science during the last three thousand years we will see that this has been its entire activity. Its entire conflict is against death, and it has been successful to a great extent.

A thousand years ago, nine out of ten newborn children used to die, and today, in countries where science has made remarkable progress, not even one out of ten newborn children dies. Among the bones found by scientists of people living ten thousand years ago, not many are seen to have lived beyond twenty-five years of age. No one lived for more than forty-five years. Not one bone found so far on this earth of any human living ten thousand years ago indicates that he was alive for more than forty-five years.

Yet today there are more than one thousand people over one hundred and fifty years of age in Soviet Russia. To live for one hundred years is now becoming an ordinary matter. You may be amazed to read in the newspapers that a ninety-year-old Russian man has married. We think the old man must be a great fool. But remember that the old man is not yet old, and that he is not doing anything uncommon. When a ninety-year-old man marries in Russia, do not compare him with the old of our country. Our old person will die twenty years before reaching that age. That ninety-year-old man belongs to a community where the maximum age is one hundred and fifty years. Till what age is a man still young when his lifespan ranges up to one hundred and fifty? Would you not fix it at a hundred at the least?

Wherever science has been successful, death has been pushed away a little further, and in recent times science has made still more progress. It does not seem unlikely that by the end of this century we will be able to keep man alive indefinitely if we want to. There will be no obstacles left to prevent science accomplishing it. Man can be made to live endlessly. That is why some thinkers of the West, and especially of America, have started to protest very vehemently that before science succeeds in prolonging the life of man we should add this rule to the constitution of the country – that every man is born with the right to die. Otherwise a very difficult situation will arise; because if the government does not allow a person to die, that person will have no right to do so.

Up to now we made rules throughout the world that nobody has a right to kill another person. But nowadays, in the whole world – especially in countries like Switzerland, Sweden and Norway, where science has been successful in prolonging man's life – people have started to agitate for the ending of life. Intelligent people have initiated propaganda campaigns maintaining that no doctor has a right to save the life of a person who wishes to die, and if a doctor saves the life of such a person, it should be considered an abuse against the fundamental right of that person, his fundamental right over his own life.

We are in a dangerous position. Suppose a man is one hundred and fifty years old. Now, he is a fool if he wants to live longer, he should wish to take rest forever, to die. But the doctors have to keep him in hospital for treatment and try to keep him alive, because at present doctors have no right to help a person to die. So they will try their best to save the man. If in spite of the doctors' efforts the patient dies, it is a different matter. So the agitation goes on to give man a right to die if he chooses.

This matter is soon going to be very significant, because no mechanism has been found in the human body which can actually precipitate death. The only reason death happens is that up to now it has not been possible to replace physical organs of the body. We are unable to replace certain parts of the body, and that is the difficulty. As we go on making progress in replacing body parts, death will not remain an unavoidable phenomenon for man. It will become an act of one's own will. Bear in mind, it will happen very soon that no man, except by an accident, will die in the course of time. So there will be fewer natural deaths and more suicides in the world. It will certainly be a suicide if a person asks a doctor to end his life. Then suicide will be a common means of death.

Since very ancient times, man has been proclaiming that death can be overcome by avidya. What the medical science of the West says today is declared in the Upanishads. They say death can be restrained so much that it is effectively overcome by avidya. The eternal within can never die. Death is of the body; then the eternal within us accepts a new body.

However, if we can keep the old body fit and active then there is no need to accept a new one, and to accept a new body seems absolutely uneconomical. It seems that nature does not know what economics is. It seems nature has no experience whatsoever of the science of economics. It gives birth to children and kills the old. Our old people are trained and experienced, and a good deal of effort went into their training, while the children who replace them are totally untrained, totally useless. It ends the lives of those who have labored for seventy years and gives birth to infants devoid of knowledge, so they have to be reared and trained. This is very uneconomical.

Economy would not allow the seventy-year-old, with all his experience, to die. A man of seventy will assume a new life after his death – and will again have to spend twenty to twenty-five years in educating and training himself, just to regain with difficulty the position he was in at the time of his death. This is all worthless. So science is busy in this direction, and makes all efforts to end this wastage. If we can save the life of an Einstein, a great wastage is avoided. If he takes three births, the increase in knowledge caused by them will not be as great as if he lives for three hundred years at a stretch, because this will be continual maturity. There will not be frequent discontinuity in between. There will not be those gaps of twenty-five to thirty years to limit that maturity. So if we keep Einstein alive for three hundred years, we can't imagine how much addition he will make to the total stock of knowledge. And knowledge is endless.

There are countless millions of cells in a small human brain, and scientists say that each cell is so capable of preserving knowledge that the information contained in all the libraries of the world could be stored in one human brain. To have so many million cells is such a tremendous potential that one individual can be the master of all the knowledge existing in the world today. That we have not yet developed that device by which we can pour so much knowledge into a person's brain is another matter. Our ways of imparting knowledge are very elementary. A child surely learns something after having been taught for twenty years – but nothing is really achieved. Having given someone twenty years of education, the most we can say is that he is not uneducated. Only this much is possible. Nothing special is achieved. Even if we were to provide education for seventy years, not much would be achieved. The stock of knowledge is gigantic and we possess neither the devices nor the systems we would need to pour it into the human brain. Hence new ways and methods are being sought after continually to develop more advanced techniques of education.

Great work on sleep-teaching is being done in Russia at present. Children are normally instructed in the daytime, and spend the night in sleep; twelve hours of the night are being wasted. So in Russia they are playing tapes into children's ears while they are sleeping so that they receive instruction during the nighttime too. Thus great efforts are being made to make sleep a medium, an instrument, of imparting instruction, and they have been successful in this to a great extent. Their hope is to be able in the near future to impart as much instruction in seven years as is now given in fifteen years, through utilizing the nighttime also.

There is another convenience to this new experiment. When the teacher is teaching the children in their waking hours, there arises a conflict between the ego of the teacher and that of the children, and this creates a great hindrance to the children's progress. There is no conflict when children are sleeping and instruction is directly absorbed. The teacher is not there and the children are also as good as not there. The pupils are in sleep, the teacher is not present, only the tape is being played. The tape feeds instruction slowly slowly into the children's brains during the whole night, and they receive it directly.

The proclamation of the Upanishad that death can be overcome by avidya, science, should be sent in writing to all the universities. The sage of the Upanishad says this is so because death is merely a physical tragedy, an accident. If we can develop the appropriate instruments and technologies, death can be pushed a little further away. There is no difficulty about this.

Up to now science has lacked the means to restore a dead person to life, but scientists hope to be able to give new life to a dead person by the end of this century. One person who died fifteen years ago has made a will of ten million dollars for the purpose of preserving his dead body in the safest way possible at least until then, or until he can be revived. A sum of a hundred thousand rupees per day is being spent to preserve his dead body in the best possible way so that there may not be even an iota of decomposition in it. The intention is to preserve his dead body in the same condition as it was in when he died, so that if we can discover the scientific key to this problem we may be able to revive his dead body and give him a renewed life.

Spiritualists are much afraid of these researches. They say, "If those experiments are successful, what will be the position of the soul?" This man's dead body can be brought to life only on one condition – that science has been able to preserve his body in good condition. This is a necessary part of the experiment, but it is not all. If his soul is wandering and has not yet entered another body, then it will enter his dead body; and I feel that this man's soul will remain wandering and waiting. He has departed after making a very valuable will. Ten million dollars is not a small amount. He will certainly wait. He will wait for another ten years, and if his body can be revived he will reenter it. It will be like reentering a house which has been reconstructed after it had fallen down.

Death can be overcome by avidya – by science – but the immortal cannot be experienced through it. The second part of the sutra is more important, and a necessary condition. It is possible that science may defeat death, and may make man almost immortal, but then, how is man going to be benefited by this change? Even after becoming almost immortal he cannot have the experience of the immortal. Even then we will not know that which is immortal in us. We may have seventy years of knowledge, or seven hundred years; we may even live for seven thousand years. But we have no experience at all of that which was there before our life, which existed before our birth and also exists after our death. If we wish to know – to experience – the immortal, only vidya, true knowledge, can help.

The Upanishads pay a great tribute to avidya, to science. It is the way to fight against death, although it is powerless to attain to the immortal. Conflict with death is a negative effort; experiencing the immortal is a positive achievement. To try to experience the immortal is the effort to know that which existed before our birth and will also exist after our death; which is at present, which was in the past and which will also be in the future. It was before this body existed, and it will still exist when this body has perished.

To know this is to attain the immortal. To go on prolonging this body's life is merely to be in conflict with death. It is a struggle about extending the distance between birth and death, whereas to go deep into the experience of that which is beyond birth and death is to discover the immortal. The Upanishads declare that immortality will be experienced through vidya. So we need to understand two or three sutras about vidya – true knowledge. What teachings about vidya can guide us now towards the immortal?

The first point is that the person who thinks he is the body is unable to move towards the immortal. So the first sutra is to strip away identification with one's body. Know it always, remember it every day. Be aware of it often, think of it often – that "I am not the body." As deeply as you understand and establish this sutra within you, that much will you move towards the immortal. Conversely, as firmly as the belief that "I *am* the body" is rooted in you, that much will you move towards avidya, towards the conflict with death. And life is such that we are reminded twenty-four hours a day that "I am the body."

If our leg is injured a little, we at once remember, "I am the body." If we are hungry we remember, "I am the body." If there is a little headache we remember, "I am the body." If there is fever we remember, "I am the body." As youth approaches we remember, "I am the body." As old age approaches we remember, "I am the body." Life constantly reminds us from all sides that, "I am the body," whereas we receive no indications from anywhere that, "I am *not* the body." And it is a point worth noting that it is the truth whose indications are not available, while it is the untruth whose indications are available every day.

But we commit a fundamental mistake in our interpretation of the indications that are present. When one thing is indicated, we take it in quite another light, and a great misunderstanding happens. The whole of life thus becomes a great misunderstanding. Indications mean one thing, but we see them in another light. When the stomach wants food, we say, "I am hungry." This is incorrect. We mistook the suggestion. The suggestion was this much only – that I have come to know that the stomach is hungry. But we say, "*I* am hungry." Nobody has yet shown how we arrived at this conclusion. How does that middle link – that I have come to know that the stomach is hungry – disappear? 'I' can never feel hungry, and yet we say, "*I* am hungry."

When there is pain in the head, I come to know that there is pain in the head. But I say that my head is aching. I tell others that I have a headache, and I tell myself that there is pain within me. There is no mistake in the bodily indications, but we make the mistake when we try to decode them. The mistake is in what we do with them.

Swami Ram always said the right thing. He always expressed himself correctly. The result was that people took him for a lunatic. The world is full of madmen – and there is no difficulty in judging a wise man as mad. Ram never said, "I am hungry." Sometimes he would say, "Listen, brother, there is hunger here." On hearing him, people would wonder whether he was in his right mind, and all sorts of difficulties would arise.

Poor Ram was expressing himself correctly, but people used to doubt his sanity. Sometimes, returning home, he would say,

"There was great fun today. When Ram was walking along the road people began to insult him." He never said, "They began to insult me"; he did not say, "As I was passing, people began to insult me." He used to say, "There was great fun today: some people on the road were making fun of Ram. Ram could see them too. I said, "Look Ram, they are having some fun with you."

It caused great difficulty when he went to America for the first time and began to address himself in the third person. In India his friends knew him well, they knew that he was a bit crazy. But in America a great difficulty arose because people could not make out what he was saying. But he was perfectly right in his statements.

The stomach becomes hungry, but *you* are never hungry. That has never happened up to now. It is not possible, because hunger is helpless before the soul, the self. The soul has no mechanism to feel hungry, it has no means to feel the pinch of hunger. Nothing diminishes or is augmented in the soul; nothing leaves the soul; nothing is lost from it to generate pangs of hunger. Something always decreases in the body because it dies every day, and due to this process of dying, you feel hunger.

You may be surprised to know that something within you dies every day; so the portion that dies has to be replaced by food. There is no other reason. Some parts within you die, so you have to replace those dead portions by living ones so that you can remain alive. Hence you lose one pound of weight when you fast for one day. What is the reason? That one pound has died and you have not replaced it. You will again have to replace it. Scientists say a person can remain hungry for ninety days. In the end this will cause great difficulty because he goes on living for those ninety days by consuming the accumulated fat in the body; but day by day, exhausting his reserves of fat, he is dying. He will grow weaker day by day, losing weight and feeling worn out, but he will continue to live.

We replace our dead elements by food; the deficiency is made good. But the soul does not die. No element of it is lessened, so there is no reason for the soul to feel hungry. There is one interesting thing to know about this happening. The soul does not feel hungry; the body does not know hunger. The body feels hungry but the soul knows hunger. This whole phenomenon is something like that story which you may have heard.

Once a forest caught fire. A blind man and a lame man were crossing the forest. The blind man could not see, but he was able to walk; he had strong legs. It was dangerous to proceed. Fortunately the fire had not spread where they were standing. The lame man was unable to walk but could see the fire approaching. Those two must have been wise people, though ordinarily such people are not. How can you expect the blind to be wise when those with eyes are not? How can the lame be wise when people with legs are not? But those two were and they came to an understanding. The lame man said, "If we wish to save our lives there is only one way. Let me sit on your shoulders. We will use my eyes and your legs. I will guide and you will walk accordingly." Hence they saved their lives.

The life journey is also a kind of deep understanding between the body and the soul. It is a journey of the blind and the lame. The soul has the experience – it experiences – but there is no happening; happenings take place in the body, but it does not experience. All experiences are felt by the soul; and all happenings take place in the body, but the body does not experience them. Hence all this trouble!

That day also some trouble must have arisen, but Aesop, who wrote this story of the blind and the lame, has made no mention of it. It was necessary for the two men to hurry, so when the blind man ran fast and the lame man looked quickly, it is possible that the blind man felt, "I can see," and the lame man felt, "I am running."

This is exactly what happens with us. It is this happening that has to be broken. Both should be clearly distinguished. Both should be separated, otherwise our wires are crossed. All happenings take place in the body, and the soul experiences them. You will begin to grasp the sutra of vidya when you separate these two. Then your journey towards the immortal will begin.

Enough for today. We shall talk again tomorrow morning. Let us now start our journey towards the immortal.

# *Animal, Vegetable Or God?*

13

*Those who are absorbed in the fulfillment
of prakriti – the manifest nature –
enter darkness,
and those who are absorbed
in the fulfillment
of hidden prakriti – unmanifested nature –
enter greater darkness.*

THE OUTWARD MANIFESTATION of existence is called *prakriti* – the material nature of the universe – visible to the eyes, touchable with the hands, knowable through the sense organs; all that with which our organs become conversant. It can be said that the visible God is prakriti; but this is the experience of those who know God. They can affirm that prakriti is the body of God. But we know only the body, we do not know that it is the body of God. Prakriti is the form of that hidden, invisible consciousness, it is the visible form of that. This fact is known only to those who know the invisible also. Otherwise we know only this much – that the visible is all there is.

The Upanishads say that those absorbed in the worship of prakriti – visible nature – enter darkness. All of us are absorbed in this way. They alone are less absorbed who offer prayers and worship in the temples. But we who are absorbed in prakriti offer our prayers and worship in the temples of the sense organs. *Upasana* – worship – also has the meaning to sit near. When you are absorbed in the taste of a thing, you are sitting near the organ of taste. When you are absorbed in sexual desire, you are sitting near the sex organ; the worship of the sex organ is going on at the time. Those who call themselves atheists are also absorbed, not in the worship of God, but in that of manifest nature.

It is very difficult to save ourselves from 'sitting near'. We have to sit near something – we can't avoid it. If we don't sit near God we will sit near manifest nature. If we don't sit near the soul we will sit near the body. If we don't sit near the spiritual and transcendental we will sit near the worldly and mundane. Certainly we will sit somewhere. The act of sitting near will go on in every condition with one single exception. I will talk about this later on.

This sutra of the Upanishad says that they enter darkness who are absorbed in the worship of manifest nature. They enter darkness because they can establish no connection with light. The worship and adoration of manifest nature is mainly due to darkness, to ignorance. Truly speaking, darkness is the basis on which being absorbed in manifest nature depends. If you wish to fulfill any desire or passion, it will be easy precisely to the degree that your mind is filled with darkness and ignorance. It will be difficult to sit near a desire if there is light – true knowledge – in the mind. The running, the searching after desires, will be exactly as smooth as the mind is filled with insensibility. Desires pertaining to all the sense organs lead us into deep sleep. If you are awake you will pass by the sense organs; and if you are asleep and insensible you will find yourself sitting near the sense organs.

The greater the unconsciousness, the nearer you will sit. Therefore the worshippers of manifest nature will necessarily be in unconsciousness. These devotees of the sense organs will have to discover various ways and means to remain in unconsciousness. Hence they must always, by and by, seek out new intoxicants. It is no wonder that they resort to drinking wine and spirits. Actually, it is impossible for a devotee of the sense organs to be away from intoxicants for long. And whenever the number of such devotees goes on multiplying, more and more new ways and means will be discovered to remain unconscious. To be absorbed in the enjoyment of the sense organs, to sit nearer to the sense organs, it is good to keep the mind unconscious and lacking discretion. It is necessary to hold the mind in trance, in insensibility, if you want to be angry or greedy or full of sexual desire. Only in such an unconscious state of mind can you sit near, and worship, manifest nature.

So you see this sutra of the Upanishad is very significant. It says, they enter darkness who are absorbed in the worship of the manifest, the visible. It also says something else – that they enter greater darkness who are absorbed in the worship of the ego. The worship of the sense organs is natural. It is a kind of worship practiced even by animals; but no animal is absorbed in the worship of *karma upasana* – that is, in the satisfaction of ego. It is necessary to understand this a bit. The worship of karma upasana is a faculty unique to man.

Suppose a man is seeking prestige. There is no direct possibility of satisfying any particular sense organ by obtaining a certain professional position. By acquiring a certain status a man may make it easier for himself to indirectly satisfy certain sense organs, but there is no direct possibility of satisfaction. The sense organs have no direct link with status. The interest or desire to seek status does not belong to the sense organs, it pertains to ego – to "I am somebody." It is true that to be a somebody will offer greater facilities for satisfying the sense organs than one has if one is a nobody, but "I am somebody" has its own absorption and pleasure. It is this interest – the satisfying of one's ego – that is meant by karma upasana.

The Upanishads say such a person goes into greater darkness. He enters greater darkness than that of animals because the interest which animals take is natural and physical. A person takes interest in eating: it is animal-like. In a sense, he is an animal. But suppose a person takes an interest in politics and goes on seeking position after position; such a person is worse than an animal. His interest is not natural at all, it is perverted. The interest derived from holding a particular post does not satisfy any sense organ, any natural organ. It is a very unnatural growth. The knot, the tumor, of ego within goes on increasing and gives him the pleasure of feeling, "I am somebody and the other is nobody." It is the interest in domination, the pleasure of power over others. It is the interest in crushing others in one's fist. It is the pleasure of crushing the necks of others.

Therefore the meaning of the worship of *karma prakriti* lies in the various ways and means designed to satisfy ego. They may be directed towards fame, towards status, towards wealth. True, a person obtains more facilities to satisfy his worldly desires if he has money. If he has no money he has to face many difficulties; but there are some people who worship money for money's sake. They do not worship it because with money they may be able to buy a beautiful woman or good food. They worship it only with the idea that they will be somebody if they have money. The question of being able to buy something does not worry them. It is not a problem for them.

In pursuit of accumulating wealth it generally happens that a person loses his capacity to enjoy the pleasures of the sense organs. Then all that remains for him to do is to take stock of his riches – to see and check his bank balance until eventually this becomes his only interest. Such a person remains absorbed in this activity from morning to evening. He neither sleeps quietly at night nor is he truly awake during the day. He is running after money and amassing it in heaps. Another person is running after fame and goes on pursuing it more and more. Another is after so-called knowledge, setting himself to gather as much information as he can. All our great network of activities begins from our desire to satisfy our ego – our feeling of being somebody.

Be aware how much less disturbance or chaos there is in the lives of animals than in the world of man, because animals are all ardent worshippers of manifest nature. They are firm devotees and cannot be drawn to any other form of worship. They want food, they want protection, they want to satisfy their sexual desires, they want sleep, and then their journey of life is over. An animal does not want more than these things. In a sense their demands are few and limited. In one sense they are very temperate – their wants are very few. They never worry about anything else when the demands of their sense organs are satisfied.

An animal has no desire to be a president. It goes to rest after eating its food, and even its demand for sexual pleasure is very limited and controlled. Except in the world of man, the demand for sexual enjoyment in the whole world of animals is periodical. There is a period when it demands sexual enjoyment, and after the lapse of that period it loses all its urge for sexual satisfaction. Man is the only animal on this earth whose sex drive is always active, twenty-four hours a day and three hundred and sixty-five days of the year. There is no limit to his urge for sexual enjoyment; he remains eager all the time. The thirst for sexual pleasure fills his whole life. No other animal is so eager for it. If it gets food, the matter ends there – no further demands. Animals have no great desire even to collect food for tomorrow, or the day after tomorrow, or for a year or two hence. If an animal is anxious to collect food, it is, at the most, for one year – and such animals are rare. Man is the only animal who not only labors to collect for his whole life, but also labors to collect for that existence after death, if there is such an existence at all.

In ancient Egypt, when a person died the Egyptians used to keep all the things required in life in the grave with the mummified body. The things kept were in proportion to the greatness of the dead person. If an emperor died, all his queens were buried along with him as he might need them after death. All his wealth, food and a great many other things were also kept there. Surviving wives were buried alive along with the dead husband because they might be useful after death! No animal worries about itself after death. It does not even worry about its death. Its expectation of time is very limited. Man makes arrangements in various forms and ways for the next world, the other world. He builds temples and gives in charity so that he may find happiness in the other world. He wants it recorded in the other world that "I have given away so much in charity, here I expect my rewards."

The worship of sense organs alone is less subtle and complex; the network of desire and worship of karma prakriti is less sophisticated among primitive people, so there is not much tension in their lives. To a large extent in primitive societies there are only the demands of the sense organs, as there are among animals. Worship of karma prakriti does not exist. As man goes on becoming more and more civilized, the satisfaction of ego instead of sense organs becomes highly valued. We give great honor to the person who sacrifices the demands of his sense organs in order to satisfy his ego. We call him a great and self-denying person who gives up worrying about food, his wife and his children in his race for position. He is pursuing status, he is pursuing prestige, and we say, "Look at this man! – how indifferent he is to his food, to his clothes, to his home affairs!" But when you look behind his activities, you will find that he is sacrificing the demands of his sense organs to satisfy his ego.

The Upanishads say such an individual goes into great darkness. He who is absorbed only in the sense organs is in a better situation than that individual. His web, his network, is not so deep and subtle because the demands of the sense organs are not many. Endless are the demands of ego. The beautiful thing about the demands of the sense organs is that all of them have few, very few, demands, they are limited. They are repetitive, but they are not limitless.

Bear this difference in mind and understand it. Those demands are repeated but are not limitless. No demand of any of the sense organs is limitless. It never happens that you carry on eating and yet your hunger remains unsatisfied. When you have satisfied your sexual desire today, it will appear again tomorrow – but also when your desire for sexual pleasure is satisfied today, all of a sudden you are completely free of that desire. Sexual desire also is not limitless. It is certainly repetitive, but it is also limited.

Ego is limitless. It does not require repetition; it requires more and more. However much you may fill it and satisfy it, it is never filled, it is never satisfied. Ego is insatiable, it cannot be satisfied. If it acquires one position, it immediately begins a campaign for a better position. No sooner does it get one position than it makes preparations for a superior position. If you tell a person, "You have been made a minister," then he immediately – that very night – begins to have dreams of becoming the chief minister. He says, "It is all right, one desire is fulfilled." Then his ego sets out immediately on its next journey.

Ego is not repetitive. Desires, passions are repeated, but because their demands have limits they become quiet when they are fulfilled. When they are awakened again, they repeat the demands. That is why animals are not inclined to worry and so never become neurotic. They do not commit suicide. They never require to be mentally examined, they don't need any psychoanalysis. No Freud, no Jung, no Adler is required by them; these are meaningless people for the animals. If you pay attention to how animals are, you will find them very quiet. Even very ferocious animals are quiet. If you have seen a tiger after his dinner, you will find him very quiet, no uneasiness at all. He is a killer, a carnivorous animal through and through, but his killing nature is there only so long as he has not got his food. No sooner has he eaten than he becomes absolutely nonviolent – he becomes a staunch Gandhian. Then he remains indifferent to the food lying before him. When the lion is resting after his dinner, smaller animals which might well be his dinner gather round him and eat the remnants of his food. But then he is not ready to kill them. When he becomes hungry the next day he will be ready to hunt and to kill, but until then the matter of killing is over. The hunger of man's ego is never over; on the contrary, it goes on increasing as you go on satisfying it.

Understand this distinction between sense organs and ego. Satisfy the sense organs and they are soon full. They will be empty again and can then be filled again. But the ego is never filled, it is never satisfied. As you go on filling it, it goes on increasing. When you throw fat in the fire to extinguish it, the fire increases instead of being extinguished; similarly all the things thrown in to satisfy the ego help to increase it. It suddenly sends up a burst of flame and goes higher and higher. So whatever is offered to ego only helps it to grow. Hence, from the moment a person is caught in the grip of ego he is more entangled than animals can ever be in uneasiness, cares, tensions and worries.

A great movement to return to nature is going on today in the West. The young men and women whom we call hippies or beatniks or dropouts are today carrying on this great movement. It is a drive to return to the sense organs. They say, "We do not want your education, your degrees, your positions, your wealth, your cars, and your palatial buildings. It will be enough for us if we get food, love and sex. We don't want all those things of yours." And I believe this is a very great happening. Such a movement on such a large scale has never happened in the history of mankind, when people have said, "We are willingly giving up the karma prakriti to return to that nature born of sense organs, the manifest nature of sense organs, desires and passions. This is enough for us, more than this we do not desire."

This shows that the network of ego-motivated activities has become so dangerous that man wants to be free from it and is willing to be like the animals. Even so, man cannot be free from ego by becoming like an animal. He can be free from ego only by becoming divine. By absorbing himself in the pursuit of the enjoyment of sense organs he will get some relief, but that network of activities will appear again. Man was living in his sense organs two thousand years ago, but ego arose from those circumstances. If we regress again today, ego will surely return tomorrow.

This sutra says they who are absorbed in the worship of manifest nature wander in darkness, and they wander in greater darkness who are absorbed in satisfying their egos. Then who can go beyond darkness? Who are they?

Two types of worship are observed. There are the worshippers of sense organs, and the worshippers of ego, and generally the ego-worshippers are against worshipping the sense organs. Suppose a person is into renunciation. Now if we can explore his mental condition thoroughly, if we can perform an exploratory operation on his mind, we will see that the secret of his renunciation is that it satisfies his ego. He has observed a fast for thirty days, so he is honored with great acclaim by the people of the town; a great reception is arranged for him. He has been able to endure fasting for thirty days.

We declare it to be an act of great self-denial; it is no small matter to remain hungry for thirty days! No, it is not a small matter.

But it would certainly be a small matter if the ego were satisfied. If his ego derived satisfaction from it a man would remain hungry not merely for thirty days but for thirty years! Ego will persuade any sense organ to go into self-denial. We have long known this secret – this trick – so if we want renunciation from someone, we start to stroke his ego.

Mankind is very familiar with this device. That is why we have honored the self-denying person. Nobody will be ready for self-denial if he is not to be honored. The truly self-denying person does not expect any respect and honor for his renunciation. If you withdraw your honoring, if you stop honoring, you will see: ninety-nine out of a hundred self-denying people will drop out. If you want to know the truth about this practice, just withdraw your honor from such people.

See what happens. A person takes only one meal a day, so people touch his feet and bow down to him. They have given that much food to his ego, and that is enough for him. He can easily let go his second meal. He will suffer in body but will fatten his ego. Thus people can be induced to do anything for the sake of this ego-worship, and almost everything has been tried to induce people to renounce in order to satisfy their egos. In the long history of mankind we find thousands of devices inducing man to do anything for the sake of satisfying his ego.

In the Middle Ages in Europe there was a great movement of holy men who whipped themselves. These men were honored in proportion to the number of times they whipped themselves, because they were subjecting their bodies to so much agony. Some of them were extraordinary people. Their only merit was that they were bleeding and tearing off their flesh by whipping themselves. Their fame spread from town to town. People declared, "This man inflicts fifty lashes on his body; that one inflicts a hundred," and so on. This was their only claim to fame; they had no other merit, but for this alone they commanded great respect. Some became great experts in self torture.

Now, you will be surprised and say, "What madness was this?

What was the reason for respecting a person who had no other merit than whipping himself?" But if you think a little about your own holy men you will know the reason. Some sadhu goes from place to place on foot – he never uses a vehicle – and that is his distinction, his mark of esteem. Another sadhu vows to take only one meal a day; another vows never to touch a woman, another remains naked.

Are these distinctive qualities worthy of merit? There is nothing special about them. Then what is the secret? You can travel on foot as much as you like: after all, the animals go on foot! No, but the ones who honor a sadhu for walking are those who can no longer do something so natural. The car owner bows down to the man who goes on foot. He feels himself insignificant confronted by this man who walks everywhere, this man who destroys his car owning, car driving ego completely. *You* may drive a car, but you have to touch the feet of this one who always goes on foot!

This walking sadhu may not be able to buy a car, it is quite a difficult thing for him to obtain; but he can walk. There were two ways open to him to hit your ego. He can either buy a more expensive car than yours, which is out of the question for him, or he can walk, which is so easy. So he hits at your ego by walking. This way he keeps up his ego. But what merit is there in walking? What transformation has happened in this person who prefers to walk? Nevertheless, we praise him. We honor him because we feel he is doing something we find too difficult to do. So we think he is performing a great, self-denying act, and we honor him.

In pursuit of honor a person is prepared to go around the world on foot. Why on foot? People can go around the world rolling on the ground to get respect and honor. There are people who do this! They go rolling along the ground on a pilgrimage to Kashi, and hundreds of people follow them on foot precisely because they have become so famous by rolling on the ground. There is no need to ask whether there is any other value to it besides this. Generally, self-denying people go on supplementing their egos by sacrificing the physical comforts of their sense organs.

I call this man a self-denying person who liberates himself from attachment to his sense organs and has no interest in satisfying his ego. That is real renunciation; otherwise there is no meaning in all those exhibitionist activities. The Upanishads are talking about people who renounce both these things. Such people are absorbed neither in the worship of manifest nature nor in that of ego. The Upanishads are talking about people who are interested in neither.

Bear in mind, the worship of the sense organs is quite obvious, but that of ego is very subtle so it is often difficult to detect the worship of ego. When a person takes great interest in food, it is obvious. But what is the interest of a person who puts on fine clothes and goes out on a trip around town? Is it not his desire that people in the town should see his fine clothes, should know that he has such clothes, and should consider him to be somebody? What is the desire of a woman who goes out wearing a mink coat worth a couple of thousand dollars? It does not have the use a coat should have. The sum of two thousand dollars bears no relation whatsoever to the coat. A coat worth forty or fifty dollars would have been all right. But what can it mean to have a coat worth two thousand dollars?

It is obvious that there is no meaning in it other than to create the fire of envy in the eyes of other women. The helplessness and inferiority of other women becomes apparent before that coat. That is the real interest, and it can be detected without much difficulty. We at once understand what is what when a person puts on a coat worth two thousand dollars. But what is the intention of a person who stands naked in a marketplace? Is not his interest also that people should see that he is somebody of note? Then there is no difference between the mink coat and nakedness. Or, we can say, to buy the mink coat one will have to work hard for a long time to earn two thousand dollars, whereas standing naked will bring the same self-satisfying pleasure derived from the mink coat, and far more easily – no need to earn a couple of thousand dollars.

The worship of the sense organs is simple, not subtle, so it is visible and obvious, while that of ego goes on becoming subtler and subtler. But be sure about yourself. Don't worry about what another person does, or why he acts so. If a person is standing naked you will not be able to know why he does so. The whole matter is so subtle that it should be considered alright if the doer himself understands his action. It is possible his nakedness may be true innocence.

If Mahavira stands naked, it is certain he is not using his nakedness in the way a woman uses the mink coat, because he had many such coats. Mahavira possessed very valuable coats. He had the material means to be somebody. So it is almost impossible for a person like Mahavira to gratify his ego by standing naked. But we cannot judge even this action of Mahavira by outward appearances; it is best left to Mahavira to decide. If your neighbor is standing naked, you cannot know why he is standing naked. It should be left to him to find out. Let him seek the cause, because this is a very subtle and deep phenomenon.

We have to go outward if we wish to satisfy the demands of the sense organs. It is not necessary to go outward if we wish to satisfy our ego. It can be satisfied from within also.

I have heard that a hermit was living alone in a very remote forest. He did not initiate anyone. A traveling monk passing by his dwelling, saw him and said, "You are very humble and modest. You have not made anyone your disciple even though you are such a great and wise man. You have been a guru to no one. I am on my way to another sadhu who has thousands of disciples."

The holy man smiled and said, "How can you compare him with me? I am a completely secluded person. I have no attachment of any kind. I have no desire even to make someone my disciple. I do not wish to nurture any kind of ego, so I do not nurture the ego of becoming a guru. I am absolutely egoless."

The traveler said to him, "I have also seen another monk as egoless as you." On hearing this, the face of the monk changed and his smile immediately vanished. He saw a competitor in front of him and his ego began to make him uneasy. In the beginning he was pleased because his ego was not challenged by the first monk about whom the traveler was talking. On the contrary, his ego was swelling with satisfaction. But the statement, "I have seen another monk as egoless as you," made him uneasy; he was upset. The mind becomes very unhappy on hearing, "Someone else like you also exists." That hermit was nurturing his ego even in that solitary place, feeding it on this feeling that, "I live a secluded life and have not accepted anyone as my disciple."

One feeds his ego with the feeling, "I have many disciples," while the other nourishes it through his pride in having none. One says, "No one is greater than I," and the other says, "I am a poor, humble person, only as good as the dust under your feet." What he means is, "There is no greater dust than me! Do not talk of dust superior to me – I am the last and the best!" It makes no difference which way you choose to feed the ego. But to understand these workings of the mind, you will have to enter deep within yourself.

So, declares the sage, he alone enters light who liberates himself from both kinds of worship – of the senses and of the ego. He has to liberate himself from the worship of manifest nature as well as from that of subtle ego.

The Upanishads speak on a very deep matter when they say that the worship of the senses does not lead you into deep darkness, because the ultimate fact is that the sense organs are given to you. They are nature, you have not created them. But ego is your invention, ego is a manufactured thing. You brought your sense organs with you when you were born.

One day you may lose interest in taste and flavor, but you will never be free from hunger; that will remain with you till you die. Hunger is a necessity. You came with sense organs into this world, and however much you free yourself from the senses you cannot be free from the necessities of the sense organs. You can be liberated from their desires but you cannot be free from their needs. You can become free from the madness of the sense organs but not from their necessities. Neither Mahavira nor Buddha nor anyone can be free from them. Food you must have, it is an unavoidable part of life.

Of course, this much is possible for one who is free from the worship of sense organs – that he ceases to be obsessed with them. This much happens – that he does not increase his desires, he keeps them to the minimum; that is, he stops when the need is fulfilled. If his body needs two slices of bread, he takes only two. He does not increase his demand. If his body can be covered with one piece of clothing he will make do with one piece only. He has no desire to adorn himself. If a cottage provides him with the rest and shelter he needs, it will be enough for him; he will not demand a palace.

Everyone has to decide for himself the nature of his basic needs; they differ from person to person. One person needs two slices of bread, another needs five. For the former, five slices will be an indulgence. So don't seek to imitate the example of others. Everyone has to search within himself, and a simple guideline to follow is that fulfilling the basic needs of the sense organs never creates worry in a person. But no sooner does a man exceed his body's basic needs and make extravagant demands than worries begin.

So consider anxiety as your unit of measurement. As soon as anxiety begins to make you uneasy then at once take note that you are demanding more than is necessary – because it is desire for the nonessential which creates anxiety. Necessities do not create anxieties at all. The unessential thing – without which we can carry on but are not willing to do so – is the cause of our cares and anxieties. So when the mind becomes worried, observe how you have been busy in satisfying demands which go beyond the needs of the sense organs.

Worry is symptomatic; it is an informer. For example, you are hungry and you start eating your food. When will you know that you are eating to excess? As soon as you feel the stomach becoming heavy, not giving any feeling of satisfaction, but on the contrary giving trouble, then you should realize that you have gone beyond your body's need. The stomach has become worried.

I told you this as an illustration. Similarly each sense organ is disturbed when it is fed more than necessary. It remains unperturbed, quiet and satisfied if it is fed according to its need. As soon as it receives more than is necessary it becomes perturbed, sick, diseased and harassed. We become very content when our hunger is satisfied, but to eat more than necessary is to invite disease and sickness. As someone once said, half the food we eat fills our belly; the other half feeds our doctor's belly. Half is necessary for us and the other half invites sickness. One remains alert and active by keeping oneself a little hungry, but overeating produces dullness; a sort of darkness descends upon the eater.

Each must decide for himself what is necessary, according to his own organic structure. The sense organs are very quick to give a warning of impending troubles and diseases. Sense organs are very sensitive and will warn you quickly that you are exceeding your needs. Remove the unnecessary; remove the nonessential.

Sense organs, then, accompany you to the end of your life; your life runs on the wheels of the sense organs. But ego is not an essential thing. It is our creation, and we can without doubt live without it – egoless. Ego leads us into greater darkness because it is created by man. It is absolutely nonessential. There is something necessary in sense organs to which we add something nonessential, and that is our trouble. Sense organs lead us into darkness due to the effect of the nonessential part, while ego is *totally* nonessential so it leads us into greater darkness. The truth is that the less the ego the deeper one lives; the bigger the ego the more petty and superficial life one lives, because ego does not allow one to go deep within. It keeps you on the surface. Why? This also needs to be understood properly.

The simple fact is that ego gets its pleasure from the eyes of others. If you are left alone in a forest, your ego will lose all its pleasure. Then to put on a diamond necklace will be meaningless: and if you do put it on, the animals will laugh at you! Even if it is of diamonds you will feel it as a burden around your neck which you will gladly remove. What can you do to your ego in a jungle? No, the total interest of ego is in the reflections created in the eyes of others and, like all reflections, they happen on the surface. These reflections surround us on all sides. Ego is like ornate fencing round a building.

It may be enjoyable, it may be beautiful, but it is created by the eyes of others.

Ego can never be created without the presence of the other – it depends on the other. That is why we always remain afraid of the other, because the satisfaction of our ego is in the hands of the other and he may withdraw his hands at any time. Suppose A greets B this morning, and does not do so the next morning. B's wall of ego falls down, his ego is hurt. His mind becomes agitated and he is preoccupied with what he should do now. Suppose his acquaintances decide to forget B. He goes out for a walk and they fail to acknowledge him; they take no notice of his presence. Then B will be as good as dead. Ego's interest and pleasure is in the eyes of others, and the eyes of others have turned away from him.

One whose pleasure is in these eyes cannot go deep within himself. He cannot live on a deeper plane. He lives only in outer coverings and garments. He alone can enter the depths of life who enters the soul, and he alone can enter the soul who forgets ego. He has to forget the eyes of others and begin to walk within his own eyes. Let him see himself. He has to cease worrying about how others look at him. Let him give up thinking about the opinions others have of him and what they say about him. He has to bear in mind this much only – "Who am I?" The question, "What do others say about me?" is absolutely meaningless. What concern have you with others? The approval of others will be of no use. In life it is not useful to have the approval of others.

I have heard: A Jewish saint called Josiah was on his deathbed, and the town's rabbi had come to him to say the last prayers for him. He asked the saint to remember Moses the prophet as he was on his way to God.

The dying saint opened his eyes and said, "Don't ask me to remember Moses, because when I am standing in front of God he will not ask me why I did not become like Moses; he will ask me why I did not become Josiah. He will certainly not ask me about Moses. He will ask me why I did not become 'that for which I sent you into the world'. He will ask me, 'Why did you not become the flower of that potential seed with which I sent you into the world?' So please do not ask me to remember Moses at this moment. The question is about *me* now."

Hearing this the rabbi said, "Do not spoil your reputation on your deathbed. People are standing on all sides, and they may hear what you are saying about Moses."

The saint opened his eyes again and said, "I lived in that madness throughout my life; let me be free from it at the time of my last breath. I am giving up that reputation now. Let me be free from this false reputation at the time of my death. Don't worry about those who are standing around me. I shall be free of them in a moment. They are not going to be my witnesses. God will not ask them their opinion about me. God will see me for what I am, so let me worry about myself."

In fact, ego is always worrying what others say about you. It is so anxious about the evaluations of others. And soul is the experience of 'what I am'. It has no concern with what others say. Others may be wrong or they may be right – that is their business.

To give up the worship of sense organs is to stop at the point of necessity, and to give up the worship of ego is to come to the zero point. If these two conditions are fulfilled, then the individual is sitting near neither the sense organs nor the ego. He sits near the soul – the *atman*. Then a new sitting-near starts – sitting near God. Really it is not correct to speak of being near God, because to be near God means to be one with God. Then we lose our identity. We cannot be 'the other' with God. As long as we are absorbed in the worship of these two – sense organs and ego – we are far away from God. Nothing else at all is to be done to be near him, to be one with him. No sooner do you give up these two religions than you are one with him.

It is like this: if a person, before taking a jump, asks, "I am about to jump to the ground, but what should I do to reach the ground?" then we will tell him, "You simply jump! The rest will be done by the ground – you don't have to do anything else." It will be enough if a person takes a jump from the roof of sense organs and ego; the rest will be done by God. Then you are not going near him; you are going *in* him. His gravitational pull is very powerful.

In our country we have named Krishna the perfect incarnation of God. The word *krishna* means gravitation – one who attracts, who draws others towards himself. The gravitational pull of the earth is very great, but you can stop yourself from being attracted towards the earth. Even a small grassblade can hold itself against this powerful attraction of the earth. It can resist it.

If you cling fast to something, then the gravitation of the earth will not be able to attract you. If you stop your clinging, if your hands are free, not grasping anything, then the earth will immediately draw you towards itself. No matter how far off, you will be drawn by it. But provided you are clinging to something you will not be drawn towards it, even if you are very close to it.

God draws towards himself the man who has let go of these two – the sense organs and the ego. Such a person enters light.

Enough for today.

# The Seed
# And The Tree

14

*It has been pointed out
that the fruits obtained by the
worship of manifest Brahman
are different from those obtained
by the worship of unmanifest Brahman.
We have heard this from those wise people
who knew and explained it to us.*

THE UPANISHADS talk about two forms of Brahman, the supreme element. The forms are two, the element is one. But it would be better to say there are two kinds of people who know, while the element is one. The one is the unmanifest original form of Brahman; the other is the manifest form of Brahman. The seed is the cause, the tree is the action, the effect. Everything is hidden in the seed, everything is manifest in the tree. So there is one seed-Brahman, seen nowhere by us. What is visible is the tree-Brahman, not the seed-Brahman. What has become manifest is seen by us; and what is hidden, unmanifest, is invisible to us. Worship can be made of both unmanifest and manifest Brahman, and in many and varied ways. The results of the two kinds of worship are quite distinct.

Worship of gods was very much in vogue when the Upanishads were sung. It is necessary to grasp well the meaning of 'gods'. In gods there is the clearest manifestation of the effects of God, of unmanifest Brahman. Thus even a stone is a manifestation. We call someone a god in whom the unmanifest shines, though he himself is manifest. We call such people incarnations of God, or *tirthankaras*, or sons of God; for example, Jesus, Mohammed, Mahavira, Krishna and Rama. Such individuals are standing in the doorway. They are manifest and seen by us from outside the door. Their faces from the front are clearly visible. They are very similar to our faces, and yet they are not like ours. Some spark of the unmanifest, some glimmer of that hidden seed-Brahman, is also in them. From all their worldly activities in life some radiance of the unmanifest shines forth and indicates the divine to us. All such spirits are divine. The meaning of the word divine is that which is visible and also radiates with the unmanifest.

The Upanishads affirm that worship, prayer and devotion to such divine spirits brings fruit, because there is something in them beyond the visible. For a person who looks hard at them in deep meditation, the visible form will disappear and the unmanifest will remain. As a result of this a difficulty arises. Suppose Rama is standing in front of his disciple; the disciple will not see Rama as a human being because he becomes so much one with the unmanifest that the visible form disappears. Rama's features disappear, and only the Brahman, the supreme, remains. So when a disciple of Rama repeats his name as a mantra – Rama-*japa* – he has no concern at all with the man who was the son of King Dasharath. Then he is contemplating only the seed-Brahman.

But one who is not a disciple of Rama does not see that part of Rama which is unmanifest. That seed-Brahman is not seen; only that part which has assumed the physical body is seen by him. Only the son of Dasharath, or the husband of Sita, or the enemy of Ravana, is seen. A friend of somebody, or an enemy of somebody – the manifest part only is seen. So when a true disciple talks about Rama and another so-called disciple also talks about Rama, they are talking about two different beings. There is no rhythm or harmony in their talk. There cannot be any communion between them. They do not understand each other because they are talking about two separate parts of the same individual.

This sutra of the Upanishad says that worshipping – sitting near – the manifest form of the Brahman where some radiance of the unmanifest form is also seen, brings its own fruits. They will be enjoyable and pleasant, or it would be better to say they will be heavenly. They will be very euphoric, but they will not be enlightening. That is why we use three words for the fruits: one is hell, the other is heaven and the third is enlightenment. One can go as far as heaven by sitting near – that is, worshipping – gods. One can experience heavenly pleasures and happiness, but one cannot rise into enlightenment; one cannot rise into bliss.

What is the difference between happiness and bliss? However deep and great happiness may be, it will surely pass away. No matter how longstanding, it will surely come to an end. So understand this distinction perfectly. Enlightenment – bliss – begins, but has no end. Heaven – happiness – begins, and ends also. Hell does not begin; it has only an end. Let me repeat this so that it may be perfectly grasped. Hell has no beginning – misery has no beginning. There may be no happiness, but it can be begun.

Hell has no beginning but it can be ended.

Heaven has the beginning and also the end. It will begin and will end also.

Enlightenment has only the beginning and no end. Once begun, it is endless.

Wherever the divine flame appears in visible, manifest Brahman, its worship and prayer can take one to heaven, to happiness. Therefore those who desire happiness are engrossed in the worship of gods. Those desirous of enlightenment are not so absorbed in the worship of gods; they turn away from gods. They do not pray for happiness because happiness can never take the place of enlightenment. Happiness, though enjoyable, will always be a bondage, and those desirous of enlightenment wish to attain to the highest form of liberation. They long for the highest bliss which has no limit, they desire that nectar which is boundless, they wish to reach that point which is the point of no return, that place beyond which there is nothing to seek.

Those who long for this point beyond which there is nowhere to go will have to go in search of the seed-Brahman. They will have to go in search of the unmanifest Brahman and not the manifest Brahman. They will be enlightened by their devotion; attaining to the Brahman they will attain to the highest liberation.

There are distinctly different outcomes to these two kinds of worship, and the great beauty of the Upanishads is that they do not reject either of them. The results, the fruits, of both kinds are clearly stipulated. They do not reject either of them but they say

those who wish to worship gods should do so with the understanding that it is a journey to happiness, and not beyond that.

In the latter part of the sutra it is declared that "We have this
from those who have known." There is one important point to
bear in mind here. Knowledge is endless. However much knowledge you may gather, it is always incomplete. It is like this: from
one shore you descend deep down into the ocean, but even though
you fathom its depth you can never know the whole ocean. It is
possible that the ocean may have known *you* thoroughly, but you
cannot know the entire ocean. There are other shores also, and on
them countless and endless travelers. Innumerable pilgrims have
entered the ocean from countless places, and it would be a good
thing if your knowledge and their knowledge were to be gathered
and blended together in as large a measure as possible.

That is why the sages of the Upanishads always declare that
what they say they have gathered from those who have known.
They blend their knowledge with that unbounded store of knowledge. They say, "We have heard this from those who know. Why
should we talk about our little knowledge? We contribute our little
knowledge into that vast, boundless store of knowledge collected
by countless people." Why should they talk separately about their
knowledge? They would feel embarrassed talking about it. They
do not even refer to it. They say this as if they themselves have not
acquired it. In an attitude of humility they say, "We have heard
from those who have known."

There are countless people, countless incarnations, and they
come from countless shores. *Tirtha* means a shore. So, the Jainas
call such people *tirthankaras*. The word tirthankara means one
who works on the shore, helping sailors cast off and put to sea.
But because the ocean is boundless, the shorelines are endless.
Because the ocean is boundless, there are countless tirthankaras.
We do not know all of them. If we look back in the past, we know
nothing of the sages who flourished before the Vedas. The refer-
ences are only to the Vedic and post-Vedic sages.

It is not that truth was not known by any who lived before the

Vedic sages, because the Vedic sages themselves often say, "We have heard from those who know." The Upanishads are our most ancient scriptures written and compiled by those who know. But the Upanishads continuously declare, "We have heard it from those who knew." The import of this declaration is that truth has always been known since time immemorial, and it has been known by so many, in such quantity, and in such infinitely varied ways, that "I cannot talk about my little knowledge! I add something to a vast reservoir." So he says, "I am telling that which has been said by those who knew it."

There is another point to remember in this matter – that those ancient wise ones who knew were never eager for originality. They were not yearning to be original. Nobody ever said, "What I am telling is the original truth; I am telling it for the first time, and nobody has ever said it before me." There is a great difference in attitude in our modern age. Today everybody wants to claim that what he says has never been said before – that he is original.

What does this mean? Does it mean that the ancient sages were unoriginal? Are people today original? No, the fact is quite the opposite. The ancient people were so undoubting, so sure of themselves, that there was no need for them to announce their certainty, while today people are so doubtful about originality, so uneasy about it, that they cannot but make a declaration of it. Modern man is always afraid that someone might say, "Do you think you are saying something new? What you are saying is nothing new to people." This simply shows that modern man does not understand the true meaning of original.

The correct meaning of the word original is not what is new but 'from the source'. Original does not mean unprecedented, the word means 'from the source'. He who knows the root is original, and many people have known it, so the word does not refer to anything new. But today people all over the world are looking for something new. Everybody asserts: "What I am saying is new," because the fear is that there is nothing special about his knowing if others have known it already. The interesting fact is that there is only one special characteristic in this world. In this connection I remember a line from the mystic Jakob Boehme: "The only thing that is extraordinary is to be ordinary."

These sages who, instead of claiming that they know, declare that they have heard from those who know, are extraordinary people. They must have been very uncommon people because they are willing to be so common. In fact, he is an ordinary person who entertains even a slight notion that he is uncommon. All ordinary people have this notion. Even the most ordinary person believes that he is extraordinary. This is a very common belief. Then whom can we call extraordinary? We can call him an extraordinary person who does not even know that he is extraordinary. He who is so humble is extraordinary.

The statement of the sage is certainly extraordinary. When the people who knew so much and knew it so deeply say, "We have heard it..." then such people must be remarkable – must be extraordinary. They must have been like zeros, like nothingness. They must have been utterly humble. They make no claim at all, either of truth or of path, and there is weight and substance in the statements of those who lay claim to nothing. That is why they often repeat again and again that they have heard from those who knew.

This mental attitude of erasing oneself, of destroying oneself totally, of rubbing out one's presence, of making oneself as if not, is related to the deepest root source of life – to pure existence. It is beyond the mind, beyond imagination or sentiments. It is transcendental.

Enough for today.

We shall meet again in the evening.


Now let us go to the root, let us go towards the transcendental.... I will tell you a few things which I remembered just now about the meditations.

About ninety percent of you are doing so fine and progressing so well that I am immensely pleased with you. But I feel sorry for the other ten percent. Do not remain in your wretched condition;

don't be one of that ten percent group. Do not throw away those valuable gifts of yours cheaply.

One more instruction about the afternoon meditation. Some of you sit here without wearing your blindfolds. You will not be benefited at all. No one should sit here without the blindfold on his eyes. Another point to remember is this: be careful about *yourself*, do not worry about others. Those who do nothing will begin to worry about others, because they are idle. So don't sit idle; be joyful, dance and laugh!

I was very happy yesterday – there was great lightness, you were very much like children. One old person was shouting like a child. He was very innocent. He was shouting, "Ma, Ma, Ma!" Be light like children. There was great celebration. It should go on increasing. It *will* go on increasing as meditation becomes deeper and deeper. If an old man becomes like a child, it means he has attained to meditation. This much for the afternoon meditation. I am completely happy with the morning meditation – it is going well.

Now I have to give one instruction with regard to the night meditation. There were two or three friends organizing the session and they were enough. But the rest who came up to involve themselves in the organizing created a lot of confusion. None of you should make self-appointments here. You are here to meditate, not to organize things. In fact it was those who sit idle who took this on themselves. They thought, "Let us go in for management." Those two or three people authorized to do this job of management will do their work – the rest have not to bother about it.

I was very sad for those sitting behind the platform as they could not meditate properly. They were disturbed by other busybodies. What difference does it make if somebody falls on me? It makes no difference! And those in meditation have not lost their consciousness, they are fully alert. They are not going to fall down. Don't start thinking that someone may rush at me or attack me. They are all in full consciousness. They love me as much as the managers do. So don't worry about all this.

They were much disturbed when they could no longer see me. That was when the trouble started, because this meditation entirely depends on my being seen. So my idea for tonight's meditation is that all those standing should be in the hall, and those who practice meditation in a sitting posture should sit behind them. This is the only arrangement required.

One more undesirable incident happened yesterday. Many outsiders forcibly entered the meeting place. This creates a great disturbance. The complete tuning which can be created in such a meeting cannot be created when outsiders come in. Even if there is just one wrong person in the hall, he will create different kinds of vibrations. So not one such person should be allowed to enter. Those in the camp who only want to listen and do not wish to participate in meditation should immediately go out of the hall when the lecture is over. They will greatly oblige us by doing so. They should not harm us.

We do not want even a single person in the hall who is merely an onlooker. He creates an obstacle, a gap. When so many consciousnesses are flowing in the same experience the whole atmosphere becomes charged, and then, if one person not so charged is among the company, he creates a discontinuity in the atmosphere. A certain portion is torn off by him. There can be no pouring of spiritual energy through that portion. Because of this, the vibrations which could penetrate through and through from one corner to the other are not being able to do so. This is why I am not at present happy with our night session of meditation.

The night meditation is the most important and valuable, and the other two sessions of meditation are meant to prepare you for this night meditation. When you are prepared after those two meditations there can be an explosion in the night meditation, but some obstacles are coming up in the program. It has not yet been accomplished. Some outsiders entered the place the day before yesterday and so it could not be done properly. It was a little better before that. We could have achieved good results yesterday, but some unauthorized people came up onto the platform and began to dabble in the management. You have not come here to manage.

And don't worry about me, you worry about yourselves. I am satisfied even if I die in helping someone, even just one person, to be successful in meditation.

# Let Us Die

15

One who knows
the unmanifest Brahman
and at the same time the manifest Brahman,
having overcome death
by the worship of the manifest Brahman,
attains to immortality
by the worship of the unmanifest Brahman.

WE CANNOT DRAW A CIRCLE without a center. The circumference is drawn all around the center. As the circumference moves away from the center it grows larger and larger. If we mark two points on the circumference there will be some distance between them, and if we draw two lines from the points on the circumference joining the center, the distance between the lines will go on decreasing as they approach the center. The distance between the lines will disappear as soon as they reach the center. There may be any amount of distance between two lines on the circumference, but as these lines approach the center, they go on coming closer to each other, and having reached the center the distance disappears altogether. At the center they are one. If we continue to draw these lines beyond the circumference, the distance between them will go on increasing as the circumference increases.

Through giving this geometrical illustration, I wish to tell you two or three things to explain this sutra. The first point is this; the element which is called the unmanifest Brahman is the central Brahman. The whole expanse of the existence comes out of it: and life – the circumference – goes on spreading out and out from this center.

After deep inquiry during the last few years, science has arrived at a new theory – that of the expanding universe. It was always believed that the universe is what it is, nothing added, nothing subtracted. But modern science says the universe is not simply that which now is, but it goes on expanding every day, just as a balloon goes on expanding if someone pumps air into it. Such is the expanse of this universe. But it is not the same as it was yesterday.

It expands by millions of miles during every twenty-four hours. Continuously it is expanding. The stars we see at night are traveling far away from one another every moment.

This is interesting: there must have been a moment when this universe was so contracted within itself that it must have been at the zero center. As you go back and back in time, the universe is found to be smaller and smaller, becoming more and more contracted. There must necessarily come a moment when this whole universe was contracted into its very center. Then its expansion began, and that process has been going on ever since. The circumference is getting larger and larger every day. Scientists say we are unable to forecast how long it will continue to expand. This is an endless expansion. It will go on growing larger and larger.

It is necessary to bear in mind another point. Science has started to use the term 'expanding universe' very recently, but the thing – the element – which is called the Brahman by the Upanishads, means the expanding. That is the meaning of the word Brahman. The meaning of Brahman is not God, but the element that is constantly expanding. The words Brahman and *vistala* – expanse – are derived from the same root. They are derivations of the same word. So, the meaning of Brahman is that which goes on and on expanding. It is not that it has expanded or spread; it is not a static condition, but it is that which is constantly expanding. The activity is going on. What happens is constantly expanding.

Even from a scientific point of view, the Brahman has two forms – one is the unmanifest, which is called *Asambhuti* by the sage of the Upanishad. The unmanifest Brahman means the zero-Brahman, the seed-Brahman. Let us imagine the time when it had not started to expand, when the seed had not broken. Then imagine the absolute first moment of expansion – and after that the sprouting, the continual expanding, the growing of the tree. From such a tiny seed, such an enormous tree will grow that thousands of bullock-carts can take rest under its shade. And from that tree will fall innumerable seeds; and from each seed will grow again a vast tree; and again each tree will propagate countless seeds, and from each seed the tree, and seeds and trees and seeds and trees endlessly. Thus a single, minute seed, through its growing process, gives birth to endless seeds. The unmanifest Brahman is the seed-Brahman, the zero-Brahman, the center point. We can only imagine this, because the center point can only be imagined.

If we ask Euclid, the greatest geometrician, he will say a center point is that which has neither breadth nor length. You could not see such a point. This is its definition – it has neither breadth nor length; and it cannot be a point if it has breadth and length, for then it becomes another figure, and there must be expansion. Where breadth and length are, there is expansion. A point is that which has not yet expanded, but which is going to expand. Therefore, says Euclid, the point can only be defined, it cannot be drawn.

When you put the smallest point on a piece of paper with the sharp end of your pencil, there immediately is breadth and length; a point can never be drawn on paper. So the point which is seen has expanded. The point which is not seen, but is defined only, is the true point. The thing which is called the point by Euclid is invisible – it has not yet begun to be; its creation is not yet manifested. It is unmanifest. Life has not yet emerged from it, but it has the potentiality for it; life is yet hidden. So this unmanifest Brahman is like the point in the definition.

This is one form of Brahman. But we do not know it. We know only the manifest Brahman – that which is out. We know the tree-Brahman which has unfolded. The manifest is not yet complete, it is becoming and becoming; it is in the process of becoming, it is constantly expanding. Our universe is becoming larger and larger every moment. To describe its increase by the day is too much – it is inconceivable. So I say it expands every second. The stars are moving away from the center at the speed of light. The speed of light is one hundred and eighty-six thousand miles per second. So in one minute it expands sixty times that distance; and in one hour, sixty times that again. And multiply this multiplication by twenty-four to know how many miles it has expanded at the end of one day.

The circumference is moving with such a tremendous speed away from the center, and this activity has been going on since endless time. Moreover, scientists are unable to determine that moment of time when this journey must have started, when the seed must have put out its first sprout in the process of becoming the tree. Nor can we say anything about the end of this journey. Science is in a great dilemma today, because it is inconceivable where and why the phenomenon of the expanding universe should end. There is no possibility of its stopping, because that would require some other impediment to its progress. Suppose I throw a stone; if it does not meet with any obstruction it will stop nowhere. But some obstruction comes up – it may strike against a tree. If it does not strike against a tree it is striking the air, and gravitation of the earth attracts it all the time. As the impetus given by my hand weakens, the gravitational force pulls it down. But if there is no gravitational pull and no obstruction in the way, a stone thrown by me, or even by a small child, will stop nowhere, because there is nothing to stop it.

Where will this universe of ours – this manifest Brahman – which is constantly expanding, stop? There must be some obstruction, some impediment, to stop it. But where will the impediment come from? Everything is within it, nothing is outside it. What is, is part and parcel of manifest Brahman. So there can be no impediment. Where can it stop? How can it stop? Will it go on expanding? Both Einstein and Planck, who did a great deal of research work around this theory, were baffled by it. At their wits' ends, they finally had to leave it a mystery. No cause, no obstruction, is conceivable that can stop it, and yet its nonstopping seems inconceivable. If it goes on expanding in this manner, a day may come when stars will be so far away from one another that one star cannot be seen from another star.

But the Upanishads talk about this phenomenon from quite a different and strange perspective, and it should be understood properly. If not today, then in the future, scientists will have to work from that perspective. But up to now it has not been the way of reasoning in the West, and there is a reason for this: the whole of Western science has developed from Greek philosophy. It stands on the foundations of Greek philosophy, and one of Greek philosophy's basic beliefs is that time travels in a straight line. This belief has led Western science into great difficulty. Indian philosophy thinks about this in a vastly different way.

Indian philosophy says all motions are circular. No motion can be in a straight line. Understand this by an illustration. A child is born, grows up and then grows old. If we asked a Greek philosopher to explain this, he would reply that a straight line could be drawn between the child and the old man to explain this happening. The Indian philosopher would reject this and say a circle should be drawn between the child and the old man because in his last days the old man reaches that condition in which he began as a child. It is a circle. Hence it is no great surprise if old people are found behaving like children. It is not a straight line but a circle that joins childhood and old age. Youth is the midpoint of that circle, it is the zenith. When youth is over, the life journey begins to return to its starting point. It is like the revolving of seasons. The Indian conception of time is a circle, like the revolving of the seasons. Summer, the rainy season and winter follow one another in a circle. In the same way morning follows evening and evening follows morning. It is a circle.

The wise men of the East believe that all movements are circular. The earth revolves, seasons revolve, the sun, the moon and the stars move round and round. Every movement is circular, no movement is straight. Life moves in a circle. And the expanding universe, too, moves in a circle. Suppose a child remains young; then a difficulty will arise. Where will its being young end? Where will life stop if it goes on expanding and does not return to the point of death?

So Indian thinking says that this manifest Brahman, in its expanding process, will pass through childhood, youth and old age and again return to fall into unmanifest Brahman. It will again be zero and void. It will return to the original source from where it began its journey. Its circle will be a huge one. The span of our life-circle will be of seventy years. There are lives that revolve through small circles. A butterfly is born in the morning and its life-circle is complete in the evening. And there are circles smaller than this, too. There are animals who live only for a few moments. They are born at the beginning of a moment and die by the end of that moment. But do not be under the impression that this animal having a life of one moment lives a lesser life than one who lives for seventy years. Do not think its life is less because it completes its circle in one moment, while yours lasts seventy years. It has its childhood, its youth, it makes love, children are born, it has its old age and it dies. In a circle lasting for a moment it completes its seventy years intensely.

But the circle of seventy years cannot be called a large circle. Scientists say that our earth was born some four thousand million years ago. We have no means to find out in which stage of its life the earth is now, but from certain considerations it appears it is in old age. The production of food is decreasing, and the world population is increasing. Death seems to be near. All things necessary for life are in deficiency. Coal, petrol and food are in short supply, all the chemicals of the earth are in short supply. The earth is getting old, so it may die soon.

What does 'soon' mean? The word soon is not to be understood from our personal point of view; if the earth has taken four thousand million years to grow old, what is another four thousand million years? But we cannot make any estimate about the earth. There are about seventy million cells in each human body. Those cells have no idea at all that you are also there, and though these seventy million microscopic cells live in your body, you do not know anything at all about them. Within your body they are born, grow up, become old, leave children behind them, and die, making their graves in your body – and yet you will know nothing about them. During seventy years of your life, millions of these organisms will be born and will die. In a similar way, the earth does not know anything about us and we do not know anything about the life of the earth. Its life of millions of years is on a circle.

It is difficult to determine the age of the entire universe, the entire manifest Brahman, but one thing is certain – there is no transgression of the law in this world. Sooner or later, the law is fulfilled. Therefore, the sage says in this sutra that there are two phases of Brahman – the manifest which is, and the unmanifest from which this whole universe was created, and in which it will again be absorbed: the central Brahman and the expanded Brahman.

"He who knows the expanded Brahman conquers both – he goes beyond it. And he who knows the central Brahman attains to immortality." But the expanded Brahman is an enclosure containing death. Death is bound to happen in it. The circle will have to complete itself. If there is birth, death will surely follow it. Then why does the sage say that such a person conquers death?

What does overcoming death mean? Do the sages not die? All the sages die. All enlightened people die. For sure, overcoming death does not mean not to die. The sage who sang that he who has known manifest Brahman overcomes death, is no more. So either he said this unknowingly or falsely – if the statement was correct he should not have died!

No, overcoming death means something else. The person who knows and experiences deeply that death is already linked with birth and unavoidable, becomes free from the fear of death. He knows that birth is the beginning of the circle and death its end. So he who knows so deeply, so profoundly that death is an unavoidable destiny, becomes free from the fear of death. Why should one fear the unavoidable? Why should one worry about what is sure to happen? Worry is only for that which can be changed or altered.

So it is interesting to observe that there was never so much worry about death in the East as in the West, and there are good reasons for this. The West feels that it has the remedy to conquer death; the East never felt it had the remedy to conquer it. If it is felt that death can be changed, then worry is bound to come. There will always be cares and worries for a thing which can be changed. There is no cause for anxiety when a thing cannot be altered. Why worry? If death is certain, if it is linked with birth, then there is absolutely no cause to worry about it.

When soldiers are on their way to the battlefield, and as long as they have not reached it, they remain worried and afraid, but once on the battlefield all their worries are over in a day or two. After reaching the battlefield, even the most timid soldier becomes a brave person. What is the reason? Psychologists are pondering over this phenomenon. This man was so afraid that he couldn't sleep at night at the thought of going into battle in the morning. He was trembling and behaving like a madman; it seemed that he would run away from the battlefield. But having been in battle, this very same man sleeps soundly.

What is the reason? As long as he had not come on to the battlefield he thought escape was possible – he could save himself, a way could be found, something could be changed. "Somebody else might be sent instead of me." But when he saw himself on the battlefield, saw bombs falling on all sides, the whole matter of worrying was over. Now there was no way out, and when there is no way out worry disappears. When the possibility of change is gone, the hope for the change also vanishes. It is the desire for change that creates anxieties and worries. When the sage says, "After knowing the manifest Brahman, the wise man conquers death," it means death holds no fear for him. If death approaches him, he is not afraid.

There is an interesting small story about Panini. He is one of the sages who compiled these sutras. He was teaching grammar to his pupils in his forest ashram one day when a roaring lion bounded in. Panini asked his pupils to listen to the lion's roaring, and try to make out its grammatical form. The lion is poised ready to pounce on anyone, the pupils are trembling, and Panini is explaining the grammatical form of the lion's roaring! It is said that even when the lion fell upon him, he continued to explain the grammatical form of its roaring. And as the lion devoured him, he expounded on the grammatical form of, "The lion kills the man."

Our immediate thought is that Panini could have run away and saved himself. Something could have been done, but people like Panini think thus – that death is certain, whether it comes today or tomorrow; then what difference does it make if it is today or tomorrow? Such people accept death unwaveringly because it is a certainty – whether it comes today or tomorrow or the day after tomorrow.

Here is the victory. In this acceptance we have accepted death along with birth. We have accepted the withering along with the blooming, the expanding. In the time of our blooming we knew that we would wither one day. On the day of our unfolding, our birth, we knew that we would one day be hidden again. The circle is bound to be complete. In such an acceptance lies freedom from death. Then where is death? Such a person has overcome death. He is free from the attraction of birth as well as from the fear of death. He is beyond both.

Bear in mind, for the rest of us death and birth are the two ends in our life, and they are outside life. Birth is outside our life, because before birth we were not. Death is outside our life, because after death we will not be. Death is the borderline. But it is not a borderline for one who knows. To him, death and birth are two happenings taking place in the midst, in the course of life. He will ask, "Whose birth? I was before, hence I could be born; otherwise how could birth take place? I was unmanifest, hence I could be manifest; otherwise how could I be manifest? If a tree is not hidden in a seed, there is no way for it to spring forth – to be born. If I die, I must be living first; otherwise whose death will it be? My birth could take place because I was before the birth. I will also be after death; then and then only, death can take place, otherwise whose death will it be?"

Death is not the end for one who knows. It is only a happening which took place in his life. Birth is also a happening taking place in one's life, it is not a beginning. The life which is beyond this circle is the unmanifest. It is hidden, unexpressed. That unmanifest life – existence – becomes manifest in birth and again becomes unmanifest in death. So one who knows this cycle of the manifest world is untroubled by it; the pattern does not cause him any unhappiness.

Suppose you are in a house. You know this is a wall, this is a door. Then would you beat your head against the wall trying to get through it? You will not try to leave through the wall. If you want to go out you will use the door. You will not sit down and regret and question why the wall is not a door. But one who does not know the door will knock his head against the wall, and that poor fellow will often bemoan the fact that the wall is not the door. If you know the door, then the wall is a wall and the door is a door to you. Thus one who knows fully the arrangement and the gestalt becomes free from that gestalt. He knows that where birth is, there death will also be found. But one who knows it incompletely – not in its full significance – comes into conflict and difficulty. This knowledge is so clearcut, so ultimate, that there is no question of any change in it. This is called destiny – the destiny of the manifest.

But we have not correctly interpreted the meaning of destiny. In fact, because we are not clear within ourselves we interpret all things in a wrong way. The person who is clear within himself interprets rightly, and the person who is unclear interprets wrongly. You have not understood the real meaning of destiny if you take it as despair.

If a person sits with folded hands in despair and frustration and cries, "It is all fate!" then such a person has not understood the true meaning of destiny. Destiny means great optimism, great hope. You find it very difficult to grasp this interpretation. The true meaning of fate is that there is now no cause for any misery. There is now no place for despair. Death is; it is unavoidable. Where, then, can there be any misery in it? Where is the suffering in that? Misery and suffering are there only as long as there is no acceptance.

Buddha used to say, "What is made will be unmade, what is had will be lost." Be aware! – in the moment of meeting our loved ones, we create our separation from them; it is bound to follow. We don't want to hear about separation. When we are reminded of separation at the time of meeting our loved ones, we become unhappy. When we think of the separation which is to follow very shortly, the joy of meeting is also destroyed. The illusion that there is joy in meeting the loved ones is at once lost at the thought of separation.

A child is born: there is rejoicing in the house and if someone says, "With this birth death has entered," we are deeply shocked and tell him not to talk of such inauspicious matters at this moment of rejoicing. But when Buddha says there is already a moment of separation in the meeting of dear ones, he is not destroying the happiness of meeting; he is only destroying the pain of separation.

Try to understand the difference between the two situations. The fool will destroy the happiness of meeting, and the wise will cut the pain of separation. The wise will think, "How can there be any pain of separation when it is already present in the meeting itself? When meeting was longed for, then separation was also desired. When death is present in birth, then how can there be any sorrow over death? When the birth of a child was wished for, death was included in that wish." The fool will destroy the happiness of birth, and the wise will destroy the pain of death.

Having known the manifest Brahman, the expanding Brahman, an individual overcomes death. He remains unaffected by the miseries, pain and suffering caused by death. Bear in mind, misery, pain and worry are the shadows of death. The person who has thus freed himself from death has no misery, no worries and no pain.

You perhaps have not considered this – that when you become worried, then death is standing somewhere near you. Suppose a man's house catches on fire; he will at once be worried and miserable. As soon as a man finds himself bankrupt, he becomes anxious and worried. Why? – because now, being bankrupt, his life becomes full of difficulties, and death has moved a little closer. When the house is destroyed by fire his life becomes insecure and unprotected – and death comes a little closer. This is the way man's mind works in such circumstances, and so he becomes sad and anxious. A man standing alone in darkness is frightened and worried because nothing is visible in that darkness, and if death attacks him he will not be able to see it. So wherever you become worried, be alert at once; you will find death standing somewhere near you. Worry, anxiety, is the shadow of death.

Whenever and wherever your mind is caught in miseries and pain, recognize at once that there is some foolishness on your part in interpreting the manifest Brahman. You believe unavoidables are avoidables; your miseries begin from the very point of the belief. You hope that that which is destined to happen may not happen, and at this point your worries begin; anguish and unease are created. No, what is to happen will happen. There is no escape from it, nothing else can happen. When you accept this mantra, when you accept this arrangement of the manifest Brahman totally, everything within you will become calm and quiet. Then there is nothing to worry you.

Hence the sage has said that there is liberation from death after knowing the manifest Brahman. But this is half the story; the sutra is not yet complete, only half so. There is still one more thing for us to know which is not said in the first half, and is very subtle and deep. As long as we are unable to see it, we are perplexed and harassed, and in our ignorance we stumble about, bumping our heads against the walls and trying to pass where there are no doors. We go on building houses of cards and drawing lines on water, and we go on weeping when we see them being wiped out and destroyed.

You know that no sooner are lines drawn on water than they begin to disappear. When you draw a line on water and try to make it permanent, is it the fault of the water, or of this line of yours, that you fail in your endeavor? Who would you find fault with? The water or the line? The man who finds fault with either the water or the line will be miserable; the man who understands his own foolishness will laugh. He will know that the line drawn on water is bound to be wiped out. It must be wiped out. If the line remains there then we are really in difficulty!

How can we understand the unmanifest Brahman when we are

not even able to understand this manifest Brahman? It is absolutely unfolded before us: is there anything more manifest than death? Yet we continually deceive ourselves. When someone dies, we sympathetically say, "The poor fellow died." It does not occur to us to regard death as a reminder of our own death.

I remember a line of a poem by an English poet. When somebody dies, the church bell tolls. The poet has said, "Ask not for whom the bell tolls; it tolls for thee." That is, without making any inquiry, know that it is for you.

Concealing a phenomenon as great as death, we behave in such a manner that if a traveler from Mars were to come and be our guest for two or three days, there are two things he would not discover about us, and these two are linked together. That traveler would not know that there is death or sex on this planet, because we keep these two concealed. Bear in mind, sex is the originator of birth, it is the first step; and death is the last step of the manifest Brahman.

The suppression of sex, the first step, begins with the fear of death, the last step. If we wish to suppress death, we will have to make ourselves forget also the process of birth, because death is linked with birth. Therefore we hide the birth process in darkness. The birth process is performed behind a curtain. And death we drive out to the limits of our villages. There we reserve a place for a graveyard, because we are very much afraid of death. We scatter flowers on the graves so that whoever passes those graves by chance may not see them. When a dead body is taken to the graveyard we cover it with flowers, so that the corpse may not appear dead but blooming. You may cover the body with flowers as much as you like, you may construct tombs as beautiful as you like, and carve names on those hard tombstones too – but the person who died is dead forever. When the person lying in the grave could not be preserved, how long will those names cut on stones last? And no matter how far away from town we keep the graves, deaths will happen in towns and not in graveyards.

We suppress sex and hide it because it is the source of birth.

Our unconscious reason for keeping it suppressed and hidden is that it is the first step. If it is unveiled and brought into the open, then death will also be unveiled; it will no longer be possible to conceal death. So it is interesting to notice that societies where sex is not suppressed become more concerned and worried about death, and the societies which have suppressed sex totally, ignoring it as though it does not exist, have suppressed death also.

I have heard this story. A Jewish child one day returned home from school having learned in school how children are born. He was much pleased with his new information and very eager to show his knowledge. As soon as he was home he asked his mother how he was born. His mother said, "God sent you."

Then he asked, "How was my father born?"

His mother said, "He was also sent by God."

The boy asked, "How was my grandfather born?"

His mother was now a little puzzled but said that he was also sent by God. The boy continued asking till he reached the seventh generation, and the exasperated mother said, "Look, can't you see there is only one answer to your question?"

Then the boy exclaimed, "What! You mean that for the last seven generations there's been no sex in our family?"

No, there is a great unconscious need to suppress sex. It is the first step of birth. If it is opened and made manifest then death will also be manifest. As long as children do not know how man is born they go on asking this question. But when they have this information they will surely ask how man dies. So you keep this first step, about birth, concealed from children, and they are always asking this question; they never get an opportunity to ask how man dies!

Bear in mind, if the happening of birth is clearly understood, then the next question cannot be any other than that concerning death. So at one end sex is suppressed, and at the other end death: look for the graveyard beyond the village limits. Thus we live in darkness between two ends, and we live in great fear. There has to be fear, because we know neither what birth is, nor what death is. When we try to falsify even the manifest Brahman which is so open and clear, then what to say about the unmanifest Brahman which is hidden and unrevealed? How can we possibly go into that?

Understand these two happenings – birth and death – properly. They are the two ends of one phenomenon. Birth is the beginning and death is the end of one and the same circle. Death happens at that place where birth happens. The happening of death and that of birth are parts of one happening.

What happens in birth? A body is created. The male cells and the female cells combine and give birth to a new composite body. Both have half the materials within them, hence their intense attraction to each other. Those halves draw each other all the time. They want to be whole, so there is a tremendous attraction between them. This is why children are being born all the time despite all religious injunctions, all rules, principles and education against sex. Preachers of celibacy come and go, but they always preach to no effect. The attraction is so powerful that all the preaching and teaching cannot touch it. This is an attraction of two halves of one and the same element. It is like breaking a thing in two parts and the parts wishing to meet each other again. When they meet a new body is created. Half the cells are given by the woman and the other half by the man.

So birth means the creation of a body from the meeting of the half-cells of man and woman. And as soon as the body is created, a soul enters that body – a soul whose desires will be fulfilled by that body, and its entry into the body is as natural and self-directed as rainwater filling holes and making puddles. The order of things is such that the soul enters a womb convenient to itself.

What happens in death? Those two merged parts of the element begin to scatter and break off. Nothing else but this happens. The link within begins to weaken and loosen. Old age means the weakening of the link. This composite body begins to decompose. The way in which the link fractures was laid down at the moment of conception. This was not determined astrologically but scientifically. In fact, when the cells of a man and a woman meet together, all this is determined.

At present our scientific knowledge about these matters is not adequate, though it is growing day by day. If not today, certainly in the future we shall be able to predict how long the intrinsic body-process of a child will last – whether for seventy years, or eighty years, or one hundred years. It will be like giving a ten-year guarantee with a watch, because the test of various parts of its machinery will tell us that the watch will be able to resist the wear and tear due to air, heat, speed and so on for ten years. Then its power to resist the wear and tear will fall away.

On the day the child is conceived, the cells of the man and woman merge together and determine how long the child will be able to bear the strain of air, water, heat, rains, miseries, pains, conflicts, meetings, separations, friendship, enmity, hopes and frustrations, days and nights and all such things. They thus determine when the link will falter in the process of bearing and resisting the strain, and when these united cells will fall apart. On their separation the soul will have to leave that body. Death and sex are the two ends of one and the same thing. The things joined by sex are separated by death. Sex is synthetic, death is analytic. Sex joins, death separates. The happening is the same, there is no difference in it.

He who knows fully this manifest Brahman succeeds in accepting it. Acceptance is the victory. You become the master of a thing when you have accepted it. Even if you accept slavery, then you become the master and no longer a slave. You will be unable to make me a slave if I remain happy even though you have handcuffed me, or if I keep on dancing even though you put me behind bars. When there is not even a momentary thought that "I could have remained free if..." but instead a simple acceptance of what has happened, then you are defeated. You have failed to make me a prisoner. I am still my own master. On the contrary, you will be my slave, because you will have to lock me up and keep a guard at the gate. If I accept this condition joyfully, if I can sing in prison while you have to stand there and keep watch with a straight face and a rifle in your hand, then who is imprisoned? Accepting totally, you remain the master even in slavery; and you are in slavery if you are not the total master of yourself. Total acceptance is the liberation. The total acceptance of any fact is freedom. When a person truly knows manifest Brahman he attains total acceptance, and thus is liberated from death.

Let us now consider the second point, though it is difficult to grasp. It is enough if the first point is properly grasped. To know the unmanifest Brahman is a matter of still deeper and more subtle experience. To know it, one has to go either before one's birth or to go beyond one's death. There is no other way except this. That is why the Zen master in Japan asks the seeker who approaches him to meditate and find out what his face was before his birth – to find his original face.

The face you have now is no more your original face than the face you wore yesterday. The face which is seen now is not yours; it was derived from your parents. This nose and other facial features, this complexion, are derived from your parents; they are not yours. If you have negro parents you inherit black, if they are English the color will be greyish. These pigments of your body are from your parents, they are not yours; so go and discover your own color. This face of yours is given to you by your parents, so try to find your original face. Borrowed faces will be snatched away. They are nothing more than masks – false faces. But because they last for seventy years we think they are our real faces. If a person is given a fixed mask, secured so firmly that it cannot be removed, in a few days he will begin to take it as his own face, because whenever he stands before a mirror he will see this mask.

A very strange experiment was performed recently in America by a white American. He decided to become a negro by changing the color of his skin to black. Living in America, he wanted to see for himself, to actually experience, under what hardship negroes had to live in his country. The white man can have no idea what hardships negroes have to suffer. How can they be realized without actually being a negro? Whatever is known otherwise will be just the knowledge of a white-skinned person.

This was an experiment requiring great courage. In the beginning, the scientists refused to help this man because it was a dangerous undertaking. But he was adamant, so by and by he persuaded three scientists to help him do the experiment. After a long treatment of six months in which injections of new pigments were given to him, the color of his skin was changed into that of a negro. His skin was now black, and curly hair was also artificially implanted.

That man has written in his memoirs: "When the scientists told me for the first time that the physical operations were successful, and now I could start my experiment, I thought of going to the bathroom to see my face. But I was not bold enough to switch on the light. I was not sure of what I would see. With a trembling hand I put on the light. I had expected that I would remain who I was – that is, the facial features would not change, only the skin color would be different. But when I looked into the mirror, I saw that not only the color was changed but I too was changed. I couldn't make out what had happened, couldn't make out who was standing before the mirror. Everything was changed.

"I had thought, having become negro-like, that I would live among negroes for six months to experience personally what they have to endure; I knew that I would not remain a negro forever – I would remain who I really am." But he has written in his memoirs that "After living among negroes for four or five days, I began to forget that I was a white American. I began to forget that I was a white man. Every day I saw my new face in the mirror. I saw photographs taken of me as a negro. Other negroes began to behave with me as if I were a negro. Walking along the road, white Americans who used to greet me passed me by without taking any notice of me. One day I went to the house of my wife and stood at the door. My wife looked at me and ignored me."

Would anyone pay attention to a negro? Do you pay attention to a servant, or a sweeper standing at your door? Who cares for them? Who looks at them attentively? They are merely seen; no one looks at them attentively. Once he went to his cobbler who used to make his shoes and polish them also. He placed his shoes on the stand to be polished. The man looked up and asked, "Are you out of your senses? Take your foot off my stand!"

He has written, "I did not then feel that since I am really a white man I should be amused at his behavior – that this is simply the way he treats negroes. No, I felt that the treatment was being given to me, a white man, and I felt offended." When the treatment wore off after six months and his skin began to turn white again, he wrote in his memoirs, "When I remember those six months, I do not feel I actually passed through such a life. I feel as if I saw some dream. That negro was some other person, a different person; I am a different person from him. We associate so much with our faces."

That face was not his. He had it for only six months. But the interesting thing is this: he believes the face which he had for six months was not his, but that the face he had before and after those six months was his. That face is also not his. His six-month face was given him by scientists, and this 'original' one he got from his parents is also not his. It is not his own.

One's own face can be encountered either before birth or after death. To seek before birth is very arduous; it is very difficult to know the unmanifest Brahman before birth. I told you before that compared to the manifest Brahman, it is very difficult to know the unmanifest Brahman. Now I tell you again, there are two ways. Regress beyond birth; go so deep in meditation that you can regress beyond birth, so that you will be able to know the unmanifest Brahman. The other way is to go further and further in meditation so that you may die and go beyond death; then too you will experience the unmanifest Brahman.

Of these two ways, the experiment with dying is easy, because it is related to a future happening. To regress is very difficult, to go forward is easy. You can take a jump forward. To go back is very difficult. To put on the clothes of childhood again is very difficult.

To return to the womb is extraordinarily arduous, because the path becomes narrower and narrower. But the loose clothes of death are easy to put on. The path grows wider and wider. Remember, the door to birth is very small; that to death is very large. To go beyond death is easy.

It is possible to go back beyond birth. There are processes and techniques to do that, but they are very difficult to practice and follow. The meditation I am talking about is an experiment with death. It is a jump into death. Through entering death willingly, it is an exercise in seeing. It is to practice being as if dead. If this happens and you enter death consciously and become as if you are not, then the face of the unmanifest Brahman will be visible. That face will be seen which is before birth and is also after death.

The processes may be two, but that center is one and the same. You can see that center either by regressing or by going forward. But the path of going forward is easy, so I insist on the path of death. I do not advise you to regress before birth to see that face; I advise you to go forward beyond death to see that face. Such a willing and accepted death becomes meditation. And if an individual wishes to live in such a death not for just a few seconds but for the whole of his life, he becomes a sannyasin. Sannyas means to live in such a way as if dead.

There was a Zen monk named Bokoju. He had entered into sannyas. Once when he was passing through a village someone started pouring abuse on him. He just stood there, hearing the abuse.

A shopkeeper who saw this said, "Why are you taking all this standing still? He is abusing you."

Bokoju replied, "I am dead. How can I retaliate now?"

The shopkeeper was surprised and said, "Are you a dead man? You look absolutely living."

Then Bokoju said, "What value will there be in my physical death? When I die, I shall die as all die; but now I am dead when alive: this has some value."

Birth happens unknowingly, and now there is no way to go into it. But death is still ahead in the future, and you can pass through it knowingly. The opportunity to know your original face through birth is now lost, but the opportunity exists to know it through death. But bear in mind that you may miss this opportunity also. If death comes as accidentally to you as birth came, then you will miss the opportunity to know. But if you prepare yourself to welcome death, if you go on dying often, then you will know.

This is the meaning of sannyas – voluntary death. To go on dying, to go on becoming as if dead. If someone abuses you, think that you are dead. What will you do when you are physically dead if someone stands on your grave and abuses you? Begin now. Begin to do that which you will do when your skull is lying somewhere and someone kicks it. This is the true significance of sannyas. Thus you shall be able to enter the unmanifest Brahman.

Otherwise you will miss the opportunity of death also. And it is not that you are missing it for the first time; you have already missed many times. Similarly, you have missed the opportunity of birth many times. This opportunity is now lost to you, and before it also many opportunities of other births and deaths.

You are so accustomed to this process that you are addicted to it. You have already gone through this one process again and again. Now you need to make a decision about whether to go any further with this process or not, since we all have the chance to avail ourselves of the opportunity of death yet again. Why not take this opportunity to enter the unmanifest!

The sage declares, "He who enters the unmanifest attains to immortality. He who knows the manifest conquers death, and he who enters the unmanifest attains to the immortal."

Remember, the immortal can be known only by entering death, because when we enter death totally, when we die in all ways and yet find we did not die, then immortality is attained. So when someone abuses you and you behave like a corpse and yet remain conscious of yourself, then you will not react to the abuse. If someone cuts your hand, or even your throat, and while it is being cut you remain conscious of yourself, then the door of immortality is open for you. He who tries to save himself from death will not achieve immortality, and he who enters death will taste the nectar of immortality.

To know the unmanifest Brahman is to find immortality, because the unmanifest is the immortal. Existing before birth and after death, it is the immortal. It is never born so it never dies. We are also the same. Only the body takes birth; it is a composite, derived from the parents. We come from very, very ancient times. We were when the body was not. On entering a body an identification with it takes place, and when the body dies it seems that, "I am dying."

When death comes unexpectedly – and generally it comes unexpectedly, with no prior intimation – it shows you a kindness. If it were to intimate its arrival you would be in great difficulty; it is an act of mercy on the part of death that it does not inform you beforehand. Suppose death were to inform you, twenty-four hours before, of its arrival: what would happen? Whatever is going to happen after twenty-four hours will surely happen, but it is difficult to imagine how miserable you would be during that period. You would be miserable and uneasy waiting for the appointment, though in fact you now have a chance to pass through death consciously. To live time second by second would be found to be very difficult. You might pass out, you might lose your senses. It may also happen – there is a possibility – that you pass this time without losing consciousness. But the greater possibility is that you would spend the time in a coma, and ultimately die in that condition. So it would probably turn out to be quite fruitless for you to receive an intimation of your time of death.

Sannyas means to inform ourselves, to understand and to tell ourselves that, "The church bell tolls for me. The corpse being taken to the graveyard is *my* body. The body burning in the crematorium is *my* body." This is why the sannyasin's head used to be clean-shaven, as was done to the heads of the dead. Formerly there were certain rites and religious observances prescribed for a man's initiation as a sannyasin. His head was clean-shaven, and his relatives used to weep and take a last bath on his account, just as they do for other people after their deaths.

Even now some of these rituals are observed, because the person entering sannyas is dying to his worldly relations and connections. The weeping of the relatives will cease in a day or two, as they see that though this man has decided to die to the worldly relatives, he is still living. This is good in a way. The sannyasin allows his relatives to pass through the pain and misery of his death in his presence; when he actually dies he will not be there to console them in their misery.

In those ancient days they used to put a new initiate on a funeral pyre. Those were very innocent days. After putting him on the pyre they set fire to the pyre. Then the guru would shout, "You are dead! Remember, you are dead!" Then the man was lifted away from the burning pyre and given a new name, and this rite declared that the old man and his old name were gone forever. Those were very innocent days, so the person who passed through this small ceremony believed that his old self was dead and he was now a new person.

Today that innocence is not there. If you are placed on a pyre you will immediately climb down. If your head is clean-shaven, you will get yourself photographed and keep the photo in your album along with your other photos. You will maintain the continuity. Man has become very clever and cunning today, so real renunciation has become rare. But there is no other way than sannyas to know the unmanifest Brahman. Even a worldly person can know the manifest Brahman, but only the sannyasin can know the unmanifest Brahman.

Enough for today. We shall meet again at night.

Now let us begin our journey to the unmanifest. Let us die.

# Only The Knowing Remains

16

*The face of that Brahman,*
*sitting in the midst of abundance of light,*
*is covered with a golden curtain.*
*O Lord, remove that curtain*
*so that I, a seeker of truth,*
*may attain to the supreme.*

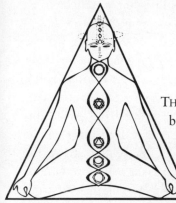

THIS SUTRA IS rather difficult to understand, but it is of extraordinary significance for many reasons. First of all, we generally believe that if truth is covered, it must be covered by darkness, but the sutra says it is covered by light; hence the prayer that God will remove the curtain of light.

This is the experience of one who has made a deep search for truth. Those who have only thought will always say truth is covered in darkness, but those who have known through deep experience will say it is covered in light; and if it looks dark, it is because of the brilliance of the light. We are blinded when the light is too intense; then the light looks like darkness because of the weakness of our eyes, they are unable to bear so much light.

Look at the sun with wide open eyes, and in a few seconds you will be in darkness. The sun is so bright that the eyes cannot endure it. So those who have known from a distance and not directly – who have only thought about it – will say that God's temple is hidden in darkness. But those who have known the experience of it will say it is hidden in light, and they will pray to God to remove that curtain. The illusion is created because our eyes are too weak to stand the abundance of light. Our being is not adequate to receive it.

As one proceeds towards truth, the light begins to increase, becoming brighter and brighter. Those who are moving further into meditation come to know, by and by, the growing illumination as their meditation becomes deeper and deeper. The Italian sannyasin Veet Sandeh told me today that there is so much light within her that she experiences rays flaring out from her, and her whole body is burning as if a sun is shining within her. The heat is not coming from without but from within, and the light is so bright that it is difficult for her to sleep at night. "When I doze," she says, "there is light and light all around."

As a person goes deeper and deeper in meditation this light becomes increasingly intense, concentrated and penetrating, and a moment comes when the intensity of light is so great that he experiences deep darkness. Only the Christian saints have named this moment correctly. They have called it, "The dark night of the soul." But this night of pitch darkness is due to the excess, the abundance of light. It is in this moment that a man begs God to remove that curtain of light, "So that I can see the face of truth hidden behind it."

It is only to be expected that there will be so much light surrounding truth that it is blinding to our eyes. It is fitting and good that truth is hidden within a circle of light. It is only our illusion that truth is hidden in darkness. How can there be darkness around truth? If darkness surrounds truth, then where will we find light in this world? How can darkness surround truth? There is no possibility, no way, for darkness to persist near light. Where there is truth there will surely be light; it only looks like darkness to us. If we ask the Sufi mystics, they will tell us that when we go deep into meditation there is not only one sun, there are thousands. So abundant is the light that it seems as though countless suns are shining simultaneously within. Naturally, we will be blinded.

Truth is hidden in light. And have you noticed? – it is easy for us to open our eyes in darkness, but it is very difficult to open them in the abundance of light. What is the difficulty in keeping our eyes open, or in opening them, on a no-moon night? But if the sun is shining into our eyes we find it very difficult to open them. The final conflict of those who approach truth is with light, not darkness.

This sutra speaks of that period of conflict. In that moment the seeker prays, "O God, remove that curtain so that I may see your true, original face." It looks quite natural if someone prays, "Take us far away from darkness; lead us out of darkness," but, "Remove this light"...? And another point of interest is the word golden used to describe the light – it is a very pleasing word. This light is like gold. It is such a light that we will have no wish to remove it. It is very difficult to ask for it to be removed, but truth cannot be seen till that light is removed. So let us understand this point.

It is very easy to give up what is bad, but real difficulty arises when the time comes to give up the good. Where is the difficulty in giving up iron chains? The difficulty arises when golden chains are to be given up, because it is hard to consider golden chains as chains. They look like ornaments. It is very easy to discard unsaintliness, but even saintliness becomes a bondage in the last stage. When it too must be renounced, great difficulty arises. In that final stage the good is also to be renounced, because even that much attachment becomes a bondage, and even that much bondage is a barrier in the search for truth. Only absolute non-attachment, absolute freedom, will do. So this seeker who has fought with darkness and conquered it, now prays to God to remove the golden curtain. It is not so difficult to fight against darkness, but there will be much difficulty when the moment comes to fight against light.

Light – and to fight against it? This is amazing. Light is so pleasant, so heavenly, so peace-giving, so invigorating, so full of life's nectar, that it becomes painful to talk of its removal. And therefore the sage prays to God to remove it: "I cannot do it myself. My mind will persuade me rather to merge with it." Remember, you will have to save yourself even from light when your meditation brings you to its ultimate brilliance. Your journey must go even beyond that. You have to overcome it, you have to transcend it. You have to be beyond darkness, and beyond light also. When consciousness goes beyond darkness and light, the duality ends and nonduality begins. Then that one is seen who is neither light nor darkness, neither night nor day, neither life nor death, who always is, and is beyond all dualities. You face a final conflict with light before that nonduality is attained.

Another way to understand it is this: it is always easy to give up unhappiness; that we can fight against. But if happiness comes our way, it is very difficult to fight against it – it is almost impossible. How can we fight against it? But liberation is impossible if we are caught in and attached to happiness. As I told you this morning, happiness will create a heaven for you, and in that heaven you will find yourself in bondage again, enticed into pleasure and love; there is no liberation here.

This prayer, this desire of the sage to remove the curtain of light and see the face of Brahman which is covered by such blinding light, reveals the final helplessness of man's mind. Man's mind has no wish to be free from light or happiness or heaven. But one *has* to be free from them. The sage is standing on the threshold. On one side is his human nature which urges him to dance with pleasure in the light, to identify himself with light and be absorbed in it; while on the other side is his deep longing within for truth, which urges him to go beyond. It is in this difficult and decisive moment that he utters this sutra, this prayer, "O God, remove your curtain of excessive light." He prays, "Please remove this delightful, heavenly form so that I may see that utter, naked truth, which is you!"

Those who live in misery do not know that happiness has its miseries. Those who live among enemies do not know that friends have their own conflicts. Those who live in hell do not know that heaven has its own troubles. How can those who live in darkness imagine that light becomes a prison?

As long as there is duality there is nonliberation, there is bondage. Then what will remain when light is removed, when darkness is removed? What is the face of truth? What is seen? At present, as far as our imagination can go, as far as our thoughts can fly, as far as our minds can reach, the utmost we can imagine is that if truth has a face it will be of light – brilliant light. Why do we think so?

Understand one or two points. We have not yet seen light. You may well reply, "What do you mean, we have not seen light? We do see light. We see light when the sun rises in the morning. We see light at night when the moon shines and there is moonlight everywhere." No, I repeat, you have not seen light yet. You have seen only lighted things. When the sun rises you see lighted things – mountains, rivers, streams, trees, people. The electric bulbs are giving you light now. You will say, "We see light." But no, you do not see light. You see the electric bulb shining. You see the people standing in its light. You see objects, not light. It is not possible to have any experience of light in the world outside. Only illuminated objects are seen, and when they are not seen we say it is dark. When is there darkness in this hall? When nothing can be seen in the hall we say there is darkness, and when objects are visible we say there is light.

We have not seen light directly. If there was not a single object in this hall you would be unable to see the light. Light hits an object; the shape of the object is seen and you think you are seeing light. If the object is seen very clearly you say there is much light, if it is not very clear you say the light is insufficient, and if it is not seen at all you say there is darkness. If you cannot make out anything of shapes and objects you say it is pitch dark. But you have seen neither light nor darkness. It is our conjecture only that there is light whenever we can see objects. In fact, light itself is such a minute energy that it cannot be seen outside.

Light is visible within because there is no object inside which can be illuminated. There are no inner objects which can be illuminated and seen by us, so when we experience light within, it is pure light, it is immediate, it is without any medium. We see two things outside – the lighted object and the source of light; and the light which is between these two is never seen by us. The sun is seen or the electric bulb is seen, and the objects illuminated here are seen; but the light between the two is not visible.

When light is seen within there are no objects, nor is there any source – it is sourceless light. There is no sun from which light is shining out. There is no lamp emitting light. There is only source-less light. When light is first seen in that objectless world, then Kabir, Mohammed, the Sufi mystics, the Baul mystics, the Jaina mystics, begin to dance, declaring what we call light to be only darkness.

Aurobindo has written, "Once I had seen within, it became clear that the thing which I had understood to be light was dark-ness. When I looked within I saw that the thing which I had con-sidered to be life was in fact death." It is indeed very difficult to receive and bear the light which, sourceless, objectless and shape-less, is born within. The greatest difficulty is that our mind tends to think, "I have reached the end of my journey, I have reached my destination."

Sense organs are not great obstacles in the way of the seeker of truth; he overcomes them. Thoughts are also not great hindrances; he goes beyond them. But our legs refuse to keep moving when the flowers of delight and the joy of achievement begin to unfold within. We feel disinclined to give them up and discard them. We find courage and daring lacking in us to go beyond them, and we think we have reached the destination. This is the moment when the sage has prayed, "O God, remove this bright light also. I wish to know that which is beyond light also. I have crossed darkness – now lead me beyond the light."

Remember this. Will and determination can help us to go beyond darkness, but only surrender helps us in going beyond the light. We have to enter into conflict to go beyond darkness; we have to struggle and fight hard. And man finds strength enough in fighting darkness, but he is absolutely weak when the occasion arises to fight against light. He is almost as if not. Determination and strong will do not work here; they are ineffectual. Only sur-render is effective.

This sutra tells us about surrender. The sage has arrived at the place where light is born. He is defeated now. He did not pray for help till now. He did not ask God to do anything for him till now. With confidence in himself he made his way to this point. Man can come this far, but those who depend on determination can never go beyond this. Only those who are prepared to surrender totally can cross this boundary.

This will be easily understood if we put it this way: meditation leads you up to the great experience of light. After this, meditation is not useful. So those who have never practiced meditation but are offering prayer are foolish – there is no need of prayer where they are. And they too are foolish who have practiced meditation and consider prayer unnecessary, because meditation will bring us to the door of light, but once there, only a deeply sincere prayer can help.

In the end you will have to pray, "I am in your hands, lead me! I have come to this point, now lead me beyond this." And remember, the man who has traveled to the limits of meditation earns the right to ask God to lead him beyond. Now, when God's grace begins to descend on him, he is prepared. He has reached as far as man can go, and even God cannot expect more than this from him. This is the utmost limit of man's ability. If now God also demands more from man, it is tyranny, it is excess.

No question of more than this arises. Now, only prayer can help, and the prayer is, "I surrender to your hands: O God, remove this curtain." Prayer is the step that brings meditation to its completion, and total surrender is the final step on the path of will and determination. You have to exert yourself as far as you can, but the moment you feel, "I can go no further than this," resort to prayer. At that moment, cry aloud for God's grace; tell him, "I have come as far as was possible on my feeble legs, but it is beyond me to go further. Now you take care of me!" This is the moment when the sage prays that the curtain may be removed and the true face revealed.

What will truth be like? What will it be like when light is also removed? It is necessary to grasp this. It is very difficult, very deep and subtle, but it is necessary to understand it a little so that it can be useful to us. I told you that in the outside world there are illuminated objects and the light source. There is no experience of light itself in the world outside. It is experienced only within, where there are neither objects nor source. And then, finally, the light also disappears.

We think there will be darkness when light disappears, that is our experience; and we might regard the sage's prayer as foolish, because how can he see God's face in the darkness which will be there when the curtain of light is removed? Remember, he has already conquered darkness; now, when the light disappears, there will not be darkness. Darkness has already disappeared long before. Facing him now is the curtain of light. What will remain when the light disappears?

When the sun sets it is evening; the night has not yet come. It is a period when the source of light has disappeared and darkness has not yet descended. That moment we are seeking to describe is the twilight which lies between day and night. That is why prayer and twilight are described by the same Hindi word – *sandhya* – they are synonymous. People began to call prayer sandhya, and to look upon sunset as the time for prayer. There are two sandhyas – one before sunrise and the other after sunset. They are midpoints; the day is over but the night has not yet come, or the night is over and the day is yet to come. That small gap between the two is known as sandhya, and we have made that period the time of worship and prayer. But the real fact is different.

This sandhya is merely a symbol of that moment of inner sandhya, when both darkness and light have disappeared. Sandhya comes when there is neither darkness nor light, there is only a peculiar kind of light known as *alok*. The dictionary meaning of the word is light. It is incorrect. Alok means that moment when there is neither darkness nor light. At dawn the sun has not yet risen but the night has already passed away. That moment of alok is in the dawn. I am referring to this as an illustration so that you may grasp the idea, because there is no other way to give you an idea of that happening within. There is neither darkness nor light. There is only alok.

As I told you, both objects and the source of light disappear when you turn inwards and only light remains. Once that light, and the darkness too, pass away and only alok remains, then both the knower and the thing to be known also disappear. The seer and the thing seen are both lost. Then it is not that the sage is standing there looking at truth, no; then the sage himself *becomes* the truth. Then the truth become the sage. Then there is neither the knower nor the known – both disappear. In alok, darkness and light and the knower and the known are no more. There is neither the experiencer nor the experience, there is only experiencing. Where there is an experience, the experience is *and* the thing experienced is. No, here there is neither the experiencer nor the thing experienced. Only experiencing remains. The experiencing sage is no more, God is no more. Differences, distinctions disappear. The lover and the object of love are no more. It is the moment of supreme liberation.

It is not that in this moment we come to know something. On the contrary, we know that we are not; and we know also that there is nothing left to know. Only the knowing remains. So the term used by Mahavira is beautiful. He called it only knowing. The knower is not, the known is not – only knowing. Both ends are gone.

It is like this: the sun, the original source, is gone and the objects receiving light are also gone. Similarly the knower – the source – is lost, and the objects known are also lost; only the knowing remains.

In the journey towards this knowing, as I told you, the first step is determination – strong will – and the second is surrender. The first is of meditation, the second is of prayer.

For one who takes both steps, nothing remains to be known or achieved or experienced.

Enough for today.

# The
# Ultimate Jump

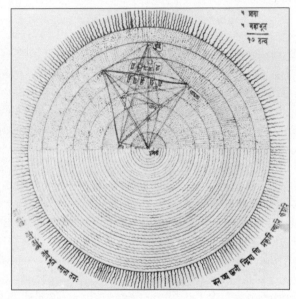

**17**

*O Sun,*
*nourisher and supporter of the world,*
*O lonely traveler in the sky,*
*O Yama, O sun, O sun of Brahman,*
*I beseech you to withdraw your rays.*
*I see your form, full of grace and goodness.*
*I am that one who is sitting in the*
*circle of the suns.*

WE ARE FAMILIAR with the one sun we see in the sky, but there are countless suns like ours. When night comes the sky is full of stars. Though we call them stars they are all suns, but being very far away they look small. Our sun is not very large. Among the countless suns it is of average size. There are much larger suns in the universe. One calculation by scientists estimates that there are about forty million suns. The experience of the sages is that there are countless suns, but the sun referred to in this sutra is that supreme sun from which all other suns receive light. The reference is to the supreme sun which is the root and primal source of light – and from which radiate all the interwoven rays in the universe. The whole of existence is the manifestation of this sun.

Remember, life, existence, is unavoidably linked with the sun's rays. At present scientists are very worried because they fear that our sun will cool down during the next three or four million years. It has cast its rays for long enough and is losing its radiation. It is now a waning star whose rays are diminishing every day. At the most, they say, it will radiate for four million more years, and one day it will be completely cold and life on earth will become extinct, because the whole of existence is dependent on the rays of the sun. The whole of existence – the blossoming flowers, the singing birds, the throbbing of life in man – is dependent on the sun's rays.

In this sutra is described that great sun with which the existence of all the suns is joined. This great sun can never be attained to by our journey and search without. As I told you this morning, our

sun is the manifest Brahman. The great sun which is being described here is the unmanifest Brahman. It is the seed-Brahman.
This whole existence is an expansion of that unmanifest source.
From it this whole universe of qualities and forms is expanding
and being created.

The sage prays here, "O sun, withdraw the network of your
rays." Many things are implicit in the drawing in of the sun's rays,
because the whole expanse of existence is linked with them. The
sage says here, "I have overcome death, O sun; now withdraw the
very spread of your existence." It is just as I told you: "I have overcome darkness, now withdraw the light as well!" In this sutra the
sage prays to that great sun to draw all the expanse of life into
itself. "I have transcended death, now I wish to transcend life also."

This is really the longing to transcend all dualities, because as
long as duality persists the other is always present, no matter what
we may achieve. However much life we may find, death will
always accompany it. It is duality, it is the other side of the same
coin. It is impossible to keep one side of a coin and throw away the
other. All we can do is keep one side turned down and the other
side showing. But the hidden side is waiting to show up, just
because it is there – it has not gone away.

Nobody can throw away the one and save the other at the same
time, but throughout his life man foolishly behaves as though this
is possible. He prays, "O God, save me from miseries, and give me
happiness." They are the two sides of the same coin. He wants to
retain happiness but does not appreciate that unhappiness will
surely follow it. He prays for honor and respect, not seeing that
dishonor follows. He prays, "I don't want death, I want life," and
in praying for life, he forgets that death is sure to follow it. In this
world when a person demands the one, he gets the other without
asking for it.

You must be willing to accept both or neither. Whoever is willing
to accept both becomes free from both; and whoever is prepared to
leave both also becomes free from both. To willingly accept both
life and death is to hold no preference for life and no aversion

towards death. Holding no preference for life, one is liberated. What happiness is there in happiness and what misery is there in misery for one who accepts both happiness and misery? Both negate each other when both are willingly accepted and a void is created.

One who says, "I am willing to give up both happiness and unhappiness," also goes beyond them. But mind persuades us to leave unhappiness and to hold onto happiness. There are ways to break this pattern of the mind: either to be prepared to accept both, or to become indifferent to both. Their polarity, their opposition towards each other, is simultaneous; they are aspects of one and the same existence. So the sage says, "Withdraw your rays, O sun, so that all of life may be drawn together and contracted inwards."

Everything goes forth from this great sun. So if we understand the longing of the sage correctly, it is this: "I long to see that from which everything goes forth, and towards which everything is drawn. I desire to see the root, the original. I long to see that from which the whole universe is created and into which the universe, in its ultimate annihilation, is absorbed; from which this vast expanse of existence spreads out and into which the great destruction draws it all back."

It is for this reason that the sun is also known as Yama – the god of death. Bear this in mind: Yama is the god of death and the sun is the god of life. But remember, death comes from the same place from which life comes. Death does not come from any other place, because the two cannot be separated. It is not that life comes from one place and death from another. If this were so we would keep life and abandon death. So the sun is called Yama also. The word *yama* is useful in other senses too. Those who named death Yama were remarkable people. The word yama means the controller. They have called death the controller of life. If death were not to control life, there would be great anarchy and confusion. Death comes and quietens all mischief. Death is rest. Just as a man sleeps and rests at night after a hard day's labor, so death gives us rest.

There would be great chaos in your life if you did not sleep for five or ten days. Your brain would be perplexed, agitated, disordered. Sleeping at night saves you from this anguish and agitation. It gives you order and refreshes you for the morning. Looking deeper into death, one sees that it is like a night's rest at the end of a lifetime of tumult and unrest – the respite from a hard life's labor refreshing you for the dawning of a new life. Hence the god of death is called Yama. He controls and brings order to life. If he were not there, life would be a puzzling and confused thing. Death is not the enemy of life. Yama declares death to be the friend of life. If death were not there, our life would be insane and chaotic.

You will be very surprised if you look at this phenomenon from other perspectives, because from its larger implications many flowers blossom – many valuable hints. If a person finds abundance of happiness and no miseries at all, he will go mad. This statement looks strange, it is difficult to grasp it. If you have happiness unmixed with miseries, then happiness will drive you crazy. It is interesting to observe that there are few lunatics in poor and miserable societies. There are far more lunatics in happy and affluent societies. At present, America has the greatest number of lunatics on this earth. What has happened?

Misery is a balancing influence, a regulator. We feel the thorns in a rosebush as enemies, but they are for the protection of roses, they are a kind of regulator. Life controls, regulates itself through polarities; through opposites the balance is maintained. If you watch an acrobat walking on a tightrope, you can see a metaphysical fact in his trick. We watch, but we fail to see. When he walks on the rope you will see him balancing himself with a long bamboo in his hands. When he swings to the left, it is to avoid falling to the right, and when he is likely to fall to the right, he swings to the left. Thus he balances, preventing himself from falling by swinging between the opposites. To maintain the balance he has to swing to the opposite side.

Death is the balancing factor of life. Unhappiness is the balancing factor of happiness. Darkness is the balancing factor of light. Material objects are the balancing factor of consciousness. This is what makes the people who called death Yama extraordinary. It is certain that they had no enmity with death. They knew the essence, the truth of death. They said, "We know that you, death, are the controller of life; if you did not exist there would be great anarchy." Think a bit. Suppose nobody died in a house for several hundred years; it would not be necessary to send anyone to a lunatic asylum, because the house itself would become a madhouse. On one side the old pass away and on the other side children are born; a balancing like that of the acrobat is going on, and will continue for all time.

Therefore the sage says, "O great sun, O Yama, you are the giver of life, you are the balancing controller of life and death. Withdraw all your rays. Withdraw your life. Withdraw your death also. I want to know the element which is beyond both life and death, which is never born, nor ever dies. I long to know that original source. I long to know that first moment when there was nothing – when there was total void from whose nothingness everything was created. I long to know that ultimate moment when everything will again be absorbed and nothing will remain. I long to know that void from which everything is born. I long to know that void in which everything is absorbed. I pray you, withdraw all the profusion of your rays."

Surely this is not a prayer addressed to any sun seen without. This is a prayer made after reaching that place within, beyond which lies the final destination from where a jump is taken into the beginningless and endless. This prayer, "O sun, withdraw everything of yours," belongs to this moment. A great courage, a final daring is required to make such a prayer, because one may think, "Can I be saved where life and death are shrunken away and all the rays of that great sun withdrawn? I too shall perish."

But the longing of the sage is this: "I may be saved or I may perish; this is no longer the question. The matter is only my longing to know the one who always is. I long to know the one who is, even when everything is lost and destroyed. I also will be lost, but I want to know that which is not lost."

Countless people during countless ages have searched for truth in this world, but nowhere in this world has such a search been made as the one made through this inner land. There is no parallel instance anywhere in this world of such an ultimate search and such a final test of courage as that dared by some of the explorers of this inner land.

Even after making long investigations I have been unable to find people who were willing to be annihilated in their quest for truth. There have been many seekers of truth in this world who made but one condition, "Saving myself, I want to know the truth." But as long as 'I' is saved, you will know only the world – samsara – because 'I' is a part and parcel of the world. If someone tells seekers such as Aristotle, Hegel and Kant, "You will be able to know truth if you search within yourselves," such people will reply, "What purpose is there in knowing such a truth? What is the use of knowing a truth which annihilates us?" Their search is with this one condition: "We want to save ourselves *and* know the truth."

Those who, seeking truth, sought also to preserve themselves, never knew the truth; instead they fabricated it. They manufactured truth. That is why Hegel wrote long books and Kant propounded deep and subtle theories and principles on truth. But there is absolutely no value, no importance, in the writing and principles of those who are not prepared to seek the self. If you ask Kant or Hegel for their opinion of this sage of the Upanishad, they will say, "He is a lunatic. What value is there if you lose yourself attaining truth?"

But the sage's understanding is profound and deep. He says, "'I' is part and parcel of untruth, a part of the world, of samsara. If I desire that this mundane existence go away, that truth come to me, and that my 'I' within remain intact, then I am trying the impossible. If this worldly existence is to go away, it has to go completely – from within as well as from without. On one side, the objects without must disappear, and on the other side, the 'I' within must disappear. The form without and form within must pass away, leaving a void within and without. Therefore if truth is to be found, the unavoidable condition for it is to lose oneself. I pray to you, O great sun, to consume everything of yours unconditionally. Withdraw your whole expanse. Return to your seed of origin. Return to that place where there was nothing, so that I may be able to know that from which everything proceeds!"

This is the ultimate jump. When a man gathers the courage for this jump, he becomes one with the supreme truth. It is not possible to be one with the supreme truth without losing oneself. Hence Western philosophers, in their attempt to seek truth, have been unable to go beyond human, worldly truth. Theirs is a search of man; it is not existential, it pertains to human beings only. The search of the sage of the East is not for worldly, human truths but for existential truths. He says, "What will you ever know about the ocean by standing on its shore? I shall know it by sinking into it." But even sinking into it we do not merge into it completely – we and the ocean still remain apart.

So the sage says, "Since this is the case, I shall become an effigy made of salt so that I can dissolve into it. I shall know the ocean by merging into it – by being the ocean itself. I shall be one with the ocean. I shall be salty as it is salty. I shall be water as it is water. I shall be a wave in its waves. I shall be an endless depth in its endless depths. Then and then only will I be able to know it."

It is not possible to know it before all this. Before this, we can have an acquaintance with it but not existential knowledge. Standing on the shore, we can only become acquainted with the ocean. To know it, we must dissolve into it.

Enough for today.

Now let us prepare ourselves to dissolve.

# At The Door Of Samadhi

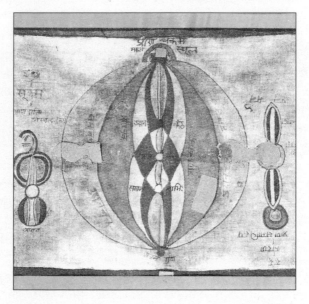

## 18

*Now let my spirit meet the absolute*
*pervading all throughout the vital air,*
*and let my body be reduced to ashes.*
*O my mind full of ego and desires,*
*now remember your past actions,*
*remember your past deeds.*

LET LIFE MERGE into that from which it was born. Let the shape lose itself in that formlessness from which it was created. Let them be one in that pure consciousness of being. Let the body be mixed with dust, let it be merged into earth. In such a moment – and there are two such moments – the sage addresses his egoistic mind full of desires: "O my mind full of ego and desires, remind yourself of your past actions."

There are two moments when this prayer may be truly offered. One is the moment of death and the other is that of *samadhi*, deep meditation. The one is when a person is on the threshold of death, and the other is when he is at the greater death — samadhi — ready to merge himself like a drop into the ocean. Most of the people who have explained this sutra have interpreted it with reference to the first moment – that of physical death. They have assumed that the sage is saying this at the moment of death, when his whole existence is going to be merged into that from where he came. But as I see it, this remembrance is not made at all at the moment of death, but at the moment of samadhi. It is not appropriate to the moment of death, because there is no precognition of death. You never know at what moment death will come. You know about it when it comes, but by that time you are already dead. As long as death has not come one does not know about it; and when it comes, the person who should know has already passed away.

When Socrates was about to die, his friends asked him the reason why he did not appear afraid, miserable or worried. Then

Socrates said, "I think this way: as long as death has not come, I am alive; when I am alive, why should I worry about death? And who will be left to worry about death when it actually comes and I am no more? I shall be completely lost in death, nothing will be left behind, and if nothing of me remains beyond death, then there is no reason to be afraid of anything. On the other hand, if, as some people say, I shall not die even after death, then there is no reason at all to worry about death."

As I said, this sutra is meaningful in two moments, either at the moment of death or at the moment of samadhi. But we have no idea at all of the moment of death – it is unpredictable, it cannot be foretold. It comes all of a sudden, at any moment. It may happen any moment, there is no foreknowledge of that moment, and this prayer can be made only when there is foreknowledge; that is, when the sage knows, "I am about to die, I am at the door of death."

No, this is not a prayer made at the moment of death. It is made at the time of the great death – samadhi means great death. I consider mortal death an ordinary death because then only the body dies; the mind does not die. I consider meditation, samadhi, the great death because there is no idea, no remembering of the body at all in that condition; the mind dies too. Hence I say that this prayer is made at the time of samadhi, because the sage is asking his egoistic and desiring mind to remember its past actions.

The second part of this sutra has been much misunderstood. The fact is that such things as these are usually interpreted for us by pundits – by our self-professed wise men. However intelligent their interpretations and explanations may be, they commit a fundamental error. They understand the words and principles of the scriptures correctly, but they do not understand at all that which is hidden unsaid behind the words and principles. The hidden essence is never contained in the actual words of religions. It is to be understood from the gaps between the words. The meaning is not in the lines but in the spaces between the lines. So those who are unable to understand the spaces, those who read only the printed words, cannot correctly interpret these great sutras.

There is a movement called Krishna Consciousness in the West. I was just looking at a book on the Ishavasya Upanishad by Swami Bhakti Vedant Prabhupad – the leader of this movement. I was very much surprised to read his interpretation of this sutra. The way he explains it is: "I am on the point of dying, I am standing at the door of death. Therefore, O God, please accept the sacrifices and renunciation I have made for you: remember the actions I have performed for you."

Not only is he unable to read the spaces between the words, he seems unable to read even the words themselves, finding other words instead. The sage is addressing his egoistic and desiring mind – there is no question here at all of bringing God in. Nor does the sage say, "Remember the actions which I performed for you, remember the sacrifices I made for you." But our business mind loves to interpret it in this way. It will say at the moment of death, "O God, remember, I have given a lot of money to charities, I have built a temple for you, I have built a dam for the village, and so on. O God, my time is over, now give me a fitting reward for all the actions and sacrifices I have made for your sake."

"My egoistic and desiring mind...." Will is the channel of our desires, of the longings of the mind. It is necessary to understand what will is so that the discussion may be easily followed. Desires arise in the minds of all of us, but desire does not become will till the ego is linked with it.

Egoistic desire becomes will. All people have desires, but these desires remain mere dreams as long as they are not linked with ego, as long as they do not become actions. To be translated into actions, a desire has to be linked with ego. Then it becomes will. Vanity – ego – is born to perform, to be. A desire to be the doer arises. You become the doer as soon as ego is united with desire.

The sage says, "O my mind full of ego and desires, remember the actions done by you." Why does he say this, and not just once but twice? Why? What need is there to remember this at the moment of samadhi or at the moment of death? The sage is just making a joke. He is just laughing at himself. At the gate of samadhi everything is passing away: the mind is evaporating, the body is passing away, the spirit is disappearing – everything is being absorbed. "O my mind, what happened to all that you were thinking about? I did this – I did that. Where are all those ideas that you were absorbed in, all those lines you were drawing on water? Gone!"

Remember, all that you have done is passing away – even you are passing away. Have a look back into the past, and remember with what pride and vanity you thought, "*I* have done this!" With what dreams you planned to do that! Remember all the footprints of your countless births and travels. No trace of them is seen today, and today you are also going to be nothing; no trace of you will remain. Today all the elements will be absorbed in themselves. Today your entire journey will be over.

So have a retrospective look, just once, and understand how great an illusion you have been living in, what dreams you have been dreaming in your madness, what hardships you have undergone for them, and how, lost in anxiety, you have lived for the sake of these dreams. And when any of your dreams were not fulfilled, think of the anguish and frustration you passed through. And remember how overjoyed you became when a dream of yours was fulfilled. Today all dreams and all achievements have disappeared, and you too are about to pass away. Looking backwards, remember all these things once more.

In great jest and joking the sage thus addresses his own egoistic will, his vain mind. That is why, I tell you, this is not said at the time of death but at the time of samadhi, because only the body perishes at the time of death; the egoistic mind does not. You travel with your mind even after death. That mind is the current of your countless births. The body falls here, the mind travels on with you. Desires accompany you. Ego travels with you. The memory of past actions goes with you. The desire to accomplish those things you could not do goes with you. Your entire mind goes with you. Only the physical body dies. Mind leaves the body and catches hold of a new body – this mind that has already caught hold of countless bodies in the past and will go on doing so.

This is why those who know do not consider death to be real death – because nothing perishes in it, we merely change our clothes. Understand this well: the body is no more than clothes, no more than an outer covering. Ordinarily we think that the body is born first and then the mind is born in it. This is wrong. During the last two hundred years Western thinking and belief has spread the illusion that the body is created first, and that the mind is then born in it, as a by-product, an epiphenomenon, as simply one quality, one attribute of the body. It is similar to what the ancient Charvakas used to say – that if you separate the ingredients that are blended to make wine, and eat or drink them separately, there will be no intoxication. The intoxicant is a by-product of the contents being mixed together. It does not come from somewhere of its own accord, it has no separate existence. It is produced by mixing a number of things together. If the ingredients are separated it disappears. So the ancient Charvakas used to argue that the body is composed of five elements and mind is produced by the union of these five elements. Mind is a by-product.

Western science is at present also in a state of ignorance in this matter, believing that the mind comes after the body, as a shadow. But in the East, those who have searched deeply into this subject maintain that the mind is first and the body comes like a shadow after it. Let us understand it in this way: what comes first in your life, the action or the desire? First comes the desire in the mind, and then it is turned into action – the action follows. But if anyone sees it from outside, he will see the action first and will have to guess about the desire behind the action. Suppose anger arose within me and I slapped you: first came anger, first came the mind, then the hand was raised and the body performed the action. But you will see my hand and the act of slapping first. Even so, you will no doubt reason that I must first have become angry. The bodily action is seen first, and as a result you start guessing what is going on in my mind. But still those workings of my mind came first, and the action of the body follows.

When a child is born we also see the body first, but those who know deeply say it is the mind that comes first. That very mind causes the body to be conceived and born. That mind creates the outline, the form of this body. It is a sort of blueprint, it is an in-built program. When a person dies, his mind goes on its journey with a blueprint, and that blueprint maps itself into a new womb. And you will be surprised to know this: we commonly believe that a body is produced when a man and a woman make love, and then a soul enters the body, but on looking deeply into this phenomenon it becomes evident that when a soul desires to enter a womb, then both the man and the woman become eager for sexual activity. Again, it is the body that is seen first, and we have to guess about the mind. However, those who have looked deeply into this matter say that when a soul desirous of entering a womb begins to wander around you, then there arises a longing for sexual enjoyment. The mind is busy getting a body ready for itself. You might not have thought of this happening.

When you lie down to sleep at night – when sleep begins to descend upon you and has almost caught you – bring your consciousness to the last thought in your mind, then go to sleep; and when you wake up in the morning and are ready to leave your bed, look back and find your first thought on waking. You will be very surprised by the result. The last thought of the night becomes the first one in the morning. In the same way, the last desire at the time of death becomes the first desire at the time of birth.

In death, the body disintegrates but the mind continues its journey. The age of your body may be fifty years but that of your mind can be five million. The sum total of all the minds born in all your births is there in you even today. Buddha has given a very significant name to this happening. He was the first to do so. He named it the storehouse of consciousness. Like a storehouse, your mind has stored all the memories of all your past births – so your mind is very old. And it is not that your mind is the storehouse of only human births: if you were born as animals or as trees, as is surely the case, the memories of all those births are also present within you.

People who have conducted profound inquiries into the process of the storehouse of consciousness say that if all of a sudden the feeling of love swells in the mind of any man on seeing a rose, the reason is that there is a memory deep within him of himself being a rose in the past, which is rekindled on feeling its resonance in a rose. It is not accidental if a person loves dogs very much. There are memories in his storehouse of consciousness which make him aware of his great kinship with dogs. Whatever happens in our lives is not accidental. A subtle process of cause and effect is working behind these happenings. Though the body perishes in death, the mind continues its journey and goes on collecting memories. This is why sometimes you see forms in your mind of which you would say, "They are not mine." Sometimes you do certain things that cause you to feel strange and say, "This has been done in spite of me." Suppose a person quarrels with somebody and bites him. Afterwards he thinks, "How strange that I could bite him! Am I a wild animal?" He is not today, but once he was; and a moment may come when his hidden memory becomes so active that he behaves exactly like an animal. All of us behave like animals on many occasions. That behavior does not descend from the sky, it comes from the store within our mind.

Our death is the death of our body only. Our mind full of ego and desires does not die then, so there would have been no opportunity for the sage to joke in this way if he were simply facing physical death. This sutra is said at the time of samadhi. There is one distinguishing feature of samadhi: its arrival can be announced beforehand. Death surprises, samadhi is invited. Death happens, samadhi is planned. Progressing step by step in meditation, man reaches to the state of samadhi.

Understand the great significance of the word samadhi. At times the word samadhi is also used to mean a grave. The grave of a sage is called a samadhi. It is rightly called so. Samadhi is a kind of death, but a profound and remarkable one. The body remains here after death, but the mind within is destroyed. At this moment of the mind's destruction the sage says, "O my mind full of ego and desires, remember the actions done by you in the past." He is saying this because the mind has deceived him in the past again and again; but today this very mind is being destroyed.

"Depending and relying on my mind I lived my life. Through victory and defeat, happiness and unhappiness, success and failure, hopes and disappointments, I believed it would be always with me; but now I see it was deceiving me. Leaning on it for support I made such a long journey, but today I find that my support is perishing – disintegrating forever. I thought it to be a sturdy boat, but today I find that it is itself water merging into the river."

In this moment the sage is addressing his mind: "O my egoistic mind, remember the actions done by you, and actions desired and intended by you. Remember the promises you made, consolations you offered. Remember how much I confided in you. Remember what you induced me to do. Remember the illusions you created in me. Remember the dreams you gave me. Remember the follies you led me into. Now you yourself are going away, and I am entering a region where you will not be. Till now you have always persuaded me that where ego is not, where will is not, there is no being. But I see today that you are going away, yet my being remains."

The mind always says, "If there is no will you will perish. You will be unable to stand up against the conflicts of life. If there is no ego in you, you will perish; you will not survive!" The mind always instigates action, determination and fight. "If you don't fight you will be wiped out." Surely, it is only natural for the sage on this day to make fun of his mind, to say to the mind, "You yourself are perishing today while I am intact. You are departing, I am not. Until now you have deceived me, telling me that I shall not be saved if you are not. But today you are leaving and I am not."

The sage makes use of this moment to joke and jest for two reasons: one is for his own mind, and the other is for the minds of those who have not yet reached the door of samadhi and are busily occupied in a thousand and one activities, whose minds are inducing them to do this and to do that, whose minds still tell them, "Your life is wasted if you fail to accomplish this, if you fail to build this palace," whose minds tell them, "You are worth nothing if you fail to accomplish this mission, this adventure."

To such people the sage is addressing his joke. He warns them to think again, because the mind is the greatest deceiver. All our deceptions are created by the mind. Each and every one of us lives in a dream world, and the mind is so clever that it does not allow us to see deep enough to reveal its deceptions. The mind is ready with a new deception before we are able to see through the previous one. Before the previous one is destroyed, mind fabricates another structure of deception and entices us, saying, "Come in here, take rest here."

If a desire were fulfilled and the mind were to allow you a single moment's interval, you would be able to see that nothing was really achieved through the fulfillment of your first desire, for which you endured so much trouble and anxiety. What did you really get? Less than rubbish! But the mind does not allow even that much interval, that much chance. The mind begins to plant the seeds of your next desire before the last one is fulfilled. When a desire is fulfilled, it is found to be useless and the interest is lost, but the mind immediately raises the germ of a new desire. The race begins again: the mind never gives you an opportunity to rest, to stop so that you can see what deception you are in. When the ground disappears from under your feet, the mind does not allow you to see the hole in its place, but offers you instead a new piece of ground on which to stand.

I will tell you a short but interesting story which Buddha used to narrate. You may have heard it, but you may not have interpreted it in this way.

A man was running through a forest. Now, a man runs for one of two reasons: either something in front attracts him, or else something from behind is pushing him. This man was running for both reasons. He was running in search of diamonds, because somebody had told him there was a diamond mine in the forest. But he was running very fast at this moment because a lion was after him. He had forgotten diamonds for the moment and was thinking of how to save himself from the lion. He ran without losing heart, but eventually reached a dead end. There was no road ahead, only a deep and dangerous pit, and no way to go back – no way to turn back, either through the forest or along the road. This is how you run, in pursuit of diamonds or to save your life, and there is no going back! All past time is gone forever. You cannot step back even an inch into the past.

This man, pursued by the lion, was also unable to return, and the road ahead was a dead end. Greatly afraid and seeing no way out, he did what a desperate person would do. Catching hold of the roots of a tree, he swung himself over the edge of the pit, thinking to climb out when the lion had gone away. But the lion, standing near the mouth of the pit, began to wait for him. The lion also has his desires! He thought, "The man will have to come up in the end." When the man saw the lion waiting for him, he looked below for a way to save himself, and there, roaring in the pit below, was a mad elephant.

We can imagine how pitiable and miserable his condition was – but not yet pitiable enough. The trials and tribulations of life are without number. No amount of conflict and upset can exhaust life's potential to create more. Suddenly he realized that the root he was clinging to was slowly, slowly giving way. He looked up and saw two rats busy gnawing away at the roots. One was white and the other black. Buddha used to liken them to the days and nights which go on shortening man's life. We can understand how great a danger his life was in now, with no escape possible. But no, the desires of man are amazing, and his mind's tricks of deception are wonderful. At that moment he saw a honeycomb above the root, from which drops of honey were falling, one by one. He put out his tongue, and a drop fell on it. He closed his eyes in great joy, and said to himself, "How blessed I am, how sweet it is." At that moment there was neither the lion above nor the elephant below, neither the rats cutting the roots nor any fear of death. In that moment he forgot all his fears, and could only feel, "How sweet!"

Buddha used to say that each person is in this predicament, but the mind goes on dripping drops of honey one after another. Man closes his eyes and says, "How sweet!" This is the situation all the time. There is death above and there is death below. Where life is, death is all around. Life is surrounded by death, and the roots of life themselves are being cut every moment. Every day, every moment, life is being emptied. Just as the sand in an hourglass slips away from one moment to the next, so our life is slipping away. But even so, if a drop of honey falls we close our eyes and begin to dream of hopes. The mind tells us, "See, how sweet it is!" When one drop is finished another is ready to fall. The mind continues to sustain us with deception, drop by drop.

So the sage says, "O my egoistic and desiring mind, think of the deceptions you have practiced upon me. Now remember this: all your past actions and all your future plans – you were the instigator of those actions, but today you meet your doom. You are at the gates of destruction, you are about to be rubbed out." At the gates of samadhi the mind becomes a void; thoughts cease to come, doubts and uncertainties of the mind disappear, the waves of the mind become calm. There is absolutely no mind. When there is no mind, there is samadhi.

I have told you that one meaning of samadhi is a grave – the grave of a saint. The second meaning of samadhi is the condition of doubtlessness, where doubts do not exist. It is worth knowing that where the mind is, there are doubts and doubts and doubts; there can never be doubtlessness. Mind is the great alchemist of doubt. As leaves sprout on a tree, doubts sprout in the mind; doubtlessness never sprouts there, it is there only when the mind is not. So when a person approaches me with a request to make his mind free of doubts, I tell him, "Don't bother about that; you will never be able to make mind free from doubts. Leave aside your mind and you will have doubtlessness."

A friend was asking me this evening, "How can I be free from greed?"

I told him, "You can never be free, because you yourself *are* greed. As long as *you* are, you can never be without greed. If you are not, greed will not be there."

Doubtlessness in the mind is never possible; it comes only when the mind is not. That is why no-mind is called samadhi – there is no doubt at all. As long as the mind is, it will go on creating doubts upon doubts. If you solve one doubt, it will give rise to another, and if someone gives you a solution, the mind will create ten doubts out of that solution.

A friend had informed me by letter that he was going to attend the meditation camp. He saw me two days ago. He had written to me that his mind was full of restlessness. After three days in the camp his restlessness has disappeared. "After three days," he told me, "my restlessness has gone away, but is the restfulness I now feel not a deception?"

I asked him, "Did your mind ever tell you that restlessness is a deception?"

He said, "The mind never said so."

I asked, "How long have you been restless?"

He replied, "I have always been restless."

His mind never questioned whether this restlessness was not a deception. And now when he has become restful for the last three days, the mind asks, "Is this peace real? Is it not a deception?" The mind is amazing! Even if God meets you, your mind will raise a doubt: "I cannot say definitely whether he is the real or an artificial one." As long as mind is, doubt will surely arise. So as long as you keep your mind you will remain in great difficulty. Even if bliss comes, the mind becomes suspicious and doubts its presence. The mind creates doubts, raises suspicions and uncertainties, and gives birth to worries and anxieties.

In spite of all this, why do we hold on to the mind so tight? If the mind is the root of all these illnesses – as those who know tell us – then what is the reason for clinging so tightly to it? For the answer, look to the sage's challenging remarks. The reason we cling to it so tightly is that we are afraid that if the mind is not then we also shall not be. In fact, intentionally or unintentionally, we have identified ourselves with it. We have come to believe, "I am the mind." As long as this is our understanding we will continue to cling to all those illnesses.

You are not the mind! You are that which knows the mind, which sees it and which is fully conversant with it. To realize this you will have to move a little away from it, you will have to stand off a little from it, you will have to raise yourself a little above it. You will have to stand on the shore to see the flow of the mind and to recognize it. How can you leave it as long as you identify yourself with it? That would be suicidal. To leave the mind means to die. So you will not be able to leave it. He alone can give it up who knows, "I am not the mind."

The first step into samadhi is this experience: "I am not the mind." This experience becomes more and more profound till it becomes so clear and secure that the mind disappears completely. It disappears like the flame of a lamp whose oil is finished. Even if the oil in the lamp is finished, the wick will continue to burn as long as there is a little oil in the wick – but now it will not burn for long. The sage is in a similar condition. He has realized, "I am not the mind," but the flame continues burning now from the little oil remaining in the wick. The sage is addressing this flame in its last burning moments, "O my egoistic mind, you promised me to be always with me and to give me light. But you are on the point of being extinguished. I see now that the oil is finished, so I ask you how long can you last now? You are completely finished, and yet *I am*." So he is telling his dying mind, "I was always separate from you, but I always identified with you. It was my delusion – samsara, *maya* – the great delusion!"

The sage is addressing himself, and as I told you, he is addressing you also. Perhaps you can also realize it. Go back to your childhood and remember how anxious you were to be top of the class: how you lost sleep at night, how much the load of examinations weighed on your mind, how you believed everything depended on them! But today there is no examination, there is no class. Go back and check up: what difference did it make whether you came first, or second or third – or failed? Today you remember nothing of these happenings. Go back and see. You picked a quarrel with someone: you thought it was a matter of life and death. Today, after ten years, that quarrel looks like lines drawn on water. Someone insulted you in the street and you struggled with the problem of how to protect yourself from his abuse. Just look: you were not destroyed. The abuse is not there now. Today you remember nothing of it. Go back and see how much importance you attached to it then. Is it that important today? No, it has no importance at all now.

Remember, the thing which you value today will be worthless tomorrow, so do not give it much importance today. Learn from your experience of yesterday, and withdraw all this value you place on the things you do now. The sage is telling his egoistic mind, on the strength of all his experiences in life, "I considered you so very important, but I tell you very definitely, at this moment of bidding you farewell, that you practiced deception throughout. It was my foolishness not to see that I was and am separate from you."

When the mind vanishes everything vanishes, because it is the nucleus to which everything is linked. The wheel of our entire life revolves on it. Therefore the sage declares that the five elements in the body will absorb themselves in their sources and everything will vanish, because the mind – the nucleus joining all together – is disappearing today.

When he attained to the ultimate knowledge Buddha said a wonderful thing. When his mind was destroyed for the first time and he entered that state of void, he said exactly the thing which the sage of the Upanishad has said. He said, "O mind, now I bid you farewell. Till now you were needed, for I wanted to have a human form. But now I do not need the human body so you can leave. Till now, needing the body, I needed its architect, the mind, too. Nobody can be created without it. Now I have my supreme abode. Now I have reached my destination. Now I have reached that uncreated house, that dwelling in my self. Now you can depart."

Such sutras are very important for seekers of truth. There is no benefit in committing them to memory. They are beneficial only if kept in the heart. If they are memorized and repeated every day they become stale. By and by their meaning is lost, and only dead words remain. But if this fact – that the mind is nothing but a deception – is clearly understood by you, then a new revolution will enter your life. I am not speaking on these sutras with a view to your memorizing what I say and becoming a pundit. No, you are already a pundit even before hearing me: there is no need to increase the bulk of your knowledge. I speak on them to give you a true picture of the realities of life. If remembering happens, let it be through the awareness that these sutras bring in throwing light on the way in which you live.

Chuang Tzu was a Chinese master. One evening he was passing with his disciples through a cremation ground. A skull knocked against his foot. He picked it up, touching it often with his head, and begged its pardon. His disciples asked him, "Why are you doing this? We always thought you were a man of wisdom. What is this madness showing in you now?"

Chuang Tzu replied, "You don't understand. This cremation ground is reserved for VIP's. Only the most important people of the town are cremated here."

They said, "Whoever they may be, high or low, death is the great leveler."

Death is a great communist – it puts everybody on the same level. But Chuang Tzu said, "No, I have to beg its pardon. Suppose this man was alive now, what would be my position?"

The disciples said, "This man is *not* alive now, so why should you worry about him?"

But Chuang Tzu took the skull home and kept it near his bed. Whoever came to see him wondered why the skull was kept there. Chuang Tzu would say, "Unintentionally my foot knocked against it. As the man is no more, I have no opportunity to beg his pardon, so I am in a difficulty. To solve the problem I have brought the skull home, and I go on begging its pardon in the hope that one day I may be heard."

Hearing this, people used to say to him, "What nonsense you are talking!"

Then he would say, "The other reason I brought it here is for it to be my constant reminder that sooner or later my skull will also be lying in a burial ground and people will kick it here and there. I do not mind that, but I am sorry I shall not be in a position to forgive anyone who begs my pardon. So a great understanding about my skull has come to me since I brought this skull home. Looking at it I shall remain calm and unagitated even if someone kicks my skull!"

This is existential understanding, it is not intellectual. The understanding has borne fruit, the person is transformed. In the same way, if this sutra reaches your heart it will bear fruit when you are doing something and your mind is urging you this way or that.

For example, this sutra should be given to a man like Morarji Desai, whose mind is constantly planning to do this and to do that. The mind goes on working like this until death, though it gets nothing from its activity. Starting his career as a deputy collector, he has risen to the position of deputy minister, but he has achieved nothing. Even if he rises further, nothing fruitful, nothing worthwhile, is ever going to come of it. The mind always keeps you in difficulty, whether it wins or loses. The mind is like a gambler. If it loses, it thinks, "Let me play once again – I may win." And if it wins, it thinks, "Now my luck is in, I must not miss it; let me play once again." If he is winning, the gambler becomes more hopeful, and goes on playing. If he loses, his mind balks at the prospect of going away defeated: "Play once more, you may win. Try again!"

So remember this sutra when the mind, like a gambler, urges you on, win or lose! And address it thus: "O my mind full of ego and desires...remember your past actions." The result of this remembering will be that your great attraction to a particular action will be lessened. Your stupidity in thinking of yourself as a doer will be smashed, and you will move closer towards samadhi. You will deepen the intensity of your meditation. Bear in mind, unconsciousness or unawareness will not do. If you go on remaining unaware and insensible to the workings of the mind, then your mind will repeat what it did yesterday.

Perhaps you do not know this, but your mind never does anything new or fresh. It simply goes on repeating what it has done before. You were angry yesterday, you were angry the day before yesterday; and after your anger the day before yesterday you repented and vowed never to be angry again. Yesterday you did the same again, and here you are again doing the same thing today. Your anger is old, and your repentance is also old. Day after day you are repeating this sort of behavior. If you are unable to drop anger, at least leave aside the repenting for it; break one of your old habits at least! But you will not do this; your anger and your repentance go hand in hand.

Man's entire life is a repetition. It is no different from that of a bullock working in a sugarcane mill. The bullock may think it is walking a great distance because its eyes remain closed as it continues walking round and round. It may think it has traveled all the earth and must be nearing its destination. Like the bullock, the mind travels in a circle. If a person keeps a daily diary, he will have to consider whether he is anything more than a machine: the same activities, the same daily routine, repeated over and over. After twenty years living together, the wife knows what her husband will say when he comes home late in the evening; she has twenty years' experience. The husband also knows how his wife will react to his excuses. Even so, both of them will go through the same questions and the same answers.

Absorbed thus in the mechanical process of the mind, the man who lives in unawareness misses all the opportunities he meets with in his life – and the opportunities are not few, but we are so clever in missing each of them. Every day there comes a fresh opportunity to be new by not repeating the old – but we repeat the old. This happens because we do not bear in mind this sutra… remember your past actions. Before you get angry tomorrow, tell your mind, "O mind, remember all the occasions you have become angry before." First, stop for a couple of seconds and remember the occasions of being angry before, and then be angry. And I tell you, you will be unable to be angry then.

Whenever the mind becomes full of desires and passions, address your mind thus: "O my mind full of ego and desires, remember the desires you have cherished in the past." Keep your old experiences in mind before embarking on a new journey, then you will not start on yet another journey through the old. Your desire will stand amazed and puzzled! This much awareness is enough to break the mind's mechanical way of working.

Gurdjieff has recorded in his memoirs that his father's last advice changed the entire course of his life. He was a small boy then, the youngest in the house. His father, who was on his deathbed, called all his sons and said something to each of them. When the youngest was called the father said, "Come near me and bend your head towards me, I want to tell you something which you should bear in mind throughout your life. I have nothing else to give you. I want you to make me one promise – that whenever an opportunity arises to commit an evil deed you will wait for twenty-four hours. Of course, you may do it, but wait for twenty-four hours before you do it. Give me this promise. If you want to be angry, be fully angry; I do not forbid you, but do it after twenty-four hours. If you want to murder someone, do it with all your heart, but wait for twenty-four hours."

Gurdjieff asked, "What is the purpose of this?"

His father said, "By following this advice you will be able to do the deed in a better way. You will be able to plan it well, and it is my life's experience that there will be no mistake in your planning. My gift to you is this experience."

Gurdjieff has written, "This one piece of advice changed the course of my life, because no one can do an evil deed if he waits even for twenty-four seconds, let alone twenty-four hours."

When you become angry, look at your watch and tell yourself, "I shall be angry after one minute." When the second hand completes one circle, put down the watch and begin to be angry. You will not be able to be angry because the glimpse and reflection of all the past occasions of becoming angry will return to your mind during the sixty-second interval. All the past repentances, all the vows taken by you, all your decisions not to do that again, all these things will reappear in front of you, and you will be unable to become angry.

But we do not wait in committing an evil deed; we only wait in doing a good deed. A friend came today and expressed his desire to be initiated into sannyas on his birthday, two or three months from now. No one waits till his birthday if he wants to be angry! I asked him, "Is it certain? How do you know where you will be on your birthday? It may even be the day of your death!"

Even the next moment you cannot trust, what to say of two or three months' time! We postpone a good action, but the evil one we do immediately in case we miss the opportunity of doing it. No, postpone the evil, and do the good immediately. You cannot trust the next moment; it may come, it may not come. If you miss the moment of doing good, the opportunity may not come again, and if you wait – even for a moment – to do an evil deed, I tell you, you will not be able to do it. One who is strong enough to wait for a moment will be unable to do an evil deed. To wait for a moment requires great strength. It is the greatest strength in this world to wait for a second when the eyes begin to turn red with blood and the fists begin to be clenched in anger.

The sage has created this sutra in order to make fun of himself – to laugh at himself as well as at all of us. Enough for today.

Try to understand a few points about meditation before we begin. The first thing is never to postpone it, not even for a second. Don't think, "I shall begin tomorrow." It is to be practiced *now*.

I have to say something about those who are sitting behind me. I had asked them to sit; it seems they thought they had simply to sit there. When I turned back and looked I found that hardly eight or ten people were participating in meditation; the rest were sitting idle. You will get nothing by sitting idle. I am puzzled to see them at times sitting idly, doing nothing, when so many around them are totally in it, inspired by it, dancing and jumping. Have you a stone instead of a heart, that nothing moves you? Are you not stirred at all, seeing so many in rapture, in ecstasy? You are very intelligent – you control your feelings so that they cannot be affected. Please let yourself go! Do not sit here rigid like stone, where so many are dancing with open hearts and minds and have become as innocent as children. Let your stiffness go; be stirred!

One more point to remember: some of you think, "We shall do it when it becomes possible for us." Ninety percent do it of their own accord, ten percent do not. But they themselves will have to break the barrier. So I tell you, those who think they cannot do it themselves should start doing it. They will have to make an effort for a couple of seconds only; it will become spontaneous from the third moment. When once the spring of water bursts forth, then water begins to flow down in a natural way. Now only one day is left, so I wish none to remain unaffected. Let all participate!

# Transformation
# Is The Test

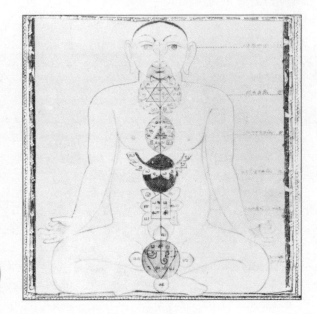

19

*Oh fire,*
*lead us to the righteous path.*
*Oh God,*
*the knower of all knowledge and actions,*
*destroy our deceitful sins.*
*We bow to you innumerable times.*

 WE HAVE SEEN STREAMS and brooks flowing down from the mountain. We know that rivers flow towards the ocean. Water runs always towards lower and lower levels in search of the lowest level, and its journey ends in ditches. To flow down is its path; its nature is to go down and down. Fire has quite the opposite nature: it always goes upwards. Rising upwards is its path, on and on upwards towards the sky. You may strike a flame anywhere, you may keep it in any position, you may hang a lamp upside down – its flame will still begin to rise upwards. Since ancient times the higher souls, the mystics, have clearly understood the upward, rising nature of fire.

Consciousness can flow both ways, like water or like fire. Generally we flow like water, seeking ever lower pits. If our consciousness gets a chance to slide downwards, we immediately drop the upwards path. Ordinarily we behave like water; but we should behave like fire, abandoning the lower levels when even a small occasion to rise higher comes before us. We should be ready to take even the smallest opportunity to spread our wings and fly towards the sky.

For those seeking an upward path, for those whose hopes were to enter a higher dimension, fire became the ideal, the symbol, for their behavior; it was regarded as a god. There is another reason why fire was regarded as a symbol and a god. When an individual begins to travel upwards, simultaneously he begins to journey within. It is exactly the opposite of the journey which is simultaneously downwards and outwards. Looking into their connotations, out-wards and downwards are synonymous; and inwards and upwards are synonymous too. You will go as far upwards as you go in-wards, and you will go as far downwards as you go outwards. Or, you go as much out as you go down, and you go as much within as you go up. From the existential point of view, up and within have the same meaning.

Likewise, from the point of view of experience, though not semantically, outwards and downwards have the same meaning. Those who decided to make an upward journey had to make an inward journey also, and as they went further within, darkness began to decrease and light to increase. So fire became the symbol of the journey within.

There is also another reason why fire became a symbol and began to be worshipped. It has one great beauty of its own; it saves the pure and destroys the impure. If gold is thrown into fire, the impurities are burned and destroyed, and the pure gold comes out brighter. This is known as the ordeal by fire – the test to destroy the impure and save the pure. The ordeal by fire became a symbol of the fact that fire will destroy that which is impure and will save and protect that which is pure. This is its natural quality. It is eager to protect the pure and to burn the impure.

There is a great deal of impurity within us – so much that no trace of gold is to be seen, though it may be lying concealed some-where within us. Sometimes some sage talks of gold, but we know only the dust and rubbish within which it lies. Some realized soul, some wise man, tells us there is gold, pure gold, within us, but when we go looking for it we find nothing but stones. So we have to throw even gold into the fire. The meaning of penance is to throw gold into fire. The word *tapa*, penance, is derived from tapa – fire. Tapa does not just mean that a person stands in the heat of the sun practicing penance. Penance means that one should pass through so much fire within that all that is impure may be burned, destroyed – and all that is pure may be left.

It is necessary to bear in mind one or two other points about fire so that it will be easy to remember its divine form, its divinity. It will be useful to understand the prayer of the sage, "O fire, lead me to the right path," and to realize why such a prayer was offered to fire. You have seen fire, you have seen water also. However low it may sink, water remains. Flowing down from a mountain it enters a valley, but it is not lost, it does not vanish. Fire rises towards the sky, but vanishes after rising only a little distance.

Truly speaking, one who makes an upward journey will vanish. As he goes up and up he is vanishing every moment; soon he will lose his ego and cease to be. He will be one with the sky. Fire remains visible for a short distance and then disappears – lost in the void, in nothingness. Water remains, however far down it may flow. The ego will surely persist on its downward journey, and if it goes very deep down it will be transformed. When ego sinks very low it becomes hard, like a stone. Bear this in mind; the ego becomes strong, frozen, hard and crystallized as you descend lower and lower, and becomes thin, weak and invisible as you rise higher and higher. Watch a flame and you will see – in a short while it has gone away. Where has it gone?

When Buddha was about to enter his final liberation, he said, "Within a few seconds I shall cease to be."

Then someone asked, "Where will you be then, when you are not?"

Buddha replied, "Watch the lamp, and ask it where its flame, disappearing into the air, has gone. I shall also disappear in that way in a short time. That moment has arrived when my flame will be absorbed in the vast sky."

There is one more secret, one more mystery, about fire: it burns everything and finally destroys itself too. After consuming the fuel, fire does not save itself. As soon as the fuel is extinguished the fire is also extinguished. Everything is extinguished, and finally no fire is left behind; it also vanishes. It would be violence if it saved itself after burning everything else, but it is love when one disappears after making others disappear. So fire is not the enemy of fuel; it is its friend, its lover. If it were not so, it would certainly save itself after consuming the fuel. It does not consume others to preserve itself; this is not the nature of fire. After burning the fuel, it burns itself and becomes quiet.

It is worth noting that fuel is preserved in the form of ashes after it has been consumed, whereas fire is not saved in any form. It is so pure that it leaves no ashes of itself behind. In actual fact, ash is formed out of impurities. Fire is simply the purest existence. It leaves no trace whatsoever behind it. It is a very arduous search for the seeker to find an ideal symbol on the outside for what happens within. The best symbol found up to now is fire. Whether burning constantly in the Parsi temples or in the religious sacrifices of the rishis, or in fire sacrifices or in the temple lamps, fire is to this day held as the best symbol, closest to the happenings within – those transcendental happenings within. This is why people consider it a god.

What is it that is considered a god? It is not simply that which is divine, because everything and everyone is divine. Everything is divine because everything comes out of the divine. The dictionary meaning of the word *devata* is one who is divine, but everyone is divine. Some know this fact and some do not, but what is there which is not divine? The stone, the tree, the river, the mountain, the sky – all are divine. Each atom is divine. So the word devata does not mean that which is divine. Why is a thing designated a god in a special additional sense? It means this: it is not only divine, but also leads others to divinity. One who turns others to divinity, who indicates the divine, who turns our longing towards divinity, is a god. That is why the sages could say the master is God. There was no other reason but this. If one is reminded by looking at the sky of that which is without form, then the sky is God. But we have difficulty in understanding this.

Those who read the Vedas today find it difficult to understand its assertions that the sky is God, Indra is God, the sun is God, and so on. They think, "What is all this madness, all this nonsense?" When Westerners first read the Vedas, they too found them difficult to understand. They said, "This is polytheism – a religion of many gods. These people have a tendency to see God in all things." But no, it is not that. Anything is a god through whom divinity is remembered, by whom one is struck with divinity, through whom the strings of the *veena* of the heart are caused to vibrate, through whom one begins the journey towards the divine.

Look at the sky. If you continue to look for some time, the form will vanish and the revelation of formlessness will begin. The sky is thus pointing towards formlessness. Shall we then be so ungrateful as not to thank that phenomenon, saying, "O God, you reminded me of the formless; I am thankful"?

Go on looking at fire – that was the purpose and meaning of the religious fire sacrifices. The offering itself is not so important in fire sacrifices; what is important is to be one with the transcendental journey of fire, through sitting near it. You see the fire leaping upwards, its flame vanishing into that great nothingness, and if at that moment you become one with that flame with a concentrated and meditative mind and lose yourself in that void, then fire becomes your god.

That is God through whom you hear the divine, through which you are inspired within to move towards divinity, through which your dormant seed of divinity is broken open, leading you to divinity. That is why the sage says, "O God, O fire, lead me to the right path. I do not know the path. I do not even know that which is meaningful from that which is meaningless. I am ignorant. Please lead me."

There is one point here which should be profoundly understood, and it is this: one who pleads to be led towards the right path is making no ordinary plea; it is extraordinary, because the plea itself is the basis of the help one needs to proceed towards the right path. This plea is extraordinary because our every intention, our every passion, our every desire, leads us to the wrong path – there is no need to pray, to plead for it. Nature has given us sufficient means for that; nature itself leads us there. If you want to go down, to degrade yourself, you need no prayer to help you. If you want to go towards darkness, nature is already helping you. Your own actions lead you to that path. Your own habits and past impressions are

already leading you towards it. It is interesting to note that nobody
has ever prayed to God to lead him to an unrighteous path. Here
God is not required; man himself is strong and capable enough to
go astray. There is no need of God's help in doing so. On the contrary, man has the capacity to lead God onto an unrighteous path!

The madness is that it is the unrighteous path which is full of
dangers, yet no one prays for God's help to take it. It should be
done thus: "O God, please help me along the unrighteous path,
for it is full of dangers!" To walk this path is to enter into much
suffering and misery and madness. It is inviting troubles to over-
whelm us. In such circumstances God's help should be sought, but
no one seeks it because everybody thinks he is capable enough to
meet the challenge. Man is strong enough to follow an unrighteous
path, but when the question of traveling the right path comes up,
he suddenly finds he is unable to do so!

The reason for man's weakness is that all his desires and passions draw him downwards, and there is no such passion endowed
by nature to lift him upwards. If he does nothing and stands still,
he will automatically slip downwards, sliding and stumbling in his
descent. The gravitational force of nature is enough to draw him
down, and with every step he will think of going lower and lower.
The whole life force will urge him downwards more and more. He
imagines there is happiness down below, and if he meets with
unhappiness in his efforts, he argues, "It is because I have not gone
far enough."

When the so-called honest people meet me they tell me, "Have
you seen how happy the dishonest people are becoming in this
world?" I call such people so-called honest people because they cannot remain honest for long, since they see happiness in dishonesty.
They cannot be honest from the depths of their hearts, and if they
appear honest it is out of fear. To be dishonest requires courage and
daring. They are weak and cowardly; they dare not practice dishonesty or treachery. But their belief that the treacherous are becoming
happy and prosperous reveals the truth – the voice of their desires is
warning them that they are making a mistake in being honest.

From within also, nature urges you to go down and down. Why? – because in descending you become more and more a part of nature. By the same token, as you rise higher and higher you go beyond nature. It is easy for nature to persuade you to descend still further because there is much rest there, and if you become like a stone there is complete rest. "Go down, leave aside your consciousness," say your desires and passions. "Give up consciousness; it is the cause of your unhappiness, so remain in a trance – in unconsciousness." That is why man takes to drink, to intoxicating drugs and a thousand other such tricks – so that he can descend easily and remain as if in a trance. There is a whole system of arrangements to help you to descend, but there is none to help you go up. And there is no bliss, no peace, without rising upwards.

This is the human dilemma, this is man's turmoil – the duel he has to fight, with all kinds of means and ways to descend but no ways set out to help him upwards. And no purpose is served without going up; without the upward journey nothing is achieved but wandering. In such helplessness, a prayer comes forth from within. When man realizes the helplessness in his condition, he prays to God. So the sage prays, "O God, lead me to the righteous path."

This does not mean that some God will take you to that path; this sort of interpretation has created many false beliefs. No God will help you. You yourself will have to go to that path; but this prayer will give you strength, will encourage you, to go on. If this prayer becomes firm and concentrated in you, if it becomes a thirst, a cry from every fiber of your being, if it becomes your breath itself crying, "O God, O fire, take me where everything vanishes and only that remains which is not I, and which was there and which will be there when I am not!" then the prayer will break open a door within you. It will be the means to take you to the righteous path, because where we deeply yearn to go, we go. Our very thoughts become our actions.

Eddington has written a very wonderful sentence, the more so because it is written by a person like Eddington. He is a Nobel prize winner, and one of the best scientists of the last fifty years.

During the last days of his life he wrote in his memoirs: "I began scientific research in my youth. Then I thought of the world, the universe, as a collection of things. But going deeper and deeper in my research work and experiencing the mysteries of nature, I have come to realize that the universe resembles more a thought than a thing. This is my last will and testimony to the world."

The same statement is the first sentence of Buddha in the Dhammapada. "You will be that which you think, so give proper consideration and reflection to your thoughts, because you cannot hold anyone else responsible for your actions; what you do today is the result of what you thought yesterday." Our own follies and mistaken notions become solid and turn into actions. Our own thoughts solidify and dictate our life. A minute wave of thought, having arisen, starts on its journey, and if not today, then tomorrow, becomes a solid thing.

All things are really condensed thoughts. What we are is the result of our thoughts. So if any prayer becomes so concentrated that it thrills every particle of your life, stirs your heart to throbbing, affects your dreams in the night, envelops your daydreams, infiltrates your sleep and becomes the obsession of your life, then the prayer is answered. No God will come to help you; but the prayer offered to the divine, wherever it is seen by us, creates in us the thrill.

This distinction should be understood properly. If you think, "My life will now be carefree. I have prayed to God, now he will look after me," then you are mistaken. Many people think like this. They think, "We have acknowledged God sufficiently by offering our prayers; we have obliged him sufficiently, now it is his duty to see that our prayers are answered." And if God fails to respond they complain against him and declare, "There is no God, it is all hocus-pocus."

No, prayer does not mean shifting our responsibility onto another. Prayer is a kind of device by which we bring a thrill into our entire life, we thrill every particle of our body. And remember, it is the device which can enter deepest of all into our hearts and bodies. If anyone becomes fully absorbed in prayer, with all his heart, then every particle of his body becomes active.

No thought goes as deep as prayer, no desire goes as deep as prayer, provided only that one has the capacity to really pray. There is not a single desire from which you cannot be freed. You can be free even from sex, which is considered the most enduring of the desires. You are not totally absorbed even in that, you are detached even from that. Some hidden portion of consciousness remains out of it. At the most it is the body that is absorbed in sexual activity; only a very small portion of the mind of a sexually-aroused person enters the action, but consciousness and the soul remain absolutely out of it. You cannot be total in sex, and that is the cause of the trouble and frustration in sexual desire. The lustful mind says, "I will sink into it totally and will derive complete pleasure from it." But it is never able to sink totally. It always finds itself *as if* sunk completely, but in fact is not able to do so – it goes to a certain limit and then returns. No sooner does it reach the moment of sinking than the moment of bursting brings it back up.

Prayer is the only happening in which man sinks totally, in which nothing is left outside. The prayer becomes total when nothing of the person offering the prayer is left outside. While praying, if you are not totally in it then it becomes a superficial act. It will not affect you, you will remain untouched. But prayer can be so profound – it becomes so – that the person offering it is lost and only the prayer remains. Then, lost in the current of total prayer, the thing happens, and the journey to the righteous path begins. The whole orientation changes. The face makes a one-hundred-and-eighty-degree turn from the downward journey towards the upward one.

This is why the sages pray to fire – it is a rising phenomenon, it burns impurities, it has no ego, and it is absorbed very soon into the sky. When someone is totally in prayer, is one with it, he becomes a flame in which there is no smoke. The smoke is there before someone begins to really pray. There is no immediate fire. There is a lot of smoke in the beginning because our fuel is very wet. In fact the fuel is as wet as our desires are many. It is like the billows of smoke that rise when we set fire to wet fuel. Do not be afraid of this. The person setting out on the journey of prayer does not witness the fire at first; he sees only thick smoke in the beginning, because we have a lot of wet fuel with us. This is why the sage has asked the fire to burn his past actions also – because these actions are the fuel that is so wet.

When is an action dry and when is it wet? Which action can be considered wet and which can be considered dry? If the action is dry the upward journey is easy, because a dry action is good fuel; and if it is wet the upward journey becomes arduous, because the fuel does not burn but produces a lot of smoke. When you remain completely detached from an action while doing it, then the action is dry. That action is wet with which you remain linked while doing it, and even after doing it. If you can be a witness while doing an action, then that action becomes dry. If you are unable to be a witness to an action while doing it, but become its doer, that action will be wet. If, while performing an action, you are full of ego and say, "I am doing it," then that action becomes wet. If instead you say, "God induces me to do this, nature gets it done through me, I am simply witnessing it," and of course if you not only say it but realize it and live in this spirit also, then that action becomes dry. And the flame of life of those who have the fuel of dry actions immediately jumps into the Brahman – the eternal spirit. But those who have the fuel of wet actions are in difficulty.

The sage knows that for all of us, most of our actions are wet. So try to make your actions dry, because prayer alone, without dry actions, will achieve nothing. Tear your ego away from actions of the past and don't let your present and future actions be bound to ego. But always bear this in mind, that no one will come to fulfill your prayer; you will be transformed only by your own prayer. Prayer is transformation. Transformation does not follow prayer, it happens in the prayer itself. So do not expect its fruit to come in the future, because the prayer itself is the fruit; and forget it quietly after you have prayed, because it is the fruit itself. It is a great achievement to pray in the right spirit. But we have mistaken notions, expecting someone else to fulfill our prayer, thinking that now we have prayed we have to wait for the fruit.

Like fire, prayer is an intensely living phenomenon. Prayer has three aspects which I shall explain to you so that you can grasp their significance correctly. The first is that when you offer a prayer you are saying goodbye to your ego; there can be no prayer if ego remains. When the sage says, "O fire, O God, show me the right path, I know nothing," he has said farewell to his ego. Prayer is the total acceptance of our humility. You cannot offer a prayer unless you become nothing.

So the first point is that to offer prayer is to demonstrate our acceptance of humility, our complete helplessness. "I declare that I am not able to do anything. I admit that whatever I did only took me downwards, whatever I did only entangled and perplexed me more. My actions have become my hell. The entanglement of my actions has become a burden, a stone weighing on my chest. I can no longer do anything. Now I pray, 'O God, now *you* are the doer, now lead me on.'" Let me repeat: this does not mean God will lead you – this very prayer will lead you. If it is done with a total heart, with utter sincerity, and if there is total egolessness, then it will surely lead you.

So the first sutra is: No ego.

The second sutra: We depend too much on ourselves.

A person once went to the saint Eckhart and said, "I am a self-made man!"

Eckhart heard him, looked at the sky with folded hands, and said, "O God, you are free of much responsibility. It is good that this man is self-made, because I was wondering how you manage to look after all the different types of people you are creating." Then, looking at the man again, he said, "Since you are self-made, you have obliged God greatly. At least God is saved from the guilt of being responsible for you."

We have great faith in ourselves. Most of us think we are self-made. This is like believing that we are our own fathers. Everyone thinks like this. All our behavior sets out to prove that we are our own fathers. The man who thinks he is his own father tries to pull himself up by his own shoelaces. We all behave in this way, and in doing so we only exhaust ourselves, break our shoelaces and injure ourselves.

No one is able to raise himself. To give up depending on ourselves is prayer. So give up this vain belief that, "I will raise myself up." Give up this confidence that, "I will make my own way and reach the destination of my journey myself." I repeat, you will have to make the journey, no one else can do it for you. But the journey only begins when this confidence is given up. This so-called self-confidence is a hindrance. No sooner is it forsaken than your energy is liberated and becomes God-consecrated. You yourself become a god. There is no other fire which will lead you; only the fire within you is able to do it.

You have enough of divinity in you to begin the journey, but that divinity will be narrowed to the extent that you have an ego. Ego will not be able to find its way, it will find the doors closed. In spite of tremendous efforts that divinity will not be able to ascend, because ego is like a stone around your neck which will drown you in the river. But forsake this misplaced confidence in yourself and you will be able to cross the river.

Have you ever observed a wonderful happening that takes place in rivers? ...But we do not observe, we are blind. The living are drowned, but dead bodies know some secret of swimming, of floating on water, of not being drowned, that the living do not know. No river, not even great oceans, can drown a dead body; it at once comes up to the surface. What is the secret? A dead body does not know anything, it is simply a dead body, and that is the secret. If a living person behaves like a dead body, then sinking is impossible – you float. No God helps you float, you simply become weightless. You become light as soon as your stone of ego is removed. Then, even if someone tries to drown you, how can he do it? We are drowned by our own selves. Confidence in ourselves drowns us. Clinging to our egos drowns us. The thought, "I shall do everything," puts us on a journey to hell.

That is why these prayers are so wonderful. Bear in mind, I have my own difficulty when I say the prayer of the sage is wonderful, because I do not consider those prayers wonderful which you do in your homes, nor even those which you start doing after reading the Ishavasya. They are absolutely bogus. To sit before the sacrificial fire throwing offerings on the fire and singing religious songs – all this is nonsense if there is no transformation in you.

Transformation is the real test.

If a person performs religious sacrifices for forty years, for his whole life, and there is no transformation in him, then in fact no sacrifice has been performed. If a person visits a temple or a mosque every day and yet there is no transformation in him, he stays where he was – then he has never entered a temple or a mosque. The temple may have been damaged a bit by his visits, but no damage is done to him, no transformation has taken place in him. He is where he was. The mosque might be afraid of him, thinking, "This man has been troubling me for the last forty years, but he himself is not troubled at all." No, it is not prayer at all. That visit to the temple is only a gesture.

I find the prayer of the sage full of meaning. It is very humble, very innocent, very natural: "O fire, lead me to the right path, because I know nothing about it, I am ignorant." If you can say with all sincerity, "O sky, lead me to the formless, because I do not know anything," you will all of a sudden find that the road is open for you. The path of knowledge opens for anyone who says, "I do not know." Such a person has taken the first step towards true knowledge. And one who says, "I know, I am a learned man," seals even the few holes which might allow him entry into the inner temple.

Prayer is the acceptance not only of ignorance but also of helplessness. No shore, no boat is seen, only the boundless ocean is visible, and its depth is fathomless. Our courage fails us. We close our eyes and imagine, think we are in a boat, but really all boats are paper boats. Such is our condition – absolutely helpless.

In a true prayer there is an acceptance of helplessness as well as of ignorance. And one who declares, "I am helpless," finds the remedy, the solution. This very declaration of helplessness is the solution. This total acceptance of helplessness is in itself our greatest and only help. The man who surrenders himself meets God. The man who says, "From now on I will walk if you bid me walk, I will rise if you raise me, I will follow you wherever you go" – this man sees his doors opening within, because he has communicated with the infinite so innocently and with such unconditional surrender that he finds himself before God.

These prayers are the keys to open the door. These short prayers are very deep in meaning and carry us very far. Keep this prayer in mind while performing your daily routine, and whenever you get an opportunity, remind yourself, "I do not know anything, I am helpless. O God, lead me." Again I emphasize the fact that no one else will come to lead you to the right path. This prayer itself will take you. In praying thus, you will be able to lead yourself. Prayer is a power, a very great power.

There is tremendous energy hidden in a small atom, but the energy hidden in these small prayers is many times more powerful than that in an infinite numbers of atoms. Pray and see; test it! The result is immediate. You will be light in no time. You will grow wings and be ready to fly high.

The burden vanishes as our heavily laden ego falls away. But we are so clever that we even fill up the prayer with our ego. Look at the person coming out of the temple after offering prayers. He looks around in pride, as if to announce to the sinners all around him his own piety at having offered prayers in the temple.

Once Mohammed asked a young man to go with him to pray. The young man could not avoid it, because Mohammed had asked him – just as you cannot avoid something if I ask you to do it! In the morning he went with Mohammed. Mohammed stood there and prayed, and the young man also stood and began to murmur something. He could only murmur.

Mohammed became very uneasy and thought, "I made a mistake in bringing this man here." But now there was no way out of it. After praying, they left. It was morning and people were still in their beds.

The young man said to Mohammed, "Sir, what will happen to these people? Though this is the time for prayer they are still in their beds. What do you think of them? Will they go to hell?"

Mohammed replied, "I do not know where they will go, but I shall have to go back to the mosque."

The man asked, "What has happened to you?"

Mohammed said, "My first prayer has become useless – I have harmed you. Before offering prayers this morning at least you were humble; you did not consider these people sinful. This is another harm done. Please pardon me, and do not come to the mosque again. Now I must go back again to pray, because now my first prayer is useless. I have harmed you by bringing you to the mosque because now you have become more egoistic and vain. The ego should be shattered by prayers, but yours has become stronger!"

Have you seen how proudly a man walks with a saffron mark and sandal paste on his forehead? He behaves as if God has given him a special license. Such people think they are God's relatives, God's family, God's chosen ones. Now they will not rest content until they have condemned the whole world to hell. Man must be considered a very strange animal when he can become full of ego even through prayer. There is no limit to his cunningness.

The essential quality of prayer is the abandonment, the death of the ego. A truly religious person cannot even say, "I am a religious person." He is so aware of his unrighteousness that he will say rather, "Who is more irreligious than I?" He will not be able to declare himself a virtuous person because he will see a streak of sin in virtue; he will see the ego in saying so. Therefore the sage says, "I do not know how many sins I have committed to burden me in my progress. I am utterly unfit, I cannot claim the right to reach the goal. I can simply pray."

So remember this sutra too, that prayer is not a claim. It is not an announcement of entitlement but an acceptance of unfitness. If you feel a little that, "I am a true claimant," then your prayer becomes polluted and poisonous. A person offering prayer finds something when he prays, "O God, it is your grace, I am not fit for it." Hence people coined the term 'God's grace'. It is divine grace. They say, "When were we ever fit? It is difficult to find people more unfit than us."

And yet I repeat, you achieve through your fitness – and not through your unfitness. But the awareness of your unfitness is the fitting prayer. The awareness of being nothing is the claim of prayer. To claim nothing is the essence of prayer. Prayer sends the fruit, but if it does not come we will say, "We were not fit to receive it"; if it comes we will say, "It is by his grace." Yet it is not achieved by his grace because he is equally graceful to all! If it is attained by his grace, it means that nepotism is prevalent here also.

A person goes to a temple, rings the bell and prays, "O God, you are the purifier of the sinful, you are the almighty," with an intention that God will be pleased and will fulfill his desires. This is just like a person who gets what he desires by praying before a king and pleasing him. That is why all our prayers are worded in courtly language. Such royal prayer is all flattery. The other word for flattery in Sanskrit is *stuti* – prayer!

No, you have not to say, "God is great." That is just flattery. "I am nothing" – this statement is enough. Not: "You are great. How can I – a humble person – propound on your greatness? How much greatness is there in my use of the word great? How can I measure you? How can I calculate your greatness? No, I can have no yardstick by which to measure your greatness. It is enough for me to measure my own humbleness. It is enough if I am able to say in my prayer, 'I am nothing.'"

I want to tell you again that nothing is obtained by his grace, and yet when someone achieves, he knows it is God's grace. Whenever someone has achieved the ultimate he has danced in ecstasy and declared most sincerely before the world that he has achieved through God's grace. And yet nobody gets anything through his grace, because you can only show grace and favor if you can also show disfavor. But his grace is perpetual, it is continuously raining.

Buddha used to say, "Nectar is raining, but some people keep their pitchers upside-down." It is not that nectar will begin to shower on the day when you turn your pitcher upright. It was raining even when you had your pitcher upside-down, it was pouring even when there was no pitcher at all. There will be no special grace filling your pitcher when you keep it the right way up. Nectar is continuously raining: to show grace is his nature – the nectar of existence is his nature.

It is continuously raining, but we have kept our buckets upside-down. Ego keeps its bucket upside-down and at the same time tries to fill it. To keep the bucket upright means to admit, "I am nothing." When the bucket is upright, its emptiness becomes manifest. What else can it manifest? When it is upside-down, its emptiness is concealed. An upside-down bucket creates an illusion of being full, because emptiness is not seen, it is suppressed. That is why we keep it upside-down. By being upright, the bucket comes to know that it is nothing but empty. There is an opening which can be filled with something.

A man's bucket turns the right way up when he knows that he is nothing, and when he keeps it upright he enters prayer. God's grace is raining and it will fill his bucket, and when it is full the man will say, "It is his grace."

If you do not keep your bucket upright, he cannot show his grace. It is by your grace that you keep it upright. To show grace to oneself is prayer. To have compassion on oneself is prayer. To be cruel to oneself is ego. To commit tyranny against oneself is ego. To commit violence against oneself is ego.

This is enough for the morning session. Now let us disperse. And kindly keep your buckets upright!

# Existence
# Is One

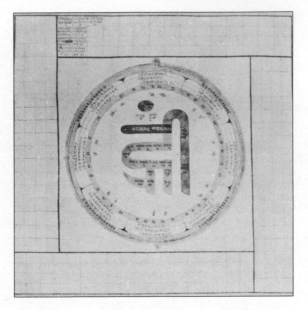

20

*Om.*
*That is perfect, and this also is perfect.*
*For only the perfect is born out of the perfect;*
*and when the perfect*
*is taken from the perfect,*
*behold, the remainder is perfect.*
*Om. Peace, peace, peace.*

IT IS THE ETERNAL LAW of existence that the end is to be found in the beginning. The end is where the beginning is. In accordance with this eternal law, the Ishavasya ends in the sutra where it began. There is no other alternative but this. All journeys are circular – the first step is also the last step.

Those who understand this law – that the first step is also the last – are saved from the useless turmoil and conflict of emotions of the mind; they are saved from those futile worries and anxieties of life. We attain to the place from where we began. The first station of our journey is also the last. Therefore we can travel in between very joyfully, because there is no other way. We will never arrive at a place where we were not. No matter how great the efforts we may make, we cannot reach where we were not.

Let us understand it in this way: we can only be what we already are. There is no other alternative. What is hidden in us will be revealed, and that which is revealed will again be concealed. The seed will grow into the tree, and the tree will again become seeds. This is the eternal law of life. The anxieties and worries of those who grasp this law vanish completely. Their threefold mental agonies become calm and silenced. Then there remains no cause for happiness – there is no cause to be unhappy when we are traveling to our destination, and there is no cause to be happy because we do not get anything at all which was not with us from the start. To give an indication, a hint, of this great law, the Ishavasya ends with that sutra from which it began.

The journeys we have made in between these two ends are various separate doors to enable us to understand this sutra, to arrive at this sutra. Each sutra was a hint to stir our remembering of that great ocean, and each shore and each holy place an invitation, a call, to set our ship sailing. If you had kept this sutra in mind, you might have observed that this sutra was hidden deep in the meaning of all the sutras. That is why it was announced in the beginning and now announces the end. I told you its meaning on the very first day. Today I shall explain its inner meaning – its essence.

You may ask, "What is the difference between meaning and essence?" Meaning is an apparent, manifest, thing, while essence is a hidden one. Meaning is the outer body, essence is the inner soul. The meaning can also be understood by the intellect, but the essence can only be grasped by the heart. Generally, the meaning is explained in the beginning and not the essence. And now, at this stage, we have looked through many doors into the temple for which this sutra is meant. Not only have we come to understand it intellectually, but we have tried to grasp its meaning by going into meditation also.

This is a unique happening. Many commentaries have been made on this Upanishad, but this is the first occasion on this earth when the commentary was accompanied by meditation. So a deep search of its manifest meaning and of its inner meaning was made simultaneously. The words of the Upanishad have been explained before, but this is the first occasion on which an active effort has been made to jump into its inner meaning – its soul. Whatever I have been telling you was with the purpose of making a diving board for you: the purpose was the jumping. This is why we entered into meditation at the end of each sutra, so that you might experience its significance by taking a jump into it.

So now I can tell you its inner meaning. You have not yet considered the meaning of these words enough; but you have done something else – you have reached silence, calm. Those who understand the words are able to know the meaning, but only those who know silence are able to know its inner meaning, its essence. If you have achieved even a little taste of silence, you will be able to understand the inner meaning into which I am about to enter.

The first thing I shall tell you about the inner meaning of this sutra is that it has declared that life is illogical. This is not said anywhere in so many words in this sutra, there is only a hint about it. Now I shall tell you what is unsaid, what is only hinted at. Wittgenstein has written a book, Tractatus, which is perhaps the most important book of this century. In it he said, "That which cannot be said must not be said: it should be left unsaid." He says further, "That which cannot be said can be shown." His meaning is that a hint, an indication, can be given towards that which cannot be said. That which cannot be said and which should not be said is the inner meaning of this sutra. What I am doing now is only giving you some indications towards it.

The first indication: Life is irrational, so those who try to seek out what life is will be wandering around death. Such people can never discover the secret of life. How do you get an indication of the irrational from this sutra? It says, "The perfect is taken from the perfect." The first irrationality is in the question, "How can the perfect emerge from the perfect?" Since there is no extra space outside the perfect, where can the perfect go?" *Purna* means the absolute, beyond which there is nothing else at all; if there is anything else, then the perfect will be that much imperfect. There is never anything outside the perfect, not even space, so how can anything come out of the perfect? And suppose it does come out, where will it go? There is no way out. But this sutra affirms that the perfect is taken from the perfect.

Not only this, but it adds another irrationality: "After the perfect is taken from the perfect, the remainder is perfect." If anyone looks at this statement from a logical point of view, he will declare it to be the statement of a madman. And if someone examines it from a mathematical point of view, it will be found totally incorrect. He will think it is written by someone who is not in his senses. This will be the opinion of anyone who examines it from the logical or mathematical points of view. But those who examine and think in this way will make the mistake which was once made in a garden.

A certain gardener invited his friend to see the beautiful roses which had flowered in his garden. His friend was a goldsmith, and he went there with his touchstone. On seeing the roses he said to his friend, "I do not believe your statement simply by seeing the roses. You cannot deceive me, I am not a child. I test gold, so to test roses is child's play. I shall test them."

The gardener asked, "How will you test the flowers?"

His friend replied, "I have brought my touchstone with me."

The gardener became nervous and thought, "I made a mistake in inviting this man!"

But by this time the goldsmith had plucked a flower and tested it by rubbing it on the touchstone. He threw the flower on the ground and said, "The touchstone has shown that there is nothing in this flower; it is fake."

The sage of this sutra will feel the same as the gardener must have felt if someone tries to understand this sutra from the logical point of view. Flowers are not tested on the touchstone for gold, and if someone tries to do so, the flowers are not at fault; it merely shows the man's foolishness. Of all the sutras of the Ishavasya, this especially has the flavor of self-realization. This cannot be tested by the touchstone of logic, and it is fully implied in the sutra that it should not be so tested. It is telling us that it is going to say something which is irrational, which is beyond logic, which cannot happen and yet happens, which should not happen and yet happens, which has no basis for its happening, which has no way of being proved – and yet it happens, and yet it is!

Life is irrational: what does this statement mean? It means that those who try to find out the meaning, the secret of life from the point of view of mathematics, logic, justice, conventions, rules and regulations, will remain without knowing it.

The goldsmith tested the flower on a touchstone. If you take that flower to a science laboratory and say, "This is a very beautiful flower," then the scientist too will dissect its every part and say, "Where is the beauty here?" He will extract its elements one by one and scatter them. Each chemical will be separated and then he will ask, "Where is the beauty?" It has juice, minerals, chemicals, and all such things, but there is no beauty in it anywhere. If beauty is not found in the laboratory of a scientist, it is not the fault of the flower; nor is it the fault of the scientist, because his laboratory is not there to discover beauty. The dimension in which beauty may be sought and measured is altogether different.

So those who think about life from a mathematical point of view can never measure it, because life is basically a secret. All our knowledge, however great it may be, is founded in ignorance; it simply hints at what remains to be known. And as we come to know more and more, we realize the depth of our ignorance. We are not able to unfold life, and if we try, we become more and more entangled.

All our efforts to unfold it are like those in a story by Aesop which I have heard. It tells how a centipede was walking along a road. A rabbit saw it and was much perplexed. The rabbit may perhaps have been instructed in a school of logic. Its perplexity was this: which of its hundred feet did the centipede raise first? And which second? Which third? and so forth. How could it remember the order of its one hundred feet? Would it not stumble while walking? It must surely be confused.

The rabbit asked the centipede to stop and answer its question. It said, "I am a student of logic and I am in great perplexity watching you. We walk on four feet so it is easy to remember the order of raising them while walking. But how do you remember the order of your one hundred feet?"

The centipede replied, "I have been walking very easily up to now; I have never found it necessary to remember the order, and I have never thought that way up to now. But as you now ask me, I shall think about it and solve your problem."

The rabbit sat there watching. The centipede tried to raise its feet but staggered and fell down. It was now in difficulty. With a sorrowful heart it said to the rabbit, "Friend, your logic has put me in great difficulty. Please keep your logic to yourself, and do not ask your question to any other centipede which happens to pass you on the road. We live in great comfort and happiness. Our feet have never given us any difficulty – they never raised this question and never argued about it. We have never thought about which foot is lifted first and which second. We do not know. This much is certain: up to now I have been able to walk. Only now, because of you, do I find myself in difficulty!"

Man's greatest dilemma is that he is in the predicament of that centipede. Man does not need a rabbit to ask the question; he raises the question himself and creates doubt and gets himself entangled. He asks himself the questions and provides his own answers. The questions are definitely wrong, so the answers become even more incorrect and misleading. Each answer gives rise to a new question. These questions and answers multiply, a great mess is created, and man becomes more and more perplexed until a moment comes when he is so perplexed that he does not know what is what. All of us are in this predicament.

Someone said to Saint Augustine, "I am much troubled by one question, and it would put my mind at rest if you would kindly answer it for me. I have heard you are a learned person."

Saint Augustine said, "You might have heard that, but now that you tell me, I am in difficulty."

The man said, "What difficulty can you be in? Difficulties are for ignorant people like me."

Then Saint Augustine explained, "I am in difficulty ever since I first heard that I am a learned person, because now I am trying to find out where this knowledge is within me but I am having no success in finding it. In error, in ignorance, I believed in it in the beginning. But now it is difficult for me to believe so. And yet, let me know your question. You have come a great distance, so ask your question. Even if I am unable to answer it, you will at least be relieved that the question has been asked. In case I am able to answer your question though, do you think questions are correctly answered by someone giving answers? But ask your question."

The man asked, "What is time?"

Saint Augustine said, "You have asked the question I was afraid you might ask. There are certain questions to which we assume we know the answers, but when they are asked, we are lost for an answer. I definitely know what time is, but when you ask the question I am in difficulty."

Until somebody asks you this question, you know what time is very well. You catch the train in time, you catch the bus in time, you go to the office in time and return home in time. So you know very well what time is. But no sooner does someone ask you the question than you are in the predicament of the centipede. You know dates, you have watches, calendars are hanging on the wall, and yet no one so far has been able to give a correct answer to that question. And the answers that have been given are like groping in the dark – nothing is established.

If someone asks you, "What is the soul?" you cannot answer, because as yet you do not know, even though it has been with you from the day you were born. Not only that, those who know say it was there before you were born. There is no difficulty about it as long as no one asks about it.

If someone asks, "What is love?" then the same difficulty arises. Everybody makes love, and even if they do not make love, they act as if they do. What a great number of love-stories there are! All stories are love-stories, and they are about love because man has not yet been able to make real love so he deceives his mind by writing stories about it. All poems are love-poems, and the person who has no love in his life begins to write love-poems. To write a poem is very easy, to make love is very arduous. Poems can be composed by rhyming lines, but love can only be made by tearing out all the lines. Poems have their own meters and rules, love is totally without meters or rules. Poems can be learned and can be composed. There is no way, no trick, to either learn or to make love. We constantly talk about love, and yet if someone asks us, "What is love?" then we are perplexed.

G. E. Moore is a great thinker, perhaps the greatest of this century. By his logical thinking he has made the greatest impression on man's mind during the past fifty years. He has written a book called Principia Ethica – principles of ethics. He has taken great pains in writing this book, working diligently on just one question: What is good? And he has labored so hard to prepare this monumental work that I don't think anyone else in the history of mankind has ever worked so hard on one book. It was prepared after the hard labor of years in which every word was weighed and written after a great deal of thinking. This logician of Oxford university, this greatest thinker, in his final conclusion has said that good is indefinable. In the end, he says that to define good is like defining the color yellow.

If someone asks me, "What is yellow?" what shall I say? I can only say, "Yellow is yellow." What else can I say? But is this its definition? Everyone knows that the color yellow is yellow. What would you do? You might pluck a yellow flower and show it, saying, "This is yellow – this is a yellow flower." But Moore objects and says, it is not the color yellow." It is like a yellow-painted wall. A yellow wall is not the color yellow. There is a yellow piece of cloth – but it is a yellow-painted piece of cloth, it is not the color yellow. Our question is, "What is this yellowness which is seen in a yellow flower, a yellow wall or a yellow piece of cloth?" Now what would you say? You might say, "Here it is, don't babble further." Moore also says this. After doing so much hard work on this subject, he says, "At the most we can say that this is yellowness." We can give an indication, a hint only; we cannot give its definition. When you cannot define the color yellow, would you dare to define God? If someone goes to Moore and asks...but the poor fellow is no more now! If he were alive, I think I would ask him – or if I happen to meet him in another life I shall ask him, "Can God be defined when you are not even able to define what the color yellow is?"

Even the most insignificant facts of life are indefinable; so when I say life is irrational, I mean it is indefinable. You can live life, but you cannot define it, and if you ever try to define it you will make the same mistake made by the sage of this sutra. He says, "The perfect comes out of the perfect, and the remainder is perfect."

This is a sort of a puzzle, a koan like those which the Zen master Rinzai used to create. These masters took great pleasure in devising koans, because hints could be given through them. When someone went to them in search of truth, they would say, "Look for that afterwards – right now I am in a bit of difficulty, and would like you to solve my problem first."

The seeker would ask, "What is your problem?" The man who has come in search of truth forgets that, "I myself have come in search of truth, how can I solve another's problem?"

When Rinzai said, "Ask your question afterwards, solve my problem first," the man would at once ask, "What is your problem?"

The person who comes to be a pupil tries to be the teacher. He forgets he has come to learn. He should say, "I have come to learn from you. How can I solve your problem? I am in difficulty myself."

But Rinzai has written, "I have played this trick with thousands of people and every time the person said, 'What is your problem? Tell me.'"

Rinzai created such problems as cannot be solved. In actual fact problems are such that they cannot be solved. No problem will be solved, because it is not manmade. It is existential, it is there in existence. If it is manmade we can solve it. Riddles are manmade so we can solve them. Children's arithmetic books have questions on one side of the page and answers on the other. No such trick is possible in life. We cannot turn a page in life to find the answer to one of life's problems. No copy of anybody's life can be useful. Who would you imitate? And how? There is absolutely no way to turn the page of life and find the answers to your problems. There are problems only, no answers at all.

Rinzai kept one particular problem ready. He used to say, "Listen, if you solve my problem, I will solve yours." The questioner felt pleased that there was a person who would solve his problem, provided he solved the other's first. Rinzai would say, "My difficulty is that I kept a goose's egg in a bottle. The young one hatched out of the egg and began to grow. I used to feed it through the mouth of the bottle. Now I want to get it out, but it has grown so much that the neck of the bottle is too narrow for it; but I do not want to break the bottle as it is very valuable. Now show me the way. The goose is trapped in the bottle, and the neck of the bottle is too narrow for it to come out. So don't say, 'Bring it out through the mouth of the bottle.' We have already tried that. If it remains there any longer it is sure to die – and you will be responsible for that!"

On hearing this most of the questioners used to become very nervous. They would say, "This is not possible. What are you telling us?" But in the event that a person said, "I shall try, I am thinking of a way out," then Rinzai would say, "Go to the adjoining room and meditate upon it. Don't take much time, because the goose's life is in danger. Meditate quickly and deeply because the goose may die at any moment." There was another exit to that adjoining room, and when Rinzai opened the door after half an hour, he always found that the questioner had run away. Then Rinzai would return and tell his friends, "The bottle is empty, the goose is out!"

Only once he got a reply from a man, but that man had not come to ask anything of Rinzai. One morning he came and sat near Rinzai. Rinzai said, "Do you want to ask me anything?"

The man replied, "Do you want to show me anything? I do not want to ask anything. If someone is eager to show something, let him show it!"

Rinzai was taken aback by the reply and thought, "This man is dangerous. He will either kill the goose or break the bottle!" But now there was no way out. Because it had become a longstanding practice, Rinzai could not help asking the man his riddle. He said,

"No, I have nothing to show. In fact, I myself am in difficulty."
The stranger asked Rinzai to tell him his difficulty. So Rinzai told
him. When he had finished, the man got up and caught hold of
Rinzai by the neck. Rinzai protested, "The goose is not within me,
it is in the bottle."

But the man said, "I am just bringing the goose out," and asked
Rinzai to say, "The goose is out of the bottle!"

Rinzai said, "Yes, it is out!"

Life is not a riddle, and those who try to make it so get into difficulty. Life is not a problem; those who make it a problem have to
seek its answer, and all the answers only puzzle them more and
more. Life is an open mystery – absolutely open in front of our
eyes and all around us. It is not hidden anywhere, it is not behind
any curtain, and yet it is a mystery.

There is a difference between a mystery and a riddle. A riddle
means that which is not open but can be opened. The mystery
means that which is already open and is still not open; that which,
though open, is still so profound that in spite of your innumerable
lives' journeys you will find that there is always something which
remains to be known. "The whole comes out of the whole, and yet
the whole remains, and when the whole is absorbed in the whole, it
remains as much as it was before." This sutra hints at the fact that
he who agrees with it can enter the mystery. And he who disagrees
with it, says it is not possible, will remain outside the door. He
cannot enter. Life is a mystery; it is beyond logic and rationality.

Rules of logic have been established by man's intellect. They are
not written anywhere in nature. Nature does not supply the rules
of logic. They are manmade and temporary, though we forget that
they are so. All our rules are like this, like the rules of games. For
example, in a game of chess there are knights and castles and so
on. There are rules governing their moves, and the players play the
game with great seriousness. The fact is, people do not seem as
serious in life as they do when they are playing chess. If a quarrel
arises between the players, there are occasions when they will fight

each other, swords in hand. The chessmen are all made of wood, yet players forget and behave like children. There is actually no knight, no castle, no king; the whole game is a make-believe!

All the rules of logic in life are like the rules of chess – they are all make-believe. There are no rules which have been given by nature or life. All have been thrust upon us by ourselves. Our rules are like traffic laws. In India people keep to the left, in America they keep to the right. If you break this law either in India or in America you will be taken to a police station. People are very strange. But one thing is certain: you have to drive either on the left or on the right, otherwise there will be chaos on the road. And in driving on the left, gradually we begin to think that there is some ultimate, some fundamental principle in it. There is nothing of the sort. It is merely a manmade arrangement.

All our rules of logic are devices, necessary to regulate our lives; but by and by we become so trapped by them that we try to apply them to the whole mystery of life. We try to ensure that our life follows them. A person becomes crazy when he makes his life follow his own rules. This is the main characteristic of a madman. I call a man healthy when he conducts himself according to the mystery of life, and I call a man mad when he tries to thrust his own rules upon his life. That is when the difficulty enters his life; and we have piled the rules up around our lives.

It will be easy to understand this sutra if we understand one or two rules of logic. One of the basic rules of logic is that A is A and cannot be B. It is okay, absolutely right, but there is nothing in life which will not change into something different. There is nothing in life which will not change into its opposite. Everything in life is fluid, all things change. Night changes into day and day into night. Childhood changes into youth and youth changes into old age. Life changes into death. Sometimes poison changes into nectar. All medicines are poison, but they are nectar for the sick. There is fluidity in life, but rigidity in rules because they are not living.

There are so many people sitting in this hall. Suppose I leave, return after an hour, and I expect you to be sitting in the same places and in the same positions in which I left you; then either I am crazy or you are. If I find you as you were when I left, then *you* are! There would certainly be some change, otherwise dead bodies must be sitting here. Living people would certainly have changed places and positions.

A dilemma rather like this situation once occurred in a certain town. One logician – and it is difficult to keep account of the dilemmas of logicians – went to a barber's shop early in the morning for his haircut. He got his hair cut. The charge was fifty paise, and the logician gave the barber one rupee. Having no change, the barber requested him to come back the next day for his change. "How can I be sure that this man will not change his premises or his profession before tomorrow?" thought the logician.

Generally logicians demand proofs. He argued with himself, "Suppose this man changes his business tomorrow? Suppose he closes his barber's shop, and opens a sweet shop instead? People will laugh at me if I say this man cut my hair. They will say, 'But he is a sweet seller!' So I have to devise some trick so that he cannot fool me."

He thought long, then he saw a buffalo sitting opposite the barber's shop. He thought, "This is perfect! It is very difficult to move a buffalo. It is a calm and settled animal – just like the rules of logic! It sits resolutely on the road, ignoring all the traffic rules. The barber could never persuade it to move. How could a barber persuade it when even a logician would fail to do so?"

He went away, having established positively that the buffalo was sitting opposite the shop. The next day he came back and saw the buffalo sitting there. Looking opposite, he saw that the mischief he had suspected was already done. There opposite the buffalo was a sweet shop. He ran in, grabbed the sweet seller by the neck and said, "I had already suspected this yesterday, so I devised a plan to confound your trickery. This is too much! You have changed your whole business to save a few paise!" The poor logician did not know that buffaloes do not follow the rules of logic.

It is not a fixed, stationary animal; during the night it had moved and sat opposite the sweet seller's shop.

Rules of logic are lifeless. Life is a living current, a flow. Those who value the rules of logic highly and try to live accordingly end up holding dead things in their hands, but those who break away from the network of logic and jump into life are able to know the mystery of life. That is why the sutra says to break all the nets of logic. I am telling you about the hint, the indication within this sutra, not about its actual words. I explained its meaning to you on the first day. This is its inner meaning. Break down all rules of logic, because if you follow them it will be difficult for you to enter life.

Plato was a very great logician who lived in Greece twenty-five hundred years ago. He should be called the father of logic. He had a very famous academy where he taught logic to his students. A wandering mystic named Diogenes once went to this academy. He was a mischievous and playful mystic; there have been very few people like him. Like Mahavira, he had even discarded his clothes. When he arrived Plato was conducting a class, explaining the principles of logic. Plato is known in our country as Afalatoon. Hence, if somebody harasses people with arguments and rules of logic he is taunted by the name of Afalatoon. Plato was such a renowned logician that if someone began to argue logically, even in a small village, people would say, "He is a big Afalatoon," even though they did not know who Afalatoon was.

Diogenes went to the academy where Plato was teaching. At that moment a student got up and asked Plato to define man. Plato said, "Man is a two-legged animal without feathers." Standing behind the teacher, Diogenes was listening, and he laughed loudly on hearing this definition. Plato looked around, and asked him, "Why are you laughing?"

He replied, "I am just going to find the answer to this definition." He went out, caught a chicken, a cock, and plucked all its feathers. He brought the cock into the class and said, "Here is your definition of man. It has no feathers, and has two legs." Then he asked Plato to come up with another definition, "And when you do, please let me know, and I will bring you another answer!"

It is said that Plato never offered another definition. He knew Diogenes was a troublesome man. He himself had seen how he plucked the chicken and brought it to him, and he thought, "Who knows what he will do next?" Diogenes went to the academy many times to find out if Plato had made another definition. At last Plato became nervous and said, "Friend, excuse me, I made a mistake in defining man in this way. How long are you going to harass me?"

Diogenes replied, "I wanted to hear you admit your mistake. Why talk about man? Even a piece of stone cannot be defined. Life is indefinable, no definition is possible of anything. I wanted you to admit your mistake. Now I will go away. I was bothered by your definition."

The rules of logic are fixed, while life is flowing. One wave changes into another wave. While you are defining a thing, something else is happening to it in the meantime. Before you finish calling a person angry, he has begun to ask your forgiveness. Then what will you do? The fact is that the anger may very well have disappeared before you finish saying that this man is angry – what lasts in this life? – so your definition will be incorrect.

Definitions are always of the past, while life is always of the present. Life is constantly changing, everything is changing every moment, but definitions remain fixed, remain established. There is no growth, no change in them. They are like our photographs. Suppose someone takes my photograph; now it will remain fixed and static, while I am becoming older every moment. Life is like a living person; definitions are rigid and lifeless. This sutra says there is no rationality, no logic, about life. Life is a mystery.

There was a Christian mystic called Tertullian. Someone asked him, "Why do you believe in God? What is the reason for your belief?"

He said, "You want to know the reason? When I looked into life, I found that there is no reason for anything. Then I thought, 'Now there is no harm in believing in God. When the whole of life itself is without reason, God can also be believed in without reason.' And if you don't believe in God and yet ask me the question, I will tell you, I believe in God because he is totally absurd" – he used the word absurd...I think it is the right word – "because I examined all the rules, analyzed them, and found them incorrect. I examined all logical reasoning and found it false. All the definitions I tested proved wrong. Whatever things I considered right intellectually, in the end proved to be wrong. Now I have abandoned the help of intellect and reasoning and becomes reasonless. I believe in God."

This is the true meaning of trust.

It means jumping into the unknown. This sutra explains what trust is. This sutra is on trust. Leaving aside all rules, all definitions and all calculations, to jump into the immeasurable is the meaning of trust. Giving up reasoning to jump into reasonlessness.

You should remember that philosophers are those who try to seek out the truth of life with the help of intellect. So far they have been unable to discover anything. They have written thousands of books, but their books are merely a play on words. They are adept in the interpretation of words and they spread their net of words cleverly and so widely that it becomes difficult to find the way out. But they know nothing, nothing at all. Those who know the truth of life are the mystics and the sages. These are the people who, rather than practicing verbal juggling, dive into existence.

Why should we try to learn from books what the Ganges is? When the Ganges is flowing, why should we not dive into it to know what it is? It may be written in books, in libraries, what the Ganges is, but should we resort to books to know what it is? Why should we not know it by actually entering it? There are two ways of knowing. If I want to know about love, I can go to a library and read books about it and learn all about it. The other way is for me to personally fall deeply into it. The first is definitely easier, so the weak resort to that path; even children can read about it. But to really know love is to pass through a great fire, through great penance, through the great ordeal by fire.

To know love and to know *about* love are two different things. There is no relation at all between them. Similarly, to know truth and to know about it are two different things. Whatever is known about truth is all borrowed knowledge, it is all stale. One who wants to know truth will have to take a jump away from his intellect.

A friend came to see me two days ago. He said, "I doubt whatever I hear. I doubt even what you say, and I shall continue to doubt what you will say. But I have some questions; please answer them."

I told him, "What will you do with the answers you get from me? Why do you want to trouble me uselessly when you are not prepared to move even a little from your position of doubting? You should live in your doubts. Why have you come to ask me? Don't ask anybody if you are determined to doubt, because whatever he says will be *his* knowledge, it cannot be yours, and you will doubt it. Existence is spread on all sides – flowers are blooming, birds are dancing, clouds are moving in the sky, the sun is rising, life is throbbing within you. Existence has endless expanse! Jump into it, know from there! It is futile to ask others – you are going to doubt anyway. But I want to ask you one thing: When will that day come when you will doubt your doubts?"

When one is determined to doubt, he should doubt the doubt itself; that way he can achieve something through his doubting. Did your doubting achieve anything up to now? If not, it is because you have not doubted the doubt itself. You have not doubted totally. Bear in mind, trust comes from two sources. Either do not doubt at all and take a jump, or make your doubting so deep that you doubt the doubt itself. Thus your doubt will cancel out further doubting and you will be empty of doubts, and out of the influence of the intellect. It is not that your intellect creates doubts; your intellect *is* your doubt.

After understanding this sutra, those who are innocent and straightforward should not doubt it; and those who are subtle and complex by nature should doubt it totally. Trust will be born from both these conditions and you will be able to take a jump.

Those who know what trust is will grasp the meaning of this sutra, and those whose trust is in reasoning will not be able to grasp its meaning, because reasoning has no place in it. Logic will not agree with the statement that the perfect comes out of the perfect, and the remainder is also perfect. But trust will agree with it, because it is very innocent and straightforward. It is a trust – a faith – in existence. It says, "Can I not have some faith in this existence which gave me the power of thinking, which gave me love, which gave me heart? Can I not give a bit of friendly trust to this existence which gave me life, awareness and consciousness? If I cannot, it is the ultimate ingratitude." This sutra demands trust and faith from us. It hints that only trust will open the door of life, trust alone will help you to reach the peak of life. This is its hidden meaning.

Finally you should fully understand what it is saying about the whole, at the end as well as at the beginning. Everything in life seems imperfect. Maybe the Ishavasya should have talked about imperfection, because then it would have been a talk on facts. No individual seems perfect, no love seems perfect; neither does any power nor any form seem perfect. Everything in life is imperfect. Then why did the sage of the Ishavasya think of starting and ending his discussions with the whole? Those who believe in realism will denounce this as unrealistic. They will criticize it as the fanciful make-believe of dreamers. Where is anything whole or perfect in this world? What the sutra hints at is the fact that wherever imperfection is seen by you, it is due to the imperfection of your capacity to see, because otherwise there is imperfection nowhere at all. In reality the imperfection is in our vision.

Our condition is like a person who looks at the sky from a window of his house. We all do it. Naturally he will find the sky cut in the shape of the window. The boundary of the window will also be that of the sky. Is it a mistake if a person who has never seen the open sky from outside his house says that the sky is rectangular in shape? No, there is no mistake, because it will always appear so if seen from a window. It would be difficult for such a person to conceive that there is no such frame on the sky.

The frame is on your window, there is no frame around the sky. It is given by you. The sky is absolutely frameless and formless. But nowhere does it seem formless, even when we go outside the house. The frame becomes a bit bigger, it assumes the form of the earth. The sky appears to encircle the whole earth, like a dome – the domes of temples are constructed on this model. Even outside in the open you are still standing inside the window – the earth is a window – so it does not make any difference. Proceed further, go around the whole earth. You will see that the sky does not touch the earth anywhere: there is no horizon, it is as false as the window frame around the sky. But even if you fly in a spacecraft you will see the sky from a particular viewpoint, and that will appear to be its boundary. No matter how extensive, it is still its boundary.

Then where can we go where we shall be able to see the formless? The sages of the Upanishads say, "There is only one place, and that is within you, where there is no window at all." Leave aside the use of all sense organs because they create frames. Our sense organs are the windows. If we look anywhere with the help of these windows, forms will be created. Close your eyes and go within; be without eyes, without ears, without hands and legs, without the body, and dive deeper and deeper within where everything is formless. There you will experience the whole.

Having experienced the whole within, the sage has affirmed that it is so, and that one who has known the whole will always see the whole, no matter where he goes, no matter what window he looks through. Even if he looks at the sky standing behind a very small window, he knows well that the frame is that of his window and not of the sky. Whoever has once seen the whole within will begin to see it everywhere. He may be surrounded by any number of windows, he may be shut in any number of prisons, yet he knows that the prisons are imposed from outside; the formless is still sitting within.

Therefore the sage begins and ends his talk with the whole. There will be no tuning, no resonance, between this sutra and ourselves if we stand with our backs to it. We and the sage of the Upanishad are standing back to back. We hear his words, commit them to memory, repeat them every morning; but if only our backs touch, then the meaning which we derive from them becomes useless.

The last thing I wish to tell you is that this whole is the only truth. It is on all sides; everything is whole. There is no question at all of the imperfect. How can the imperfect be? Who would create it? God alone is; there is no one else who can make imperfection. God alone is, so who would draw the boundary? Boundaries are always made by the presence of others. If you think the boundary of your house is made by your house, then you are mistaken. It is made by the neighbor's house. It is not made by your house on its own, it is always made by the presence of others.

God is always alone, existence is always one, the flow of existence is always one. There is no other at all. Who would make the boundary? Who would make the imperfect? No, it is impossible; existence is limitless, existence is absolute. But we will only know it when we are able to catch a glimpse of it within.

One who has tasted even a drop of the ocean within is able to know the mystery of boundless oceans. The whole comes out of the whole, and is absorbed in the whole also; and in between comes the imperfect which is created by the frames of our intellect, by our sense organs. Give up these frames, go a little beyond them. Then you will be established in the whole, and one who has been thus established in the whole will be able to understand the hidden meaning of the Ishavasya.

Now, at the end, let us start on our journey within. As it is the last day, I want to tell you two or three things. First, during this six-day experiment I have brought you to such a point that I now ask you to add one small thing to it. There will be a great explosion if that is added, so be prepared for it.

When you look at me, gaze fixedly, do not blink your eyes, and at the same time, with each out breath make the sound Hoo, Hoo! This sound of Hoo, Hoo will hit powerfully on your dormant kundalini. The Sufis have researched deeply into the sound Allah Hoo! They start with the sound Allah Hoo, then by and by the word Allah is dropped and only Hoo remains. Shout Hoo forcefully, and as you do so, your navel will contract. Let your Hoo strike powerfully below the navel. This will make your navel contract completely and strike against the kundalini. It is the place where the kundalini is. It will be hit hard.

Ninety percent of us are now in that condition when the sound Hoo will strike so hard that the energy within will start rising up like a flame of fire. When it rises up I shall make a sign to you with my hands. Then go crazy! When I lift my hands upwards you will experience the energy within rising – rising like a flame of fire. You will feel that all your life force is rising; you will feel transcendence. Then begin to shout loudly, to dance, to jump, with all your might.

# *About The Author*

Most of us live out our lives in the world of time, in memories of the past and anticipation of the future. Only rarely do we touch the timeless dimension of the present – in moments of sudden beauty, or sudden danger, in meeting with a lover or with the surprise of the unexpected. Very few people step out of the world of time and mind, its ambitions and competitiveness, and begin to live in the world of the timeless. And of those who do, only a few have attempted to share their experience. Lao Tzu, Gautam Buddha, Bodhidharma...or more recently, George Gurdjieff, Ramana Maharshi, J. Krishnamurti – they are thought by their contemporaries to be eccentrics or madmen; after their death they are called "philosophers." And in time they become legends – not flesh-and-blood human beings, but perhaps mythological representations of our collective wish to grow beyond the smallness and trivia, the meaninglessness of our everyday lives.

Osho is one who has discovered the door to living his life in the timeless dimension of the present – he has called himself a "true existentialist" – and he has devoted his life to provoking others to seek this same door, to step out of the world of past and future and discover for themselves the world of eternity.

Osho was born in Kuchwada, Madhya Pradesh, India, on December 11, 1931. From his earliest childhood, his was a rebellious and independent spirit, insisting on experiencing the truth for himself rather than acquiring knowledge and beliefs given by others.

After his enlightenment at the age of twenty-one, Osho completed his academic studies and spent several years teaching philosophy at the University of Jabalpur. Meanwhile, he traveled throughout India giving talks, challenging orthodox religious leaders in public debate, questioning traditional beliefs, and meeting people from all walks of life. He read extensively, everything he could find to broaden his understanding of the belief systems and psychology of contemporary man. By the late 1960s Osho had begun to develop his unique dynamic meditation techniques. Modern man, he says, is so burdened with the outmoded traditions of the past and the anxieties of modern-day living that he must go through a deep cleansing process before he can hope to discover the thought-less, relaxed state of meditation.

In the early 1970s, the first Westerners began to hear of Osho. By 1974 a commune had been established around him in Poona, India, and the trickle of visitors from the West was soon to become a flood. In the course of his work, Osho has spoken on virtually every aspect of the development of human consciousness. He has distilled the essence of what is significant to the spiritual quest of contemporary man, based not on intellectual understanding but tested against his own existential experience.

He belongs to no tradition – "I am the beginning of a totally new religious consciousness," he says. "Please don't connect me with the past – it is not even worth remembering."

His talks to disciples and seekers from all over the world have been published in more than six hundred volumes, and translated into over thirty languages. And he says, "My message is not a doctrine, not a philosophy. My message is a certain alchemy, a science of transformation, so only those who are willing to die as they are and be born again into something so new that they cannot even imagine it right now...only those few courageous people will be ready to listen, because listening is going to be risky.

"Listening, you have taken the first step towards being reborn. So it is not a philosophy that you can just make an overcoat of and go bragging about. It is not a doctrine where you can find consolation for harassing questions. No, my message is not some verbal communication. It is far more risky. It is nothing less than death and rebirth."

Osho left his body on January 19, 1990. His huge commune in India continues to be the largest spiritual growth center in the world attracting thousands of international visitors who come to participate in its meditation, therapy, bodywork and creative programs, or just to experience being in a buddhafield.

# Osho Commune International

The Osho Commune International in Poona, India, guided by the vision of the enlightened master Osho, might be described as a laboratory, an experiment in creating the "New Man" – a human being who lives in harmony with himself and his environment, and who is free from all ideologies and belief systems which now divide humanity.

The Commune's Osho Multiversity offers hundreds of workshops, groups and trainings, presented by its nine different faculties:

Osho School for Centering and Zen Martial Arts
Osho School of Creative Arts
Osho International Academy of Healing Arts
Osho Meditation Academy
Osho School for Love and Conscious Living
Osho School of Mysticism
Osho Institute of Tibetan Pulsing
Osho Center for Transformation
Osho Academy of Zen Sports and Fitness

All these programs are designed to help people to find the knack of meditation: the passive witnessing of thoughts, emotions, and actions, without judgment or identification. Unlike many traditional Eastern disciplines, meditation at Osho Commune is an inseparable part of everyday life – working, relating or just being. The result is that people do not renounce the world but bring to it a spirit of awareness and celebration, in a deep reverence for life.

The highlight of the day at the Commune is the meeting of the White Robe Brotherhood. This two hour celebration of music, dance and silence, with a discourse from Osho, is unique – a complete meditation in itself where thousands of seekers, in Osho's words, "dissolve into a sea of consciousness."

## For further information:

Many of Osho's books have been translated and published in a variety of languages worldwide. For information about Osho, his meditations, books, tapes and the address of an Osho meditation/information center near you, contact:

Osho International Foundation
P.O. Box 2976
London NW5 2PZ, U.K.

Osho Commune International
17 Koregaon Park
Poona 411001, India

Chidvilas Incorporated
P.O. Box 17550
Boulder, Colorado 80308
U.S.A.

# THE MUSTARD SEED

### COMMENTARIES ON THE FIFTH GOSPEL OF SAINT THOMAS

A startling new vision of Jesus emerges in these discourses on the sayings of Jesus according to the Gospel of Thomas, one of the scrolls found in the Dead Sea area near Qumran.

In the great fabric he weaves and counterweaves, Osho uses the rich threads of Eastern traditions of mysticism and enlighten-ment and imparts fresh meaning to this controversial fifth Gospel. With obvious delight and love, a living master bridges the twenty centuries since Jesus and reveals the deeper meaning and beauty of words relived here and now.

The Mustard Seed is especially powerful for those brought up in the Christian tradition.

*The disciples said to Jesus:*
*"Tell us what the kingdom of heaven is like."*
*He said to them: "It is like a mustard seed – smaller than all seeds,*
*but when it falls on the tilled earth it produces a large tree and*
*becomes shelter for all the birds of heaven."*

IN THE OSHO SERIES ELEMENT PUBLISHING PRESENTS

# THE HEART SUTRA

The Prajnaparamita Hridayam Sutra was given by Gautam Buddha directly to his disciple Sariputra two and a half thousand years ago. Now interpreted by Osho for today's seeker, these discourses are significant, vital and penetrating.

"*I salute the Buddha within you,*" Osho begins this series, and calls us to awaken, to find out who we are – to find the Buddha within us.

In addition to speaking on the Heart Sutra, Osho responds to questions from visitors and disciples on a variety of subjects including innocence, experience, suicide, intelligence, prayer and meditation.

"*...These are the most important sutras in the great Buddhist literature. Hence they are called The Heart Sutra; it is the very heart of the Buddhist message.*"

Osho

*"Osho is the greatest incarnation after Buddha in India; he is a living Buddha."*

**Lama Karmapa,**
late head of the Kargyupta Sect

# NO WATER, NO MOON

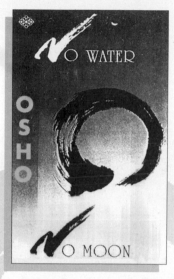

Each chapter of No Water, No Moon opens with a story, a Zen tale of spiritual insight. Using these stories as illustrations, Osho isolates the obstructive attitudes and conditionings we carry (judgments, knowledge, rationalizations and politics) that prevent us from seeing the world and ourselves through fresh, clear eyes.

This book is a guide to unburdening the heart, to opening, to entering the authentic search for one's true, natural being. Osho speaks in depth on how to make oneself available for spiritual transformation through an innocence and wisdom known only to one's inner heart.

No Water, No Moon has a powerful capacity to jog the reader into reaching towards his own inner depths.

*"I found No Water, No Moon one of the most refreshing and cleansing and delightful books I could imagine. It is a book which will never cease to be a comforting companion."*

**Yehudi Menuhin**